Winging It

Winging It

The Making of the Canadair Challenger

Stuart Logie

Macmillan Canada
Toronto, Ontario, Canada

Canadian Cataloguing in Publication Data

Logie, Stuart, date.
   Winging it: The Making of the Canadair Challenger

ISBN 0-7715-9145-4

1. Canadair Challenger (Jet transport).
I. Title.

TL686.C36L6 1991   338.4'762913349'0971   C91-094516-0

1 2 3 4 5 JD 96 95 94 93 92

Cover design by Wolf Schell
Cover illustration by Mike Tomalty

Macmillan Canada
A Division of Canada Publishing Corporation
Toronto, Ontario, Canada

Printed in Canada

To Loretta

"The excitement in this business lies in the sweep of the uncertainties."

John Newhouse,
"A Sporty Game"

CONTENTS

CHRONOLOGY

1941   Canadian government and Canadian Vickers set up production facilities for amphibious aircraft.

1944   Canadian government takes over the aircraft operations from Vickers and creates Canadair Limited.

1946   Canadair is sold to the Electric Boat Company of the United States.

1953   Canadair Ltd. reaches a peak of $144 million in sales and 11,800 employees.

1965   Canadian Department of National Defense notifies Canadair of its intention to buy military aircraft "off the shelf" from foreign manufacturers.

1968   Canadair Ltd. reaches $151 million in sales.

1973   Industry enters a slump. Canadair chief engineer Harry Halton proposes a small jet as the way to find new markets.

1974   The Canadian government purchases de Havilland and announces its intention to purchase Canadair as well.

1975   Bill Lear and his LearStar design find their way to Canadair.

1976   Government takes over ownership of Canadair. Canadair signs an option to build the LearStar with Bill Lear.

1977   Bill Lear disassociates himself from the LearStar program and the LearStar becomes the Challenger. The U.S. government deregulates the aviation industry.

1978   First Challenger 600 completed.

1979   Challenger 600 flight testing begins in the Mojave desert. Grumman, a major competitor, launches the Gulfstream III.

1980   Canadair launches two derivatives: the Challenger 601 and the 610. Challenger 1 crashes during flight testing. Late in the year the Challenger 600 is certified and begins deliveries.

1981   The Challenger 610 is cancelled; the 601 is rushed into production.

1982   First flight of the derivative, the Challenger 601. Word of soaring program costs prompts a government inquiry that results in a cap on corporate borrowing. The borrowing limit is exceeded and the Canada Development Investment Corporation takes over the company.

1983   CBC's *fifth estate* reveals the Challenger's problems to the nation. Executives resign or retire and the largest corporate loss in Canadian history is declared.

1984   Government reorganizes Canadair and assumes the massive debt. The Conservatives sweep to power and try to find a buyer for the company.

1986   Canadair sold to Bombardier Inc.

1989   Bombardier launches the Regional Jet program, to build a stretched version of the Challenger 601.

1991   First flight of the Regional Jet.

ACKNOWLEDGEMENTS

This book would not have been possible without the generous cooperation and patience of the man who built the Challenger, Harry Halton. Indeed, once Harry Halton approved the writing of the Challenger story, doors which had been closed to writers previously were now opened.

Some of those who opened their doors to the author were: Jim Taylor, Peter Aird, George Turek, Andy Throner, Jim Tooley, Beth Kearns, Ron Pickler, Doug Adkins, John Mackenzie, Antoine Guerin, Bob Wohl, Jacques Ouellet, Carl Ally, Dave Hurley, Bill Juvonen, Joel Bell, Mike Lavoie, Albert Blackburn, and Larry Robillard. Their personal contributions, which among other things helped to establish the long-ago conversations used in this book, were significant in many ways and very much appreciated by the author.

There are a number of books that provided the author with useful background material which the author wishes to acknowledge: Richard Rashke's book on Bill Lear, *Stormy Genius* (Houghton Mifflin, 1985); Roger Franklin's book on General Dynamics, *The Defender* (Harper & Row, 1986); Gordon McGregor's autobiography, *The Adolescence of an Airline* (Air Canada, 1970); Ron Pickler's profile of Canadair's products, *The First 40 Years* (Canadair Ltd., 1985); and John Newhouse's superb profile of the aviation industry for *New Yorker* magazine, "A Sporty Game" (The New Yorker, 1982).

Special thanks to Keith Meredith for proofing the book for technical errors, and for providing valuable insight into the sometimes arcane ways of the aviation industry. A heartfelt thanks to Macmillan Canada editor Susan Girvan who, with skill and tremendous patience, took a massive and somewhat confusing manuscript and turned it into a great book, and to Macmillan Canada publisher Denise Schon who believed in this book from the very start and took a chance on a first-time author. Thanks also to Catherine Chase at Canadair for her cooperation in providing the author with photographs for this book; to Wolf Schell for his excellent book jacket design; and to Ron Levine for his author photo.

Finally, an acknowledgement of sincere gratitude to the author's family and friends who provided tremendous support over the two years spent writing this book.

Stuart Logie

PROLOGUE

Regrets

O nce every week for nearly five years Fred Kearns, former president of Canadair, and Harry Halton, the company's former chief engineer, met for lunch at the Jockey Club, a posh restaurant in the Westmount Square complex in downtown Montreal. They spent their time reminiscing about the years they spent together at Canadair, but the conversation would eventually turn to one period in particular: the time they launched the most daring aircraft program in Canadian aviation only to see it nearly destroyed by corporate mismanagement, government inattention, public cynicism and plain bad luck. Kearns and Halton felt that history had been unkind to them and to their program, particularly since the program was proving itself to be the success story they had always predicted.

Indeed, history has been unkind to them. To this day Canadair is remembered as the company that came up with the largest single corporate loss in Canadian history. Canadair's employees were known as the engineers and tradespeople who could spend money like there was no tomorrow but couldn't drill a hole straight. But nothing could be further from the truth. Since the dark days of 1983 Canadair has emerged as one of this country's largest and best-run technical enterprises, and its success is mainly due to the vision of one man: Fred Kearns. As for the corporate loss, tremendous sales expectations were defeated by a brutal business cycle, not because Canadair had produced a bad product. Without Kearns's vision, his courage to take risks and his determination to overcome all the odds and objections, there very well might not be a Canadair today. There would certainly not be a Challenger, nor a CL-215 water bomber putting out fires around the world, nor a CL-289 military drone system, which in 1989 secured the largest single export order this country had seen to date. But Fred Kearns was only human, with the usual human limitations. When he launched the Challenger aircraft program in 1976 with a handful of engineers, a line of credit at the bank and a company that had never produced a civilian jet aircraft, he unleashed a maelstrom of complex forces, and at times they were beyond his control.

This story is not an apology for Fred Kearns. It is the story of one of Canada's most misunderstood technical achievements. The Challenger aircraft is a success story. It was developed and certified for flight in one of the shortest schedules the industry has witnessed. By 1991 more than 250 airplanes had been delivered around the world, and the product is consistently rated one of the best in its class. A new model, the 50-passenger Regional Jet, based on Harry Halton's original Challenger design, will put Canada in an exclusive club—we will be one of the world's most technologically advanced countries supplying commercial airline products.

Fred Kearns made some mistakes in his time, but launching the Challenger program was not one of them. Still, the Challenger program is the Canadian success story that very nearly came apart before it had a chance to prove itself to the world. Kearns's one regret was that success did not come quickly enough nor as easily as he had hoped.

1

One more kick at the can

C hristmas 1974. Times had been tough before at Canadair but never this tough. The company was in a free-fall, and it seemed there was nothing that could be done about it.

Fred Kearns and his wife, Beth, walked arm in arm through the factory. Fred dreaded this moment. It was the annual employee Christmas party, where all the staff members and their families mingled and talked about the year that was—and 1974 had not been a good year. Business was at an all-time low. A shrinking military market and an economic recession had picked away at the company's prospects until there was hardly anything left, and this was having an effect on the employees. The mood at the party was bleak, even hostile. Since 1968 more than seven thousand Canadair employees had been let go, and the two thousand who remained felt they were working for a company without a future. Many had known Canadair as their only employer. They depended on the company to help them pay down their mortgages and clothe their children. Many called the employees—who ran the gamut from tradespeople to highly educated engineers—the Canadair family. In 1974 it seemed the family was destined to disintegrate under the stresses of bad economic times and industrial upheaval. It was up to one man to keep the family together: a shy and genteel accountant named Frederick Ronald Kearns, president of Canadair. He desperately needed to find something that would give this family a future. If he didn't, he might be remembered as the man who let the country's largest airplane manufacturing company go down the tubes.

Canadair began as a war baby. At the start of World War Two, the

1

Allies recognized an urgent need for a long-range flying boat for maritime patrol and for search and rescue and Canada was given the mandate to build one since its industry had experience in the area of building amphibious aircraft.

In 1941 the Canadian government made a deal with Montreal ship builder Canadian Vickers, which had produced a number of amphibious aircraft, to build the PBY-5A Canso flying boat under a license from its San Diego designer, Consolidated Aircraft Corporation, later renamed Convair. Even by today's standards the new operation was large for Canada: $23 million (in 1941 dollars) in equipment and buildings, and more than ten thousand people. However, Vickers's ship-building activities became so heavy it could not manage both operations efficiently, and in 1944 the government decided to take over the aircraft division. They immediately placed it in the hands of a newly created management company headed by a former Vickers aircraft division general manager, Benjamin W. Franklin. Franklin called the management company Canadair Limited and ruled it as if it were his very own company.

When wartime production ceased it was clear that, despite a proven ability to manufacture, though not design, wartime aircraft, Canada's fledgling aircraft industry had failed to inspire confidence. Members of the Canadian government, including C.D. Howe, Mackenzie King's minister of supply, were expecting a boom in postwar commercial aviation. Howe had drafted plans for the creation of Trans-Canada Airlines (TCA), the precursor of Air Canada. At first the new airline would use wartime DC-3s built by the Douglas Company, but it would eventually need a longer range aircraft to provide transcontinental service. The RCAF also required a new transport airplane. Howe envisioned the building of a large four-engine transport to meet the needs of both the RCAF and TCA but he didn't have a Canadian company in mind to build this new airplane. Instead, he intended to select Boeing of Canada in Vancouver, the Canadian subsidiary of the Seattle-based company. Canadair was slated to get a small military contract to build parts for the Avro Lincoln bomber, the successor to the Lancaster. Compared to the TCA/RCAF aircraft program, this was mere table scraps.

Franklin, as senior executive of Canadair, went to Ottawa and vigorously protested Howe's plans. Franklin knew that Canada's other wartime aircraft companies—Victory Aircraft, Fleet and Canada Car—had more than enough capacity to handle production of the Lincoln bomber on their own. Canadair, he argued, should be taking a shot at the commercial market. Franklin wanted Ottawa to take a gamble on the company.

Franklin had no small measure of politics on his side. When Ottawa had created Canadair and situated it on a potato farm in the village of Cartierville near Montreal's north shore, it had created one of the largest industrial concerns in the province of Quebec and in the country. Overnight thousands of jobs were created. To give a major aircraft contract to an American subsidiary located in British Columbia would have had political repercussions. Howe agreed to let Franklin come up with a proposal.

Franklin had experience with U.S. aircraft manufacturing, and because of this he decided to break with tradition and build an American-designed rather than a British-designed airplane. He knew that the Douglas Aircraft Company, which was based in the United States, was pinning its hopes for the postwar commercial market on the DC-6, a larger version of the wartime four-engine DC-4. The DC-6 would have new engines and a pressurized cabin—an innovation in aircraft design. The DC-6 was still in the development stage at the time of the RCAF/TCA contract. Franklin decided to build a hybrid: he would make a DC-4 with a number of the DC-6's advanced features added to it.

Christened the North Star, the Canadair-built version of the Douglas Company DC-4 had problems from the start. First they had difficulty in designing and producing the pressurized cabin. Canadair had moved so quickly that the Douglas Company had not yet perfected a design for a fully functioning pressurized cabin for the DC-6. Canadair underestimated the difficulty of the job, and because of the ensuing delays had to make a deal with TCA to deliver unpressurized North Stars, then supply pressurized versions when they were ready.

Not all the problems were Canadair's fault. C.D. Howe had insisted that Canadair use parts built in the Commonwealth so instead of using the Pratt & Whitney R-2000 radial engine that powered the American-built airplane, Canadair was obliged to use the British Rolls-Royce Merlin. This was a noisy, less advanced engine which had propelled Lancasters and Spitfires during World War Two. The Merlins were more powerful and cheaper than the Pratt & Whitney R-2000s, but they were also a lot heavier. The airplane required significant design changes to compensate for the weight difference.

The Merlin's performance also fell short: the noisy engine was not designed for long term use and soon had reliability problems as its valves and pistons quickly wore out. TCA President Gordon McGregor's struggling debt-laden airline was saddled with expensive and time-consuming engine repairs thanks to the Canadair-built aircraft in its fleet.

McGregor had a low regard for Canadair because of the delivery delays and also because of the way it handled the engine noise problem. He called the airplanes "noisy North Stars" because the 24 engine exhaust stacks blasted hot, noisy air directly at the cabin windows. Canadair had a contractual responsibility to reduce the noise problem but eventually gave up, claiming that neither insulation nor redesign would solve the problem. Meanwhile, a TCA mechanic in Winnipeg came up with a new design for a crossover exhaust manifold. The design proved to be very effective, despite Canadair's belief that it would never work, and from that point on McGregor took a dim view of the aircraft manufacturer. To add to McGregor's frustration, Howe gave Canadair the contract to manufacture the TCA-designed manifolds.

The accumulated difficulties made the North Star a public embarrassment to the government. The media lampooned the plane and blamed Canadair for the mess. Opposition politicians in Ottawa called on Howe to do something about the situation, suggesting Canadair be turned into an auto manufacturer or made into a government warehouse. The situation was a personal embarrassment for Howe, who had listened to Franklin's pleading for a shot at the commercial market. Howe had given Franklin a kick at the can, and Franklin had blown it. Now he would pay the ultimate price. Franklin was fired and the company was sold to the Electric Boat Company of Groton, Connecticut, in the fall of 1946. EBC, later renamed General Dynamics, owned the company until Ottawa bought it back in 1976.

In retrospect, the sale of Canadair to Electric Boat was the best thing that could have happened. Canadair needed the entrepreneurial guidance and businesslike discipline of a private-sector commercial enterprise. EBC, founded in 1900 by John Phillip Holland, the inventor of the submarine, was much smaller than Canadair at the time of the sale. But EBC had a leader, John Jay Hopkins, who recognized good business opportunities, including an offer from a foreign government anxious to unload what seemed to be a public liability.

Hopkins was a self-made man, a chubby millionaire lawyer who had amassed his fortune in oil, mining and railroad interests before being drafted by EBC's board of directors. Hopkins saw significant commercial possibilities in the emerging postwar order. He was one of the first to recognize the beginning of the modern military industrial complex that would provide continued security in an insecure and increasingly bipolarized world. Hopkins was determined to become a major player in the new world order. To do that he needed to turn EBC into a diversified defense-industry company. An accomplished player on Wall Street, Hopkins launched a tax-free dividend of preferred stock that made EBC flush with the cash necessary to go into the airframe industry. EBC's opportunity to do that came when the Canadian government, convinced after the North Star episode that its citizens lacked the know-how to run sophisticated industries, let it be known it was prepared to nearly give away its $22 million Canadair facility for $10 million. Hopkins leaped at the offer.

Ironically, Hopkins had more faith in Canada's citizens than did their own government. He maintained much of Canadair's management and actively recruited other Canadians from de Havilland, Avro, Boeing and Douglas. One of them, H. Oliver West, was made Canadair president and proved to be an excellent choice. A short, unimpressive figure with a penchant for order and control, West was the executive vice president of Boeing and distinguished himself as Boeing's top operations man during hectic wartime production. Once at Canadair, West began a drastic overhaul of production lines. Parts deliveries were improved in terms of quality and schedule by reforming the company's supplier base. New engineers were drafted from anywhere they could be found, often from the ranks of desperately poor but highly educated European war refugees making their new home in Canada. It was also West who went out with his chauffeur and collected the hundreds of pieces of authentic early Canadian furniture that still grace Canadair's impressive executive offices, Mahogany Row, and which remain the largest single collection of such furniture in the world. (Why the pine-furnished offices are called Mahogany Row is a mystery.)

West's effect on Canadair was remarkable. The North Star's reputation improved and new orders flowed in. Although the North Star's improvements came too late to make it a commercial success, it is worth noting that the North Star became the workhorse in TCA's fleet and served longer than any other aircraft purchased by the airline in this period. From 1946 to about 1960, almost fifteen years in which TCA operated a fleet of some two dozen North Stars, only two fatal accidents occurred during more than five billion passenger miles, making the North Star one of the safest airplanes with one of the highest utilization rates in the world.

In 1949, three years after it was sold to EBC, Canadair suggested that it be allowed to develop an aircraft from operating specifications furnished by TCA, assuming that government money would be available for such a project. C.D. Howe's lack of enthusiasm was exceeded only by McGregor's. Both men would tell Canadair that the combined needs of TCA and the RCAF would not be enough to justify the expense of tooling up. The thought that Canadair could sell outside the country was never mentioned.

Disappointment over the lack of Canadian support soon faded as Canadair found a place in Hopkins's vision of the newly emerging military-industrial complex. Berlin was blockaded. China fell to the Communists. The Russians exploded an atom bomb. The world war had ended, but a new war, the Cold War, was just beginning. Hopkins's vision was being realized, and military business began to flow into Canadair.

In the 1950s Canadair came into its own as an important military aircraft contractor. It handled an order from Ottawa for a two-seat jet trainer, the T-33, built under license from Lockheed. Canadair went on to build more than 650 of these aircraft. But the aircraft program that put Canadair on the map was the F-86 Sabre jet fighter built under license from the North American Aircraft Company.

More aircraft were produced by Canadair during the Sabre program than in any program before or since, more than 1,800 in all. Although built initially to be used as the United Nations' front-line attack plane for the Korean War, the F-86, a pilot's airplane because of its great handling characteristics, became a popular war plane during the colonial wars and freewheeling arms trading and profiteering that flourished during the 1960s. The F-86 was used in Portugal's wars in Mozambique and Angola and in Rhodesia's civil war. The

Sabre may have marked the company as a maker of weapons of destruction but it also established Canadair as a competent and innovative aircraft manufacturer. Canadair took advantage of an opportunity to put the Sabre into a supersonic wind tunnel, a device that uses large fans to replicate the movements of air at high speeds, for tests at Langley, the U.S. Air Force's research and development center and developed a vastly improved war plane at minimal expense. It also developed an advanced understanding of the latest developments in aerodynamics research. The Sabre became one of the best bargains in the military business, and Canadair had shown that it could take someone else's design and make it significantly better, something the company would do again and again.

Canadair's star rose dramatically. By 1953, the company had more than $144 million in sales and 11,800 people on the payroll, its highest levels of sales and employment. To the surprise of many, the Canadian defense establishment, once suspicious of Canadair's capabilities, embraced the company with military transport contracts and a flow of defense research money. The American defense establishment, which rarely bought outside the United States, placed orders for Canadair's Sabres and jet trainers even though comparable aircraft were available from aircraft manufacturers based in the United States.

The new-found faith in Canadair did not include the belief that the company could design and build its own aircraft from scratch. In the late 1950s when the Canadian government decided on its military aircraft needs, it again bought a foreign airplane in exchange for industrial offsets. That meant Canadair would continue to build someone else's airplane under license and could forget about ideas of developing a Canadian-designed and Canadian-built military aircraft. In 1959 the Canadian military selected the Lockheed F-104 Starfighter. As a result, the experimental engineering development (or "skunk works") of a Canadair-designed supersonic fighter stopped. More advanced development work also stopped on another supersonic fighter, the Avro Arrow.

H. Oliver West's success at turning Canadair around in the early 1950s was remarkable, but unfortunately for West his success led him to overreach himself. To the delight of Electric Boat's directors, more than three-quarters of EBC's profits came from Canadair. It was clear to West that Canadair was riding a wave of success based solely on military contracts and that wave could crest at any moment. He felt that EBC could not necessarily be counted upon to support the company in new commercial directions. West hatched a plan that was nothing short of audacious: Canadair would buy its parent. He never got a chance to test the idea. West had cancer, and it wasn't long before Hopkins was on his way to Ottawa by private plane (an overhauled DC-3 from Canadair) to tell C.D. Howe, Canadair's biggest customer, that Hopkins was dumping his Canadian president and would be taking over the presidency himself.

When Fred Kearns joined Canadair in 1949, the company's surge in military aircraft production was just beginning. Kearns started humbly enough in the guardhouse working as a timekeeper, the lowest possible rung on the accounting department ladder. By 1961, the year Kearns was made executive vice president, the boom was over. West's prediction a decade earlier—that the military business would not keep Canadair going indefinitely—had finally come true. The United States had reinstated the policy of buying at home, and Canadair's military business began to shrink dramatically. By 1965 the situation had become serious.

That year Canadair president J. Geoffrey Notman and his young executive vice president went to a special meeting called by Canadair's biggest customer, by now nearly its only customer—the Canadian defense department. The meeting was a turning point: in no uncertain terms, Notman and Kearns were told that the climate had changed under Prime Minister Lester B. Pearson. Peace was breaking out everywhere, and Canada was not going to be in the defense business anymore. There would be one more fighter aircraft for Canadair to build, the CF-5, and that would be the end of it. After that, the Canadian government was going to buy off the shelf.

The increasing sophistication of modern warplanes made them extremely expensive, and the technology that went into building the planes had become subject to export restrictions. Canadair was lucky to get the CF-5 from the American defense contractor Northrop; other U.S. fighter-aircraft manufacturers had turned down Canadian government requests to build under license outside the United States. U.S. manufacturers didn't want to sacrifice jobs for export sales. The message to Canadair was that it had better look for other sources of revenue.

While this came as a shock to Canadair, the company was not completely unprepared. From the days of West, the company had been dabbling in the commercial market. Success, however, had been hard to come by.

In the 1950s Canadair had obtained the rights to the Bristol Britannia aircraft designed in Britain by Bristol Aircraft PLC. The first Britannia derivative was the Argus CL-28, built under contract from Ottawa for the RCAF. The second derivative was a military transport, the CL-44-6, the Yukon, also for the RCAF.

Both Notman and Kearns had seen a commercial application for the Yukon, a large four-engined aircraft, in the emerging air-cargo business, and they prepared a business proposal. Some government money was obtained to develop a version with a tail that swung open at the rear and allowed the loading and unloading of cargo pieces up to 85 feet in length. The result was the CL-44D and it was an innovative design. Notman also mounted a strong lobby effort to get TCA to buy some of the airplanes. Having gotten the government to invest in development, Notman thought Canada's publicly owned airline could be counted on to justify the expense with an order. This created a tussle in Ottawa. TCA argued against the plane, saying that the air-cargo business was not a money-maker, and besides, equipment acquisition was best left up to the operator, not the owner, of the airline. Canadair lost the tussle, and the CL-44D never went into the TCA fleet.

However, three cargo airlines—Flying Tigers, Seaboard World Airlines and Slick Airlines—did come forward as eager customers. Cheap, big and reliable, the CL-44D proved to be the competitive edge that kept the three companies alive in a very difficult market. The planes were tough, so ruggedly built that when one accidentally landed in Boston harbor, a National Transportation Safety Board inspector commented, "Who built this airplane? Bridge engineers?" Strong as she was, the plane never really got a big share of the market. Unfortunately for Canadair, it was not the right time to launch another propeller-driven barge of an aircraft. In the late fifties nobody at Canadair thought the development of commercial jet aircraft would proceed as rapidly as it did. But more importantly the company was disappointed by an air-cargo market that, as TCA had warned, never materialized. Seaboard, for example, was in such rough shape that Kearns eventually had to second his top finance man, Peter Aird, to the company to put its house in order or else see the customer go bankrupt.

These factors went against the cargo CL-44D. No sooner had Canadair hit its stride with the production of the CL-44D than the program was canceled. Only 35 aircraft had been built. The cancellation came after a proposed swap of military aircraft for CL-44Ds fell through in 1963. Under the deal, the U.S. air force was ready to trade two hundred CL-44Ds for used F-101 fighters. A U.S. Air Force general was ready to come to Ottawa to ink the deal when a ruckus broke out in the Conservative caucus of Prime Minister John Diefenbaker. In a typically Canadian dispute, Ontario MPs protested the fact that Quebec would receive the lion's share of the deal. Diefenbaker consulted his top adviser in these matters, Doug Belyea, the chief of the Department of Defense Production in the Department of National Defense (DND). Belyea recommended against the swap and Diefenbaker nixed the deal just before it was to be signed. In the end, Canada bought the F-101 fighters and sold the United States nothing.

It was heart breaking for the company. The cancellation dramatically cut the fortunes of Canadair. As well, because of the CL-44D's high Canadian content, the fortunes of the whole Canadian aircraft product industry were affected. It was an example of Canadair's lack of political savvy. Had the company pointed out more forcefully that Ontario aircraft-component manufacturers would have benefited from the deal, the program might have been saved.

The news in 1965 that the Canadian government was going to cut its military commitment significantly came as a tremendous blow to Notman, then in the last year of his presidency at Canadair. His inability to improve the company's commercial activities was linked with the failure to sell TCA the CL-44D. Now the military was telling Canadair it was not, after the CF-5, going to buy airplanes from Canadair, either. The government tried to soften the blow with a promise of money for new equipment for the CF-5 and export financing, since Canadair would now be looking at international markets in order to survive. Between 1967 and 1968 the government fronted Canadair the largest amount in the company's history to that point for a modernization program, some \$12.5 million. This was intended to keep the company competitive as it sought subcontracting business from the larger U.S. aircraft manufacturers. Indeed, Ottawa thought Canadair had only one role with a future—as a subcontractor for other aircraft programs.

There is no underestimating the significance of the government's decision. Canadair owed its existence to the defense establishment. There were occasions when the defense establishment prevented Canadair from considering commercial opportunities by insisting on absolute priority in the shop. During the 1950s, between 75 and 95 percent of the company's revenues routinely came from Canadian defense work. Relations were not always easy between the company and its number-one client. Canadair people viewed the military, with its constant turnover of staff, as a transient, faceless customer who asked dumb questions yet walked around like it owned the place, which in some measure it did. Canadair suffered the military people with a haughty arrogance, which is not uncommon in the engineering culture but which did not help matters any, and the relationship deteriorated further after Notman and Kearns visited Ottawa in 1965. While the military business accounted for a large part of the revenue, it contributed little to profit. Despite popular impressions to the contrary, in military work margins were just as slight as in commercial, if not slighter; the only virtue was that the margin was guaranteed in writing. As military business began to shrink at Canadair, the company had less and less time for its military customer. Canadair was shifting its focus toward commercial opportunities.

This shift represented a considerable challenge. And since Notman wasn't going to be around to force this tremendous change on a company set in its ways after a generation of activity, the challenge to make Canadair a more commercial operation was left to Kearns, who took over from Notman in 1965.

A man of few words who preferred to smoke his pipe in quiet and spend his free time with his grandchildren, Kearns seemed an unlikely choice to lead an aerospace company in a rough-and-tumble business dominated by barnstorming fly-boys and genius engineers. He was the sixth of twelve children, the son of a feed-mill operator from a very Catholic Ottawa Valley family, and he brought something unique to the trade—an ability to keep the faith. His Catholic upbringing had taught him the value of a dollar earned and the necessity of getting along with others in the pursuit of one's dream. Kearns's dream was to restore his company's future, and to do so he knew he would have to place his faith in the abilities of others. Since Canada's chronically floundering aviation industry seemed not to believe in its own ability to take risks and succeed, Kearns knew this would be the challenge of his career. It all boiled down to a question of faith. He believed that Canadians could master the forces of technology and business and create new opportunities. Indeed, his shyness belied a trait that few recognized, that Fred Kearns ranked with the country's most daring entrepreneurs.

In later years, Kearns may have seemed remote, even cold to those who did not know him. To his friends, however, he was Fred, the silent and strong executive whose cheerful enthusiasm, unflagging optimism, courage and ability to lead others made his shyness all the more astonishing for what it concealed.

Kearns got his first job in the Estates General office in Ottawa. He lived in a boardinghouse on Elm Street, where he got to know the Robillard family, who also hailed from the Ottawa Valley. Larry Robillard, an RCAF pilot who much later went to work for Canadair and Fred Kearns, remembers giving Fred his first thrill ride on a motorcycle. Larry's mother remembers Fred's red hair, his cheerfulness and his readiness to help anyone who asked for it. "Everyone liked Fred," she said.

World War Two was on, and Fred volunteered for the Royal Canadian Air Force. His four brothers were already in the service, one of them listed as missing in action following a bombing raid. Larry Robillard was a pilot in the 144 Canadian Spitfire Wing under the direction of the highest-scoring Allied pilot, J.E. "Johnnie" Johnson. Robillard one day got a letter from his mother conveying a request from Mrs. Kearns that Larry look out for her young Fred, an impossible task given the many different wings then in operation in the war. But to Robillard's astonishment, Fred Kearns showed up one day with kit bag in hand, the latest recruit for the 144 Wing. Throughout his life, it seemed, Fred Kearns was blessed by strange fate.

As the youngest member of the 144, Kearns flew 140 missions and succeeded in taking out his share of enemy aircraft and ground targets. On his fourth sortie he crashed his Spitfire and walked away with a wide grin on his face; on his fourteenth he did the same thing.

Always cool, always with a smile on his face. When the war ended he was transferred to Wing Intelligence where he ferried aircraft. That's when he crashed his third airplane, an Auster, in a cabbage patch. Again, he emerged unscathed and smiling. In the face of danger Kearns steadfastly remained an optimist.

Kearns returned to Canada after the war and took a commerce degree in accounting at McGill on a war vet grant. He was passed over for a job at the Canadian division of International Business Machines but Jim Tooley, who was then Canadair's comptroller, was impressed with Kearns's Spitfire experience and thought it made a good qualification for accounting at Canadair.

Kearns kept up with his flying buddies. In fact, he ended up working with many of them. Fred was a member of the RCAF Auxiliary, or the Aux as it was called, and every weekend Fred and the boys would get together and fly old Harvards and a new single-engine jet airplane, the de Havilland Vampire. This particular auxiliary, the 401 City of Westmount Auxiliary Squad, met at St. Hubert Airport south of Montreal, where they wowed the gals with their flying antics. Fred crash-landed another airplane, his fourth, and walked away with that grin on his face. Eventually Jim Tooley put the screws on Kearns to pay attention to the company's books rather than the logbooks, and Kearns became first and foremost a company man. He wasn't far from his friends, however; nearly every one of the City of Westmount Auxiliary pilots was employed at Canadair.

Inside Canadair, Kearns's self-confidence and drive impressed Tooley, who eventually recommended Kearns as his replacement as vice president of finance. At the age of 37, Kearns became the youngest VP in the company's history, and Canadair's president at the time, J. Geoffrey Notman, saw in Kearns the man who would someday succeed him. Notman promoted him to the executive vice president level, effectively making Kearns his right-hand man. It would soon be up to Kearns to take the company in hand and lead it into the future.

When Fred Kearns took over the presidency in 1965 he wasted no time seeking new opportunities for the company. That year he snared a major subcontract from Lockheed to produce components for what would be the largest (and among the most expensive) transport

aircraft in the world, the C-5A; the following year Kearns launched
the CL-215 water bomber program, another frustrating commercial
venture with great potential; the CL-41 basic jet trainer program was
in full swing; and the CF-5 fighter built under license from Northrop
was tooling up. By 1968, Kearns had managed to revitalize the
company: $151 million in sales, a new company record and more than
nine thousand employees. Unfortunately, Kearns, ever the optimist,
had bitten off more than he could chew.

Since the late 1950s, after the winding down of the Sabre program,
Canadair had been actively seeking subcontract programs to pick up
the slack and pay for the overhead. In 1965 Canadair got its largest
subcontract in a deal with Lockheed to produce 81 sets of structural
components—shipsets—for the C-5A Galaxy, a super-large military
transport designed and built to meet a United States Air Force
requirement. Lockheed managed the program badly, and it nearly
ruined Canadair. Lockheed had underbid the competition by planning to build an enlarged version of another Lockheed aircraft, the
Lockheed C-141. Lockheed was so confident it could knock off the
plane with few development costs it had agreed to do the program on
a multi-year fixed-price basis. It was a tremendous risk since the
contract was based on nothing more than a preliminary or "up-
front" definition. Lockheed didn't realize that a vast number of
changes would be required, and they would obliterate the up-front
definition the costs had been based on. It takes time and money to
make changes, and the USAF began insisting on expensive changes.
The program became a financial nightmare.

To Lockheed's dismay the Galaxy turned into a completely new
aircraft instead of the C-141 derivative they had planned to produce.
It was a poor time for Lockheed to find itself at the start of a new
aircraft program. The Vietnam war effort had savagely depleted the
supply of engineers, suppliers and skilled labor. Resources were so
scarce it was feared U.S. President Lyndon Johnson might impose
ration quotas to protect the war effort. Lockheed, which was also
doing development work on the L-1011 jumbo passenger jet,
searched aggressively all over the world for engineering talent as well
as suppliers.

Canadair won the bid to do subcontract work on the program and
Lockheed heaped work on the company. Lockheed had hundreds of

British engineers, all of them living and working in England, design-ing the wing components Canadair was to produce. Canadair set up a British subsidiary, CL Designs Ltd., to handle the process planning and tool-design work. Soon the Galaxy program was also a technical nightmare. As it became apparent that the scaling up of the existing model wasn't working, the weight of the Galaxy shot up and designs changed almost hourly. Change traffic—the flow of changes to drawings—swamped Canadair. Some design changes were so desper-ate and some requirements so loopy that suppliers like Canadair found them unproducible.

The C-5A was a terrible burden on Canadair financially as well as technically. At one point Lockheed owed Canadair nearly $40 mil-lion and the day-to-day survival of the company was assured only when Canadair's owners, General Dynamics, stepped in and guaran-teed a first loss of $20 million for the company. Later, Lockheed would admit liability and make up all the losses.

The mounting complexity of the Galaxy subcontract also dis-tracted Canadair's engineers from other programs such as the CF-5 fighter program. This was the last major Canadian defense aircraft procurement program Canadair ever saw. The Northrop-designed CF-5 was selected by Ottawa as a compromise airplane because of a schism within the Department of National Defense as to what should be the best next-generation RCAF airplane. To some in DND, the CF-5 better suited the requirements of Canadair than the require-ments of DND, since it was a lightweight and comparatively un-sophisticated fighter. While the plane may have suited the require-ments of Canadair, the production of the CF-5 was a bag of trouble for the company. A customer for the CF-5, the Netherlands govern-ment, wanted movable leading-edge devices. Although Canadair had made leading-edge devices for the F-86 Sabre, it didn't have the manufacturing or quality-control experience to put such devices on the CF-5, an airplane Canadair engineers concluded shouldn't have such devices in the first place. Northrop, the airplane designer, didn't provide any answers—and it didn't help Canadair when the company had trouble producing the airplane's complex electrical systems, either. A company with little experience in licensing out production of one of their own aircraft, Northrop provided minimal support during Canadair's difficulties.

Kearns's third gambit was the CL-215, the other Canadair airplane Kearns could claim he had brought into this world. Of all the products Kearns was struggling to deal with, the CL-215 water bomber, launched in 1966, was the sentimental favorite of many. The big yellow bird was a truly unique airplane, a flying fire engine designed by Canadair in conjunction with a committee of forestry experts. She could swoop down, fill her gut with water from a lake or river and race to dump the load on a fire. She was built tough to withstand both the wild hot-air turbulence shooting up from a raging inferno and the dramatic change in flying characteristics when a load of more than a thousand gallons of water was dropped in one and a half seconds. The airplane was known to have sliced an eight-inch hardwood tree like a piece of straw with its wing, taking only a slight chunk out of the leading edge. Pilots who flew her had an abiding respect and affection for the airplane, which had the graceful lines of a railroad boxcar.

While she was beautiful in the eyes of some, the CL-215 also ran into difficulties right from the start.

The program's first problem was in certification. The Department of Transport (DoT) sent Walter McLeish to certify the airplane. McLeish came from the Central Experimental Proving Establishment, where Canada's Armed Forces test new acquisitions, and was an experienced aircraft evaluator. But he had never certified an airplane before, and decided to make an extremely thorough job of it. He wanted Canadair to certify to the tougher U.S. Federal Aviation Regulations (FAR) "utility category" certification rules instead of the "restricted category", a Canadian Transport category, Canadair wanted to certify the water bomber to. In the opinion of McLeish, the higher level of certification would make the airplane more attractive to the market, a decision that was up to Canadair and not the Department of Transport. But more importantly, making Canadair certify to the "utility category" meant that flight-loads testing or structural static testing would now be required. What Canadair expected to be a fairly simple flight test and certification program instead turned into a profoundly complex evaluation of every aspect of the airplane's design. Canadair was outraged because, among other things, the new demands boosted development costs by several million dollars. It damaged relations between Canadair and DoT for years to come.

The water bomber's launch customer (typically the first large order for an aircraft program) also became a problem. The Quebec provincial government, along with the government of France, was the airplane's launch customer, and a crisis erupted when, without notice, Quebec said it was reducing its order from fifteen airplanes to ten, then later down to five. Ostensibly the reason had to do with the CL-215 engines, overhauled war-vintage piston engines purchased from a supplier in the United States. Quebec had contracted the respected U.S. aviation consulting firm Dixon Speas Inc. to do a study on the CL-215, and the study came down very hard on the reliability of the engines. Canadair dispatched its top salesman, Ron Pickler, to Quebec to try to resolve the issue. What Pickler discovered was that the issue had less to do with the engines and more to do with public relations.

"Do you realize that you are the first senior person I have ever seen from Canadair?" said the surly deputy minister responsible for Quebec's fleet of airplanes. Pickler soon concluded that the problems were due to a bureaucrat who was miffed at his treatment by Canadair.

These hurdles were small compared to one hurdle the airplane never succeeded in overcoming: the U.S. market. As of 1991 not one CL-215 had been sold in the United States despite expensive marketing efforts and an obvious need for greater forestry protection in the United States. The failure to penetrate the market was Fred Kearns's biggest disappointment in the program and it was certainly not for want of trying. The U.S. Forest Service and the Air Tankers Association formed a relationship to stop the CL-215 at the border, and Canadair was never able to overcome the opposition.

Aerial attacks on forest fires in the United States are carried out with two types of air vehicles, the helicopter hauling huge buckets and the airplane fitted out with water tanks. Over the years airplane and helicopter operators have made a nice business converting older rotor and fixed-wing aircraft into aerial tankers and chartering them to the Forest Service. The CL-215, with its ability to scoop water on the fly, posed a serious threat to this business, and the operators, with the support of the forestry service, moved decisively to shut the airplane out of their territory.

In 1970 Fred Kearns thought he had a break. A CL-215 was at the Cincinnati Air Show, and a couple of forestry service officials said they would be interested in seeing a demonstration of the airplane. CL-215 salesman Ron Pickler had wined and dined these officials, and they seemed genuinely impressed with Pickler's claims for the yellow bird. Kearns was told of this, and he responded by immediately setting up a demo in neighboring Idaho where there were some brush fires out of control. But when Pickler showed up at the demo, the forestry officials he had warmed up the night before were stone cold. They said the forestry service had changed its mind. The demo was off.

A furious Kearns called up Roger Lewis, chairman of General Dynamics, Canadair's owner, to complain about this. Lewis was sympathetic and suggested that Kearns send the airplane to California. The state was being ravaged by some of the worst fires in its history. Santa Ana conditions, a combination of dry winds and no rain, had turned parts of the state into a tinderbox. A cigarette tossed carelessly into the brush under these conditions could create a devastating inferno in minutes. With such a serious situation, Lewis reasoned to Kearns, nobody would turn down a helping hand from a state-of-the-art flying fire engine. Lewis obviously wasn't fully aware of the forces lined up against the airplane.

Kearns dispatched the plane to California, where it soon ran into opposition. It was decided that the airplane could be used only in Los Angeles County, an area not controlled by the Forest Service and the tankers. The county's director for civil protection, Captain Al Trefethen, was very keen on seeing the airplane in action and gave Canadair the green light. The airplane, piloted by Yves Mahaut, a top pilot from Quebec's air service, did a super job of killing deadly fires and in one instance saved 75 horses that local fire officials had abandoned to the fire. Canadair's yellow bird gave quite a performance. But the next day, with fires worse then ever in other parts of the county, Captain Trefethen said the CL-215 would have to leave.

Canadair was ready for a fight. Kearns sent salesman Ron Pickler and test pilot Doug Adkins, another member of the City of Westmount Aux, to meet with the head of the California division of the Forest Service. The only way the airplane could stay to continue fighting fires, the head of the division told them, would be if it operated with ground-loaded tanks and not as an amphibian. Pickler and Adkins shook their heads in disbelief. "Otherwise, I'll get the governor to order you out of the state!" the official shouted.

The next day, as a reluctant Canadair technician started to bore holes in the fuselage for the ground hoses, it started to rain. The fires began to go out, and so did Canadair's hopes of showing, let alone selling, its CL-215 water bomber in the United States.

Four months later a board of inquiry into the fires of that season issued a report. Canadair had been present at the board of inquiry and had made a very effective presentation. The board's chairman told Canadair that the company would be hearing from them. They did. A copy of the report was sent to Canadair, and it didn't contain a single reference to the CL-215. Instead, it recommended that a U.S. airplane manufacturer be asked to submit a design for a proposed amphibian aerial fire fighter.

There was, however, one very successful CL-215 marketing effort in Spain, a timely deal that came to be known as the wine-for-water sale and that got a 15-airplane production run going. Peter Aird, Canadair's chief financial officer, was in Madrid to close a deal on a sale of two CL-215s when he was invited out to dinner by Spain's minister of agriculture. To make conversation during the dinner, Aird, who is no great wine drinker, politely remarked on the good quality of Spain's wine. The minister perked up.

"I've got warehouses full of the stuff and I can tell you we have a real problem trying to sell it abroad," the minister said.

Aird thought about this for a moment, then asked how many airplanes Spain would be able to buy if Canadair arranged a dollar-for-dollar swap of wine for airplanes.

"You couldn't make so many airplanes, that's how much wine we have!" the minister replied.

When Aird returned to Montreal he contacted Quebec Premier Robert Bourassa and told him of the possibility of doing business with Spain. Was he interested? Very much, said the premier. Bourassa sent a top emissary to Spain and within months a deal was concluded to sell Spain eight more CL-215s in exchange for the purchase of an equivalent dollar value of wine over eight years by Quebec's liquor commission. Spain's share of the wine market in Quebec today is due to this deal. The deal couldn't have come at a better time—it was the early seventies and Canadair was desperate for business.

Kearns could keep CL-215 production going only as long as there were firm orders; no orders, no production, and the CL-215 became an on-again, off-again program. Selling a flying fire engine requires a

customer with money and a rather sophisticated sense of forest
conservation. Interestingly, apart from Canada, the typical CL-215
customer is a country with very limited forest reserves to protect;
Italy, Greece, Yugoslavia, Spain and France all bought the airplane.
To its credit, Canadair learned to manufacture the airplane despite
the stop-start problem. What helped was the decision to use only
inexpensive and uncomplicated manufacturing tooling, called "soft
tooling," on CL-215 production. Even with few sales, the program
didn't lose money and never really hurt the company.

None of these initiatives could sustain Canadair's boom times for
very long. Within five years the company had dropped from an
employment level of nine thousand and sales of $151 million to less
than fifteen hundred employees and $40 million in sales. In the early
1970s Canadair was barely meeting the overhead. By 1975, number
crunchers were running around chipping away at whatever could be
cut or sold in order to keep the overhead down. General Dynamics
wasn't able to help very much since its own aircraft facilities, in Fort
Worth and San Diego, were losing money. By this time Canadair was
no longer the major source of income for the American parent.
General Dynamics had swallowed a number of very large defense
contractors in the United States. Time had shown that Canadair had
been a bit player in Hopkins's drive to turn his company into a
preeminent defense-industry contractor. Nevertheless, GD did make
an important contribution to Canadair: it helped to pull Canadair's
tiny CL-89 missile program out of the fire at the last minute. Without
the experience of this program, Canadair probably wouldn't have
been able to design and build a new jet. The program was the heart of
the company's engineering capability, and its success remains another tribute to Kearns's vision.
    The CL-89 was a reconnaissance drone missile and is still used in
the European theater. The drone, which contained photographic
equipment, was designed to be launched from a mobile launcher, fly
over a designated area and return to safe territory, then land with the
aid of a parachute. It was an extremely complex military program
involving three governments and state-of-the-art technologies. In the
early sixties, GD's money-making Pomona missile division, an industry leader, lent Canadair some of its engineering talent for the CL-89

program and became involved during the engineering and reliability reviews. GD's contribution proved critical in making the CL-89 a successful product. In fact, the CL-89 was in many ways Canadair's most important program in those lean years. Despite its small size, the CL-89 had all the complexity and sophistication of a much larger aircraft program. And if Canadair's people could build the CL-89, then they would likely be able to build the company's next aircraft. The CL-89 kept the company's top engineering talent busy, and defense development dollars kept the accounts books breathing.

At the urging of the program's chief engineer, Harry Halton, Kearns protected the program from many of the direct hits others were taking in those cost-cutting days. Initially Kearns resisted the idea of keeping high-priced talent on a program that gave the factory very little work to do. He didn't fully appreciate the significance of what was being done. When he realized that the program contained the company's best engineers in weights, aerodynamics and electronics—the heart of a technical enterprise of this nature—he defended the program vigorously before GD's board and chief executives, some of whom would have preferred the engineering department to disappear altogether and Canadair to buy its technology from GD with Canadian government funding.

Under Chairman David Lewis, Roger Lewis's successor, GD was not interested in paying for development in another country when the company could do the work in San Diego or Fort Worth. Fortunately, Kearns had an ally at GD: Ed Heinemann, the corporate vice president for engineering and one of the top airplane designers in the United States. Heinemann was a close friend of Harry Halton, and he shared Halton's and Kearns's view that Canada and Canadair needed an indigenous aerospace capability if both the company and the Canadian industry were to continue to operate, a legitimate concern during the dramatic period of declining activity for the Canadian industry.

This decline in Canada's aircraft industry, particularly the airframe sector, did not go unnoticed by Ottawa. Bureaucrats and politicians watched with alarm as the Canadian aircraft industry shrank in the post-Vietnam war era. The country's airframe industry, consisting of de Havilland, Canadair and McDonnell Douglas Canada, was 100 percent foreign owned, and the owners seemed at best indifferent, at worst menacing. Hawker-Siddeley, the British company that owned de Havilland, had warned its Canadian subsidiary it would not fund the building of a new aircraft, this after de Havilland announced intentions to develop the DASH-7 commuter. The reason was simple: the DASH-7 could compete with one of Hawker-Siddeley's own airplanes. The warning would have been a death knell for de Havilland, since it was unlikely the world was going to take many more de Havilland-built Twin Otters. To survive, the company needed to build a new aircraft for new markets.

Fortunately for the Canadian industry, the 1970s were years of economic nationalism under Liberal Prime Minister Pierre Elliott Trudeau and the government was not about to watch foreign companies strangle or dismantle Canada's airframe industry. In 1973 the government began devising a rescue plan. Ottawa negotiated an option with Hawker-Siddeley to buy de Havilland, then gave de Havilland $75 million to develop and build the first two DASH-7 prototypes.

And what about Canadair? Fred Kearns began what would be the selling job of his life, to persuade the government to buy Canadair and fund a new airplane program to secure the company's future. Kearns knew that under GD's current chairman, David Lewis, there would be little chance of launching the new aircraft program Canadair needed. Kearns was also fed up with GD's branch-plant mentality, which had left Canadair's top management underpaid and despondent at the lack of activity. Canadair needed an owner that would give them the money and the tools to get back into the game. Ironically, Canadair was looking for exactly the same thing it had found when it was acquired by Electric Boat Company nearly thirty years before: entrepreneurial owners willing to gamble on a vision.

Convincing the government to buy Canadair was not difficult. Politically it was unthinkable that Ottawa would save Ontario's de Havilland and neglect Quebec's Canadair. Kearns had the support of Trudeau ally and Liberal Cabinet minister Jean-Pierre Goyer. The Canadair plant was located in his riding, and he lobbied Trudeau on the need to buy Canadair. The bureaucrats agreed it would be a good idea to acquire Canadair since GD was profoundly indifferent to Canadair and could probably be talked into letting it go for much less than it was worth. Kearns's only problem with all this was that some bureaucrats believed that if both companies were to be saved, then the government should rationalize the industry, making one the main airframe manufacturer, the other a parts supplier.

The nod to acquire Canadair came in early 1974. In March, Industry Trade and Commerce (ITC) Minister Alastair Gillespie called GD's Chairman David Lewis at the golf course and told him that the Canadian government was about to announce it would acquire de Havilland in June. Ottawa, he said, would also announce its intention to acquire Canadair. "I just wanted you to hear it from me first," Gillespie told Lewis, who was between rounds. The government purchase of Canadair was extremely complex and took nearly two years to complete. In the eleventh hour, two things happened that nearly scuttled the deal.

A senior Canadian government bureaucrat named Jim Howe was a strong free enterpriser who objected to the government's long-standing policy of supporting the aviation industry through grants and other subsidies. He and others in government believed that if Canada was to have an aviation industry, then that industry should exist without the benefit of government support; it should find support in a commercial market. This group assumed that both de Havilland and Canadair wouldn't make it on their own. They proposed that the firms be dismembered and sold off.

Howe, who worked as a floating economist, reflected the elitist thinking of a number of Ottawa mandarins who looked down on Canadair as nothing more than a bucket shop populated by tradespeople. These mandarins, McGill- and Harvard-trained lawyers and economists working in Finance, Treasury Board and Privy Council, didn't know the aviation manufacturing business. Government policy was mostly involved with the airline business, specifically Air Canada. As for manufacturing, economists were hired to advise bureaucrats and ministers on industrial issues, and Howe's opinion seemed to matter. He was, after all, a self-made man who had become a millionaire at a young age and epitomized free enterprise and the entrepreneurial spirit.

Kearns wasn't hoping to hold on to the company's position as an aircraft manufacturer for sentimental reasons. Since his first days as president, when he had witnessed the company's fading future as a military contractor, Kearns knew that the subcontractor role would make Canadair entirely dependent on the whims of the prime contractor. The loss of control would mean that during bad times, when business was needed most, prime contractors could yank business away from the subcontractors and do it themselves.

Meanwhile negotiations continued, and Kearns pressured Ottawa not to give in to Howe's thinking. Fortunately, the politicians did not share Howe's view of Canadair; indeed, there was a growing realization in the Cabinet that Canada's aviation industry was at a crucial point and thousands of jobs were at stake. Still, it took considerable arm twisting by Kearns to get Ottawa to show its commitment to keeping Canadair in the airplane business by placing an order for fifteen CL-215s. With this new life for the CL-215 program, Kearns was satisfied that Ottawa supported Canadair's right to stay in the aircraft business, at least for a while.

A second, less serious hiccup came in the last hours of negotiations. It had to do with the $20 million line of credit guaranteed by General Dynamics to cover a first-time loss for Canadair, given in the dark hours of the Galaxy C-5A program.

The GD credit was going to pass over to Canadair, and ITC said it would guarantee the line of credit with Canadair's bankers by a letter of comfort signed by the minister. The letter of comfort was not a formal guarantee approved by Parliament but simply a letter from Privy Council on behalf of a minister. Canadair's principal banker, the Royal Bank, said the letter was not acceptable; it wanted nothing less than a formal guarantee passed by Parliament. Canadair didn't take the Royal Bank's threat seriously, but as the deal was about to be signed, the bank's vice president and branch manager in Montreal, Jimmy Walker, reminded Canadair of what the bank had said earlier: no parliamentary guarantee, no credit. The Canadian Imperial Bank of Commerce, which had been Canadair's sole banker until the account was split with the Royal, picked up what the Royal turned down, and the problem was solved. As far as the CIBC was concerned, the letter of comfort was as good as a guarantee, and the letter of comfort became Canadair's prime instrument of debt financing.

On January 6, 1976, after 30 years of foreign ownership, Canadair went back into government hands. The price had come down from $104 million two years earlier to $38 million, not a bad deal for Ottawa on the basis of Canadair's fixed assets.

Canadair's days as a military contractor were almost at an end. With no new products coming to market, with almost nothing in development that could be considered a money-making proposition and with few workers, Kearns had to justify the government's decision to purchase Canadair and keep it intact or risk seeing the company reduced in stature and stripped of its strengths. Canadair had faced this prospect a number of times before. Kearns had to find a good commercial program, then persuade Ottawa that his company could handle it. To some, the idea of Canadair, a company on the wane, launching a completely new commercial aircraft program was crazy.

In the aviation business, a new aircraft program is the biggest game in town. Launching such a program from scratch continues to be a billion-dollar crapshoot, a business risk almost without peer. There are few businesses where lead times—the time it takes to develop a product and get it to the market—can be more than five years. A lot can change in an economy in five years, making the gamble prohibitively risky.

Aviation has a freewheeling style of doing business. Sometimes companies defy sound business practices in order to succeed. Still, it is a serious and important business driven by a highly educated and motivated industrial elite. There is no single industry so involved with technology, none more obsessed with quality and reliability, and few that can consume as much capital yet yield so little profit. (In most cases investors must face a total risk that exceeds their company's net worth.) And in the aviation industry, cutthroat competitiveness brings the swift extinction of the loser.

Even though Canada is one of the world's largest users of aircraft (fifth in the world in terms of fleet size), the country is a marginal player in the game of new aircraft programs. In the decade before 1975, the industry's annual sales averaged $1.7 billion a year, a little less than 0.5 percent of Canada's gross national product. The aircraft industry in Canada is small compared to industries in the United States, Britain and France. As far as airframe makers go, de Havilland and Canadair were the only serious Canadian concerns. One got by making propeller transports, the other survived on military offsets negotiated by the government. Canada had never produced a Canadian-designed commercial jet aircraft. Fred Kearns wanted to change that. The future of the company depended on it.

When the deal to sell Canadair to Ottawa was in the last stretch, de Havilland's president, Bundy Bundesman, called Kearns to chat. He told Kearns he had been in touch with Carl Ally, an aviation marketing man who was representing Bill Lear, designer of the world-famous Learjet. Ally and Lear had a proposal for a commercial program, and Bundesman had suggested Ally talk to Kearns. Kearns waited for Ally's call with a good deal of optimism and hope. If Ally had something, Kearns would shortly be on his way to Ottawa, just as Franklin had been many years before, asking for one more kick at the can.

2

King Lear

B ill Lear started to weep.
Twenty-five Learjets, the little jet planes that changed the face of corporate aviation, were lined up in precise order like Prussian officers. They were in front of the Lear Avia hangar at the airport in Reno, Nevada, with their bug-eye windshields and long, skinny noses arrogantly poking the air, though the addition of huge ribbons and bows had given them a slightly ridiculous cast. They were the honor guard for the seventy-third birthday of the man who created them, Bill Lear, considered by many to be the last of the great aviation pioneers. His friends and family were throwing him a little bash. It was more like a coronation of a king, in this case King Lear, king of the business jet.

Inside the hangar, Lear stood before the crowd of friends and admirers. Normally a blustery figure, Lear was uncharacteristically quiet, silently battling his swelling emotions and groping for words. Moments earlier he had learned that he had been named man of the year for 1975 by the National Business Aircraft Association. The reason: his Learjet helped change an industry. Lear, a man with an imposing physical appearance, was visibly moved by this burst of praise and recognition, and silently the King of the Corporate Jet began to weep.

King Lear. Enfant terrible. Stormy genius. Wild Bill. Few men in the history of aviation attracted as much attention as William Powell Lear. Perhaps it was because many of the great leaders in the formative years of the industry were engineers who quietly went about their business. Not Lear. With nothing more than a grade-school education, a genius for electronic gadgets and an indomitable spirit, Lear sought to be a legend in his own time. A jack-of-all-trades, he had a hand at designing anything and everything, from the hamburgers in the Lear company cafeteria to sophisticated electronic components on military aircraft. Before he died in 1978, Lear had invented scores of successful (and some unsuccessful) products and had some 150 patents in his name. He invented the miniature inductance coil, which was the basis of the car radio, and was a founding partner of the Motorola Corporation. He invented the eight-track tape-recording system. During the Vietnam war every bomber, transport or fighter aircraft carried at least one piece of Lear-designed equipment, from gearboxes to transmitters. Lear's greatest achievement in fighter-aircraft technology was the development of the autopilot, a device made of gyroscopes that send signals to the motors and actuators that move the airplane's various control surfaces—the rudder, elevator and ailerons—thereby providing control to the airplane in all three axes. The U.S. Air Force called it a miracle of engineering, and it earned Lear the prestigious Collier Trophy, the Pulitzer prize of the aviation industry, and had made Lear a man of prominence at 48, at the beginning of his career. His most noted success, the Learjet, was yet to come. It was the Model T of corporate aviation, and for three decades it remained the most popular business jet in the world and broadened the appeal of business jet aviation.

But there was a flaw in the legend. Lear, an unyielding autocrat, was not a businessman. All his life Lear was the boy genius with a youthful contempt for order, restraint and control. Says a close friend of Lear, "There were two Bill Lears: one that could make things happen, the other a little boy having a great time." He did make things happen, but the restless Lear had trouble keeping them going. He was an artist out of place in a high-risk industry that viewed continuity, routine and predictability as matters of survival. Lear did have his place, however, as a great promoter of technology in a period punctuated by scientific and engineering advances. Lear found practical and profitable ways to apply technology in order to make money. He was very much the high-technology entrepreneur. Yet Lear was also the wild-eyed researcher who had to experiment, create and explore. His tendency to experiment didn't allow for much of the stuff that makes business possible. Business concerns bored him—and so did his personal fortune. By his seventy-third birthday, one of aviation's most creative and productive contributors to the growth of aviation had not achieved as much wealth as might be expected. He had some patent royalties, a few houses and some money in the bank. Lear's desire was not fortune. What he really coveted was fame. He wanted his name known the world over.

His birthday party was a farewell of sorts, a last hurrah for the man who had accomplished much and was now expected to retire quietly. However, the Lear story was far from over. Inside the old body the little boy lived on, as vital as ever, and Lear wasn't ready to call it quits. The LearStar executive jet, a venture Lear embraced after the failure of an attempt at a steam-driven bus in 1974, was to be the swan song of a prodigious mind that had amazed and infuriated the aviation industry for nearly thirty years. The LearStar, no more than an idea to marry airframe and engine technologies, was very much on Lear's mind the day he was feted by his friends and made man of the year by the business aviation industry.

Ironically, the industry that made him man of the year wouldn't touch his latest idea. The American aviation industry had unanimously turned him down when he went knocking on doors looking for someone to build the LearStar. The industry knew Lear very well, and knew from experience that the man did best on his own. He must have known, at 73, that his quest for a partner in the United States was a long shot.

Lear didn't have the money or access to capital necessary to launch the LearStar on his own. Eventually he looked outside his native country for a backer. What he had to offer, aside from the idea, was his name, a valuable asset he didn't underestimate. The name carried power and influence in the business of corporate aviation; an airplane with the Lear name would always get a look from the market. If a company wanted to get into the corporate jet business, it couldn't lose if it had the Lear name on its product. Lear was determined to find a backer. A dead steam bus was not how he wanted the legend to end. He was going to have one more fling with his greatest passion, aviation.

The event that had turned Lear from designing aviation gadgets to building airplanes took place one day in the early 1950s. Lear was flying his Lockheed Lodestar, which dated from World War Two and which the U.S. Air Force had given him for tests of his innovative autopilot, when the airplane's engines began running hot. Ignoring the fact that the twin-engine propeller aircraft was way past its prime, Lear decided to have his engineers overhaul the aircraft. Lear found ways to make the old plane fly faster and better. He stripped out the interior and put in carpeting, paneling, a toilet and a bar. With the addition of new furniture, Lear had one of the nicest corporate airplanes in the country. A few months later, the president of Fairchild Corporation took a ride in it and liked the airplane so much he bought it on the spot for $200,000. Naturally Lear bought two more Lodestars and converted them. They, too, sold quickly, and like a number of other people in the business of converting and selling airplanes, Lear realized he was on to something: a growing market for business aircraft.

After converting several more Lodestars for corporate clients, Lear decided the Lodestar needed to be redesigned. He brought together a group of young maverick aircraft designers, including Ed Swearingen, considered one of the brightest in the field. They redesigned the Lodestar and christened it the LearStar. When they finished with her, the LearStar could fly 100 miles an hour faster at cruising speed than the Lodestar and had an extended nonstop flying range of 3,800 miles. It was the fastest twin-engine transport with the longest range then in production. And at $650,000 a pop, it was also the most expensive. After the LearStar was certified in 1955, Lear's company began converting all the Lodestars it could find; there were still between two and three hundred Lodestars and Venturas, the military version, available.

Lear knew he would have to come up with a plan for another airplane model or his days in the aviation business would be over once all the Lodestars had been converted. He began thinking of a completely new airplane. In 1959 one of his sons, Bill Jr., came up with the precursor to the Learjet. And it came all the way from Switzerland.

After World War Two a Swiss aircraft designer, Dr. Hans Studer, had developed the P-16 fighter bomber. Six prototypes of this precisely tooled aircraft were built with the idea of selling them to the Swiss Air Force. Two of them, however, ended up at the bottom of

Lake Constance, and the P-16 became known as the Swiss Submarine. When Bill Lear and his family moved to Switzerland in the late 1950s, they met Dr. Studer, who hadn't given up on his P-16. One day Dr. Studer asked Bill Jr., who was also a flier, to test the P-16. Bill Jr. was so impressed with the sturdy little airplane that he brought drawings of the P-16 to show his father.

Lear was immediately taken by the idea of a jet airplane as the follow-up act to the propeller-driven LearStar. In the P-16's design, particularly the straight, narrow wings for high-speed flying, he saw his next airplane. In 1959, Lear hired Dr. Studer to turn the P-16 fighter into a hot-rod corporate jet.

This was going to be a corporate airplane unlike any other. For one thing, it was going to be a pilot's airplane. The cockpit would be large and comfortable, while the passengers would sit in near prenatal positions in a stark cabin interior without the benefit of even a bathroom. It would fly higher, faster and farther than any other business aircraft. Lear called it the SAAC-23. SAAC stood for Swiss American Aviation Corporation, the name of the Swiss-based company Lear formed to build the airplane, and 23 represented the Federal Aviation Regulations Part 23 certification regulations the airplane would comply with. Lear boasted he could sell more than six hundred of the aircraft, which at the time was more than any other business aircraft had sold. But by 1962, the year Lear promised to have the SAAC-23 flying, the airplane was still on the drawing board.

The problem was that Lear was a self-taught radio engineer, not an aeronautical engineer or a business manager. The LearStar had been a conversion program, and converting was a much simpler enterprise than developing a completely new aircraft. The new program had three quarreling chief engineers and little direction. The Swiss government, which had helped Lear with grants to start up, was unhappy because Lear had imported the chief engineers for the project.

At least one of those imported engineers, a former Cessna chief engineer named Henry Waring, saw the problem. Lear had to get production out of Switzerland and to the States, preferably to Wichita, where 65% of the world's airplanes were being built at the time. Switzerland was a leader in precision tooling and engineering, but it was not an airplane-producing country, and its engineers didn't have the same working habits as Wichita.

Wichita was an airplane center and a hub of aviation expertise. Its aviation industry dated from the turn of the century when a bunch of brash fly-boys and designers arrived for a design competition and stayed to set up one of the world's earliest and busiest aviation centers. In 1962 Wichita wasn't so busy, and employment in the industry had dropped by nearly half during the preceding five years. Excess capacity meant that Wichita would be very sweet on having Lear locate there. Low on money, still two years away from first flight and anxious to get the Learjet-23 (he abandoned the SAAC name) off the boards before he went broke, Lear agreed. He moved, lock, stock and fuselage, from Switzerland to Wichita.

When Lear moved his company into the new building in Wichita in early 1963, he had only $12 million to cover the design, production and certification of the Learjet. Critics said it would take at least $100 million to build the new business jet from scratch. To do it for less, Lear decided to skip an important production step. Airplane manufacturers at that time usually built a prototype of an aircraft with soft tooling, refined it, and only then acquired the expensive hard, precision tooling to manufacture the aircraft. Lear, certain his design would fly, went straight into hard tooling to save money and time. Every aircraft manufacturer who knew about Lear's program knew he was taking a big risk.

The Learjet was not a designer's dream. It did not have an innovative aerodynamic structure, since Lear couldn't afford the time and money for the extensive wind-tunnel testing such a design would require. The best the designers could do was give the Learjet body, or fuselage, sleek lines. The wings were more than a decade old in terms of aeronautical design. For all its sleekness, the Learjet was still going to be a fairly common aircraft from an aerodynamic point of view. But its conventionality made it relatively easy to build, and Lear succeeded with the first airplane.

All through the development period of the aircraft Lear pushed his finger into every aspect of development and was convinced of the rightness of his decisions. He ruled with a mixture of fear and inspiration. He harangued his employees and scorned his critics. He was also reckless. Lear was particularly proud of his high-tech windshield and knew that pilots, who often made the critical decision when it came to selecting a corporate aircraft, hated feeling claustrophobic in the cockpit. Lear had a 270-degree-view windshield developed by a Plexiglas company he had found. He was so convinced that his chosen windshield would do the job that he took the pilot's seat behind the glass during a certification test. During the test, dead chickens were fired from a cannon to simulate the impact of a bird at 450 miles per hour. Nobody dared tell Lear he was taking a stupid chance, yet nobody wanted to see him and the program smashed to pieces if the windshield failed. While he was sitting in the cockpit, someone from the team called to Lear to say that the president of the United States was on the telephone. Lear went to get the call; it would not have surprised him if it was the president, but it turned out there was no one waiting on the line. The chicken was served up for the test. It smashed through the windshield, passed through the cabin and shot out the back of the fuselage. When Lear returned and saw what had happened, he went back to the telephone and gave the windshield supplier hell.

If Lear had died while Learjet #1 was being developed, it can be assumed there would not have been a Learjet #2. So it was that Lear found himself on the ground on October 7, 1963, when the first Learjet made its maiden flight. Staring into the sky over Wichita while test pilot Hank Beaird took the plane through its paces, Lear knew his gamble—skipping the prototype stage—had paid off. The Learjet was finally on its way.

Lear got the Learjet Model 23 certified with the Federal Aviation Administration (FAA) ten months after first flight and saved a tremendous amount of money in the process. Although it was a long time in development, the Learjet's certification program remains something of a record in the industry, particularly for a brand-new airplane. There were a few reasons for this. The Learjet 23 was the first jet of less than 12,500 pounds to be certified. Lear broke new ground in this area and set some of the standards. It was the smallest civilian jet ever certified by the FAA and Lear had little trouble getting a certification tailored to his vision of this new class of transport. Moreover, the FAA gave the Learjet an easy time because few people in the agency believed that anybody would want to buy such an airplane. And when an FAA flight test team crashed the first Learjet into a cornfield after inadvertently leaving their wing spoilers extended, Lear's certification suddenly became top priority for the embarrassed FAA. In addition, Lear maintained unremitting pressure, including threats—and sometimes he made good on those threats—to call anybody and everybody involved in the U.S. aviation industry. The pressure succeeded in intimidating the FAA to hurry up the process.

The result was a certification program that was remarkably fast and inexpensive, and considering that the certification process can consume as much as a third of a commercial airplane's development budget, it gave Lear a tremendous advantage. He used this certification schedule for his model in planning subsequent aircraft, but he would never again come close to getting certification in ten months. With the Learjet 23, he had been plain lucky.

Despite the good luck at the FAA, the program still cost Lear much more than the $12 million he began with, and by the time the Learjet was certified he had exhausted his line of credit. There wasn't any money left to produce the airplane. He decided to go public, a difficult decision for a man who likes to have complete control. Claiming he had orders for sixty-three aircraft worth $30 million, Lear easily raised $5 million through a share offering and managed to retain majority share control of the company. Within a year Lear stock went from its $10 offering price to $83. Lear was flying high. Soon he began talking about the next Learjet, Model 24, a heavier version of the 23, and the Lear Liner, a 28-passenger intercontinental jet.

Within two years of the first flight in 1965, the Learjet 23, which experienced pilots loved to fly because of its hot-rod qualities, began showing up on fatal crash statistics. The aircraft was difficult to fly and did not forgive pilot error. Within one three-month period there were three fatal accidents and five landing mishaps. Learjets everywhere were grounded for two days by the FAA, and Lear stock began to tumble. His competition, the Jet Commander built by Rockwell, was waging an intense ad campaign at the time, and Lear didn't need challenges to the Learjet's airworthiness. To counteract the publicity, Lear sent a Learjet 23 to circle the globe with his son John and test pilot Beaird at the controls. The airplane flew a perfect flight plan and established 18 world records.

But nothing could help Lear beat a more serious set of statistics. By the mid-1960s the economy was in a tailspin. Every aircraft manufacturer was hurting. Lear might have weathered the recession, since he was still selling more aircraft than the competition, but in the years leading up to the slowdown he had launched many more businesses and new programs than the company could support. When the full force of the recession hit in 1966, Lear's company was in a state of near collapse, and he had no choice. To keep the company alive, he would have to sell it. And he did. He sold the company to rubber magnate Charlie Gates for $20 million, and suddenly Lear was out of the aircraft manufacturing business after soaring in it for only a few years.

Lear was not the first to design a small passenger jet; Lockheed and North American (later purchased by Rockwell) had each designed small passenger jets, but they were larger and slower than the Learjet, and were destined for military or very large corporate operators. Lear was the first to design and market a jet affordable to a wider market. It took Cessna's tremendously successful Citation jet a full decade to outnumber the Learjets operating worldwide (1,346). Even in 1990 the Lear name was synonymous with corporate aviation and private jets. It is firmly established in the lexicon of the wealthy.

Nearly a decade after selling his company, on that June day in 1975, surrounded by supporters and two dozen tarted-up Learjets, Lear was determined to make a comeback in the aviation world before he slipped the surly bonds of this earth. But after a year of looking, Lear had yet to find the right partner, indeed any partner for his LearStar. His best hope rested with one man: Carl Ally.

A year before Lear's seventy-third birthday, at the National Business Aircraft Association conference in Los Angeles, Carl Ally had been making the rounds. A stocky, spectacled, chain-smoking veteran fighter pilot of two wars, Ally was hunting for work. He was an advertising man, a promoter whose killer instincts in war translated nicely into a marketing operation catering to aggressive, even belligerent business aviation clients. With Ally, the marketing campaign began with the gloves off.

In Ally's line of work, the NBAA was where the action could be found. Since the early fifties the NBAA had consisted of aviation entrepreneurs who, as Lear had done, converted military and airline equipment for business use. In the beginning it was small-scale stuff. A DC-3 could be bought for $100,000, fitted out like an aerial palace and sold for $500,000. Every year the airplane converters would get together to swap information, share some drinks and tell some tall tales. That changed in 1959, when a company called Grumman began selling the first aircraft designed specifically for business use, the Gulfstream I.

The 1970s boom in business aviation was preceded by an era of marginal activity, and the market was no more than a private domain created in the earliest days of aviation by the captains of industry who could afford such luxuries. It included people like Henry B. DuPont, who owned the first aircraft certified in the United States, when the government began to do that sort of thing, in 1927. It was a Buhl-Verville J4, which DuPont used for business travel. Wider use of aircraft for business began in 1936, when 10 wealthy businessmen got together to finance the development of a new airplane to take them on fishing trips. Henry Morgan, Marshall Field and C.V. Whitney, among others, formed a syndicate to help the fledgling Grumman Aircraft Engineering Company, which was then developing an amphibian airplane, the Goose. Later, as the Goose became more sophisticated and comfortable, it began to be used as a business aircraft. The Goose could land anywhere there was water, an important characteristic as there were very few airports at the time.

Everything changed after World War Two, when the flood of cheap and roomy DC-3s came onto the market and the number of airports available for aviation jumped as a result of the war effort. Grumman's little airplane was obsolete. The company came up with follow-ons to the Goose, specifically the Widgeon and the Mallard, but the company soon saw that the growing executive or business-aviation market wanted conventional aircraft. Wisely Grumman also figured out that this market would soon tire of the old DC-3s, and so the Grumman Gulfstream G-I executive aircraft program was launched. The launching of a completely new aircraft specifically designed for the corporate operator made it possible for other airplane manufacturers to undertake the large expense of designing and building an aircraft for that market. Business aviation began to emerge as a big-time operation.

In 1974 the industry was booming while other sectors of the aviation industry were in the doldrums. Aircraft technology was improving dramatically, the demand for newer and better aircraft was growing considerably, and the market segment called "general aviation" (which did not include military or airliner aviation) was seeing its golden years. The move to corporate airplanes was stimulated by the decline in airline schedules that started with the 1973 fuel crisis. Suddenly it was harder for the executives of multinational and multi-based corporations to get around. Company leaders who could afford them began to recognize the benefits of corporate aircraft.

Carl Ally showed up at the Los Angeles NBAA hoping to interest business aircraft manufacturers in more than his marketing skills. He had an idea for the next generation of airplane. He thought the time had come to build a supersonic executive aircraft. Advances in aeronautics had put the technology within reach, and Ally had a survey of business aircraft operators that showed a significant interest in having a high-speed aircraft capable of flying longer distances than currently possible. The idea of building a high-speed intercontinental business jet had been floating around for nearly a decade. In 1967 Pan American Airlines' Business Jet Division, which marketed Dassault's French-built Falcon jet in North America, put out feelers to see if any business aircraft manufacturers were interested in developing a new business jet capable of flying from coast to coast or even continent to continent. It turned out they were not interested, mainly because they were involved in launching new but shorter-range jets. A decade later, after these shorter-range jets had found their place in the market, discussion in the industry turned again to developing a longer-range business jet.

But Ally was convinced that high speed meant supersonic speed. At the NBAA, Ally would soon be convinced otherwise. That's because the King of the Corporate Jet was there, as well.

"Sweetheart! How are you?"

Ally felt a strong tug on his arm and turned to find a beaming Bill Lear. Ally first met Lear in 1963 when he had been invited to Wichita to have a look at the Learjet program. Ally was impressed with the Learjet and suggested, naturally, an aggressive advertising campaign aimed directly at Lear's competition, the Jet Commander. Lear had been demure. "I don't want to rock the boat here in Wichita," Lear had wisely told Ally. Ally stayed in touch with Lear over the years but never got involved with him professionally. That was about to change.

"I've got a great idea and I want to talk to you about it!" Lear said.

"No," Ally protested. "I've got the great idea and I want to tell *you* about it."

The two went to a quiet place to talk, and it became clear to Ally that what Lear was talking about was the long-range business jet. When Lear finished, Ally gave his pitch for the supersonic business jet. Lear dismissed the idea with a wave and a warning that supersonic transport would always remain too expensive and too elitist. At heart, Lear was not an elitist—he was a self-trained, self-made individual with the beautiful charm of the common man and the character of a real American. He found it difficult to get excited about such an expensive project. Lear thought of airplanes for people like himself, simple folk with a mission. He knew the Learjet had been a success because it was affordable.

Lear hoped to repeat the same trick in an airplane with two eminently exploitable technological advances. First, a new generation of jet engines—the high-bypass engine—was coming onto the market, and second, there was a new aerodynamic design for airplane wings. Put together, these breakthroughs would allow an airplane to fly farther on less fuel than anything that existed on the market. The combination of more power and less drag gave the idea a beautiful simplicity. It would be state-of-the-art, yet because it would be more efficient, it would be better value. It would capitalize on the oil crisis, which made the price of fuel, the number-one operating expense, a major concern to all aircraft operators, private and commercial. In fact, business aircraft owners were already showing increasing readiness to trade up to a more fuel-efficient airplane. There weren't, however, any new airplanes to trade up to. Despite the breakthroughs in aviation technology, there hadn't been a new jet model introduced since the early sixties when Lear, Dassault and Grumman had all come out with corporate jets. Lear knew that the time was ripe for a new business aircraft.

As Ally listened to Lear's pitch, he thought the LearStar could be a winner, but not the way Lear envisioned it. Lear was still fixed on his original Learjet design, something sleek and fast. It was a repeat of a design that had already found its market, and there was probably not much room left for growth. Ally knew that the market wanted business aircraft to look more like commercial airliners, which flew farther and had more room, and he urged Lear to reconsider the design, to focus on the class of jets dominated by Grumman and Dassault, the "big bird" class of business airplanes.

"If this airplane is going to carry people on longer flights you can be sure those people are not going to like being squeezed into a mailing tube," Ally told Lear, referring to the Learjet's narrow body design.

"Look, Carl, wall-to-wall girls is no substitute for getting there," Lear replied.

Ignoring this, Ally saw something in Lear's new idea. "You've got something here, and what you've got is an intercontinental jet." (Ally later realized Lear was talking about the same jet Pan Am had considered for development several years ago.)

Ally promised to help Lear find a backer for the aircraft. First, however, he wanted to know more about the new wing technology. After the conference Ally and Lear went to visit an aeronautical engineer named Richard Whitcomb who had been working on a design for a more efficient wing, called the supercritical wing. Convinced by Whitcomb that the supercritical wing was more than just theory, Ally embraced Lear's idea completely and forgot about his supersonic business jet. The LearStar was something better. It would meet the growing demand for airliner comfort on an intercontinental business aircraft. "Airliner comfort" at that time meant flying in a Boeing 747 wide-body aircraft. Obviously a business jet could not be so wide, but at least it could be wider and more comfortable than the competition. The only aircraft with the big-plane characteristic was the top-of-the-market Gulfstream II, an expensive aircraft that had neither the supercritical wing nor the high-bypass engines. If a new airplane based on Lear's idea was to be launched, it would have to deal with Grumman as its main competitor, and Grumman was already considering launching an improved model that would be capable of flying intercontinental. Time was of the essence.

Lear called up a friend, aeronautical engineer Larry Heuberger, and the three of them began banging out some specifications for the new jet. If it was to beat a potential threat from Grumman it had to be lighter, just as roomy, more fuel efficient and cheaper, and it had to come onto the market first. It would hold fourteen people. It would fly across the ocean. And it would cruise at 600 miles an hour. It wasn't much more than some drawings, really a wish list, but a roughly hewn and inelegant LearStar 600 began to take shape.

Finding a backer was the biggest problem, and Ally feared that the LearStar would be just another idea to die on a sheet of paper. He had visited or contacted all the serious manufacturers by 1975, and was turned down everywhere. One of those companies was General Dynamics of St. Louis, the behemoth defense contractor.

The last thing GD wanted was another commercial aircraft program. Its San Diego aircraft division had been responsible for the colossal financial failure of the Convair 880/990 aircraft program, at $425 million the largest corporate loss in American history at the time; it beat out Ford's loss for the Edsel, and as a result the 880/990 earned the moniker the Flying Edsel. The fiasco nearly caused the collapse of GD, and while the San Diego division lived on as a component builder for McDonnell Douglas's DC-10 airliner and Lockheed's C-5 military transport, both contracts ran over budget, fell behind schedule and cost GD pots of money.

GD's Fort Worth military aircraft division wasn't in much better shape. After the end of the ill-conceived F-111 program in 1972, which GD's chairman Roger Lewis called a multimillion-dollar example of Murphy's Law, the future of that facility hung in limbo for three years until it took a shot at a defense contract to build the F-16. The prototyping was expensive, and the strain on GD's fiscal resources was showing. Things were so bad that, unknown to Ally, GD was in the process of parting with the company's former jewel, Canadair.

Ally hadn't sensed a flicker of interest anywhere until he ran into Bundy Bundesman during de Havilland's takeover by the Canadian government. Bundy was at the Paris Air Show in 1975 to promote his new commuter aircraft, the DASH-7. The de Havilland company was better known than Canadair to people like Ally and Lear because of the worldwide success of the de Havilland Twin Otter. Ally approached Bundy with the LearStar idea, but Bundy said he wasn't interested.

"We've never built a commercial jet aircraft and I don't think we're about to start now," he explained. "But I've got a friend who's made to order. He needs something like this. I'll arrange a meeting. His name is Fred Kearns and he's president of Canadair."

On the surface it appeared unlikely that one of the industry's most illustrious entrepreneurs would find much in common with a sleepy Canadian military contractor. Yet each had something the other wanted. Lear wanted a company to build his new business jet, and Canadair desperately wanted a new product that would keep it alive. A business jet with the Lear name on it might be just the ticket. It was an improbable alliance, the stormy genius teaming up with a military contractor languishing in the doldrums. But it was Lear's only hope for seeing the LearStar made into a reality.

3

The birth of the LearStar 600

T he huge Canadair parking lots were half empty in November 1975 when Carl Ally wheeled his rented car into one just off Laurentian Boulevard. From the outside, Canadair's facility in suburban Montreal hadn't changed much since the heady days of World War Two, when it had been erected in a farmer's potato field. The wartime gray-painted shingles and sash windows made the place look dowdy and antiquated and every bit the military contractor languishing long after the war ended. Ally was taken through the front doors and down Mahogany Row to be introduced to Canadair's top executives by de Havilland's Bundy Bundesman. Pleasantries finished, Ally gave his pitch.

"Gentlemen, I would like to talk to you about the next generation of executive travel, the LearStar 600," Ally began.

As far as presentations go, this one wasn't very flashy. Mostly talk and a few drawings. There was no market research, apart from Ally's dated Pan Am survey, which indicated interest in a longer range executive jet. Canadair's executives were not overly impressed with the survey, since they believed that a pilot or airplane owner would naturally be in favor of an airplane that would fly farther and faster than what was available on the market. There were letters from companies stating a requirement for an executive jet with range and weight specifications similar to the LearStar. (They were letters from Learjet customers who wanted to see a larger Learjet.) There were inquiries from the newer regional airline operators for a 30-passenger regional jet, which didn't yet exist. Finally, and this interested Canadair's president, Fred Kearns, because it involved a business he had wanted to break into since the days of the CL-44D, there was an up-and-coming air freight company called Federal Express, which was shaking up the courier business with a revolutionary strategy. Ally said FedEx was genuinely interested in buying 40 of the LearStars to replace their fleet of the smaller French-built Falcon jets. All together, Ally boldly predicted, there was a market for a thousand LearStars over the next decade. It was a wild guess. As one Canadair person commented later about Ally's presentation: "It was done by the seat of his pants."

The pitch complete, Ally was given the plant tour. He was delighted by what he saw. In contrast to its antiquated-looking exterior, Canadair's plant contained some state-of-the-art precision manufacturing equipment, including the numerically controlled five-axis milling machines acquired for the Lockheed C-5A subcontract. They were expensive, the best machines around to produce precision components for an aircraft. To Ally's delight, they stood idle. In fact, most of the plant stood idle. He didn't know it, but Canadair's engineering staff was almost completely idle, as well. Apart from the missile and water bomber programs, there wasn't any engineering work going on. Engineers, who keep track of their activity with work-hour sheets, were scrambling to find an hour here and an hour there to charge to a job instead of charging to overhead. Nobody wanted to be counted as overhead, the kiss of death for job security. Even not knowing this, Ally could see that Canadair had overhead problems and needed the LearStar as much as it needed Canadair. He was optimistic and went home feeling that he had finally found someone to build the airplane. The next day Fred Kearns tried to find out if Carl Ally's idea had any merit.

The overheated air, saturated with the sickening odors of hospital food and antiseptic, greeted Fred Kearns as he entered the fifth floor of the Jewish General Hospital in Montreal. He knew the smell from experience. The stress of being the president of Canadair had once landed him in hospital with such a life-threatening heart condition that the owners of Canadair, General Dynamics, nearly had him replaced. He survived and kept his job. This time it wasn't Kearns who was sick but his chief engineer and good friend Harry Halton. Halton was in bad shape, the unfortunate victim of an operation that had gone wrong and left him a paraplegic. Kearns found a feverish but alert Halton sitting up in bed when he entered the room. This was no mere bedside visit to a sick friend. Tonight they were going to make a pact.

He pulled out Carl Ally's line drawing giving three views of a small jet and handed it to Halton, who recognized the drawing and smiled. "So Bill Lear is also thinking of a new 30,000-pound jet airplane," he said with a slight smile; Halton had been telling Kearns for two years that a 30,000-pound jet was exactly what Canadair should build. The timing was right, he had said. Bill Lear, the flamboyant designer of the Learjet, the most popular business jet in the world at the time, also thought the timing was right.

"Can we build it, Harry?" Kearns asked.

"Yes, Fred, we can build it."

"Are you sure we can do it?"

"Of course, we can do it."

"Well, let's shake hands on it."

They shook hands. It was the informal go-ahead to bet the future of Canadair on a new jet program. After Kearns left, Halton told his wife, Steffi, what had happened.

"What?" she cried. "You nearly died the other night and now you've got a 102 degree fever! How the hell could you guys be so crazy?"

Was it destiny or just coincidence? How could it have been possible that Bill Lear and Harry Halton, Canadair's chief engineer, had been both thinking about the same kind of airplane? Was it simply that the time had come to develop this new airplane, and that if Canadair didn't do it someone else would? What is certain is that the technology was there and that such an airplane had been on Halton's mind a full year before Ally described the LearStar to Canadair.

Halton had been thinking of a business jet as a possible commercial venture for Canadair since the company took on a subcontract in 1972 to supply Avions Marcel Dassault of France with components for a prototype of a new 150-passenger commercial airliner Dassault was planning to build, the Mercure. The Mercure program was an engineering success and a marketing failure for the French manufacturer, known for building the Mirage fighter jet, one of the world's best fighter aircraft. It was the last venture for Dassault in the commercial airliner business; for Canadair's part, it cost nearly $11 million in Canadian government development money. Dassault was enjoying some commercial success with a smaller business jet it had come out with in 1963 called the Mystere, later named the Falcon Fan Jet for the U.S. market, the same jet Federal Express wanted to replace with LearStars in its air freight business. If Dassault could go from building fighter jets to successful business jets, Halton reasoned, why couldn't Canadair?

Halton's vision of a new business jet had come into clearer focus and gained some urgency in 1973 when Canada's aviation industry was squeezed by a shrinking market. That year the industry experienced its lowest level of sales in more than a decade, and indications were that the situation was going to get worse before it got better. It was decided that the industry needed to take a hard introspective look at what it could do to reverse this decline, and in 1974 Canada's aerospace companies met at the Château Montebello in Quebec for a two-day conference.

It was at this gathering that Halton, speaking for the Canadian airframe sector and Canadair, said he saw a commercial opportunity in a new generation of small civilian jet aircraft, one that would use the new developments in engine and aerodynamic design technology. Halton was short on details as to what the airframe would look like save for one, that with a fan engine, it would have a maximum gross takeoff weight of 30,000 pounds. What Lear and Ally proposed was very nearly in that range.

The question was, could Harry and his engineers build this kind of airplane? Halton certainly thought so.

Harry Halton was born in Czechoslovakia in 1922 to one of the original Pilsener brewing families of Bohemia. Halton was the only child, and when Germany invaded Czechoslovakia in 1939 Harry was sent to school in England. He never saw his family again; they were wiped out by the Germans in the Holocaust. Halton got into the aviation business almost by accident. An electrical engineering graduate from Northampton Polytech, Halton went to work for a medium-size outfit that in peacetime produced electrical equipment for racetracks and the London subway. During World War Two, the company joined the war effort and Halton found himself designing and making primitive avionics equipment for most types of British wartime aircraft. After the war Halton, his wife, Steffi, and their young son emigrated to Canada where Halton landed a job at Canadair in 1948, a year before Kearns joined the company.

By 1975 Halton had been promoted to executive vice president. His rise through the ranks was based in large part on his ability to manage the many different disciplines of aeronautical engineering and make them work on a single product. He had an unusually charming management style. While other senior managers in aviation tried to move things along by shouting louder, Halton would feign ignorance and approach issues as if he had just walked in off the street. This method elicited the thinking of his engineers without patronizing them. Aviation engineers are a breed apart professionally. They sit in their corner working over sheets of paper that are absolutely incomprehensible to the layperson. They deal in a realm of knowledge that is extremely difficult to manage. Halton always recognized this and treated his engineers sincerely but firmly. He respected their abilities and learning and approached them with the attitude that their skills had to be drawn out of them with seduction and charm. He routinely surprised his engineers by following up an innocent query with a devastatingly accurate display of his understanding of a problem. Halton had earned the respect of nearly every engineer who worked for him.

Halton was certainly one of Canadian aviation's brightest stars by 1975. His breadth of experience and understanding of the aviation business was formidable and had been gained almost entirely at Canadair. He was also something of an aberration. Usually the engineering department of an aviation company would be headed by an aerodynamicist. Almost certainly an aerodynamicist would take charge of a new airplane program. Halton wasn't an aerodynamicist; he was an electrical engineer. He always defended his credentials with the argument that an aerodynamicist couldn't be trusted. He felt that the field of aerodynamics was so arcane it was easy for the aerodynamicists to persuade management to make business decisions based on questionable engineering arguments. Halton believed in systems, not in fancy designs.

Halton's education on this matter came when he was heading the CL-89 missile program in the late fifties. It was by far the most complex program ever undertaken by Canadair, an engineering-

intensive project, and Halton and the other engineers were having a
lot of trouble getting their missile to fly straight. In a panic they called
General Dynamic's missile division for help. Irv Buckler came up
from GD's Pomona missile division. He was a brilliant engineer with
a keen understanding of what was being called "systems engineering."

At the time Canadair knew what systems engineering was, to a
degree: it was the part of the program that made sure all the components of a product worked together. However, Canadair treated
systems engineering like any other discipline in the program, like
aerodynamics, electrical, weights. That, said Buckler, was all wrong.

"You guys think systems engineering is some sort of separate
discipline," Buckler told Halton one day. "It isn't. It's a way of life,
and until you understand it's a way of life that permeates the whole
engineering department, you're just not going to make it."

Halton got the message and from then on worked to make systems
engineering a religion in the company. It wasn't easy, and Halton
often found it difficult to instill the idea in his people. Each discipline
had to understand it had a responsibility for making the system work
as a whole rather than have an outside group worry about systems
engineering. The difficulty lay in the fact that Canadair employed a
whole generation of British engineers for whom this idea was alien.
These engineers came out of the era of the designer-based program,
where the designer of the product, usually an aerodynamicist, made
sure all the systems worked together. As aviation programs became
more complex, this tradition of designer-run programs became obsolete. Indeed, Canadair's engineering talent lagged behind the rest of
the industry in this respect, and Halton had a considerable challenge
in bringing his people to the new ways of thinking.

The stocky electrical engineer with the odd European accent
proved his ability to pull together all the elements of a complex
technical enterprise. What Kearns proposed would be Halton's
greatest challenge and a not-to-be-missed opportunity of a lifetime.

When Kearns came to Halton's bedside in 1975 with a drawing of a
new airplane, Halton knew that Canadair did not have the best
reputation in the Canadian aviation industry. He was friendly with
most important people in the industry, and he was acutely aware that
Canadair had a credibility problem. Compared to de Havilland,
Canadair was the flaky twin brother. De Havilland was considered a

successful company because it stuck with what it knew, propeller-driven small aircraft, and made a business out of it. By contrast, Canadair had been into everything and stayed with nothing. Canadair designed and built a world class jet trainer, the CL-41 Tutor, the first company-designed, company-built airplane, then dropped out of the trainer business. It got into the cargo transport business with the CL-44D then dropped out after only a short run. It built the CL-84 tilt-wing aircraft and, with the end of the Vietnam War, got out after making four prototypes. Canadair also built the anti-submarine warfare (ASW) CL-28 Argus, a world-class ASW aircraft, and then stopped production. The CL-215 water bomber was an on-again off-again program. The CL-89 missile program would have come to an end if Halton hadn't decided to use the program to preserve his engineering staff and to initiate work on a second-generation product.

Everything Canadair tried to get into in the way of a new business had failed to carry over the long term. De Havilland, on the other hand, seemed to be blessed. While Canadair struggled to get into targeted markets, de Havilland sold airplanes into markets it had never imagined when its products were in the planning stage. The Twin Otter was never designed as a small transport for commercial airlines, yet there were more flying as commercial transport than in the intended market, the U.S. military. The best that could be said about Canadair was that it did a good job of building other people's products for limited markets. No wonder Halton worried about the reaction to the news that again Canadair was thinking of trying to target a new product to a new market.

Despite the reaction of the industry and the relative unpreparedness of a company at the low end of a cycle, Halton was confident that Canadair had the talent and experience to pull off a new airplane program. Of the 250 or so engineers at Canadair Halton had targeted for protected status, nearly all were still with the company. Kearns was offering Halton more than just control of engineering; he was offering global control of the program, from conception to delivery. This would be more than Halton had handled before. His skills in management were mostly in engineering-intensive projects, not in manufacturing-intensive areas. When Kearns asked Halton if he could build the LearStar, Halton could only hope so, because he knew of Canadair's manufacturing capabilities largely by reputation.

Halton's hopes were grounded, however, in a genuine belief that the company's manufacturing division had a first-class reputation.

He knew that Canadair had learned a great deal from some of the best companies in the industry, from Boeing, Douglas, North American and Lockheed. Canadair's drawing system used the Douglas Santa Monica system; Canadair learned about transonic aerodynamics from North American on the F-86 Sabre program and from Lockheed on the supersonic CF-104 Starfighter; autoclave technology from Bristol; quality assurance from Boeing; power controls from North American; modern bonding technology from General Dynamics and Lockheed; composites from Lockheed. The list of knowledge and technology transfer was extensive, and in terms of manufacturing technology Canadair was way ahead of de Havilland. Canadair was a far more productive company than de Havilland, thanks to a superior manufacturing capability. It also produced successful high-technology spin-offs. CAE, the large manufacturer of flight simulation equipment, did a very nice business in airborne magnetic anomaly detection equipment for defense forces in half a dozen countries; CAE got into the business after the Canadair engineers who developed the technology for the RCAF jumped to CAE.

Canadair had always tried to maintain an active research and development team and to keep it working on experimental design. With the help of the Defense Industrial Research program out of Ottawa (killed by Defense Minister James Richardson during cost-cutting measures in 1974), Canadair was able to keep a highly trained team of about a dozen aeronautical engineers working on various experimental projects. Among Canadair's research and development workers during that time was a group developing computer methods to study transonic aerodynamics and high-lift systems for a new wing design for high and low speeds. This work was a continuation of the ground-breaking aerodynamic research work done by U.S. government aeronautical engineers, which Canadair had gained access to and later applied to the Sabre warplane program. This sophisticated aeronautical design experience would prove to be one of Canadair's best design assets for developing a new generation of aircraft. As well, Canadair had a very strong subcontractor network in place. To the dismay of its union, Canadair as prime contractor always kept at least a modicum of work with its network of subcontractors. If the company wanted to start up a large program, it had good subcontractors to rely on.

Halton did not harbor any serious doubts about Canadair's ability to take on a new program. After Kearns's bedside visits in the winter of 1975, Halton contemplated the challenge that would lie ahead of him if Kearns decided to proceed. Any way he looked at it, it was the biggest risk to be taken in a high-stakes industry. And success depended on the ability to get the aircraft designed and built right the first time.

Most aircraft designs are the result of evolution. A company develops a sound airplane and discovers later, when the technology has advanced, that a similar design incorporating these advances will make a better airplane. This is called the derivative process. The North Star was a derivative of the DC-4, itself a derivative of the DC-3. But the LearStar 600 would be a completely new airplane, and Canadair would begin with a clean sheet of paper. It was the biggest challenge in the company's history: new wings, new engines, new airframe, new systems. Halton was well aware that fifteen years earlier, the A.V. Roe Company of Toronto had collapsed after attempting the same challenge with the Avro Arrow. Airplane design and production were changing dramatically thanks to new technologies, and despite Lear's claim that the airplane should be relatively simple to build, in Halton's mind the LearStar was shaping up to be a huge technological gamble.

Halton knew of at least one successful example of such a challenge. Donald W. Douglas was an exceptional American designer in the 1930s who had an opportunity to bid on a large order of aircraft. Douglas assembled a collection of recent advances: new engine cowlings that offered better performance, all-metal frames, retractable landing gear, internally braced wings and wing flaps. He put them together and came up with the Douglas Commercial One, or DC-1. It was followed quickly by the DC-2 and later the DC-3, which revolutionized world air transport and for a long time was the most successful aircraft program in the world.

If Halton needed to find a reason to overcome the pain of his sudden illness, the LearStar 600 was it. It set him humming. This was what he had been waiting for, the opportunity to build a completely new airplane. It was the dream of any aviation engineer who wanted to lead his industry. The risk lay in the likelihood that he wouldn't be given the luxury of perfecting the technologies in a third version, like Douglas.

The people who actually build the airplanes, the tradespeople who drill and bend the metal out of blocks and sheets and shape it into an object of grace and sometimes even beauty, say that the basic idea of the airplane hasn't changed much since the first all-metal airplanes. Almost every advance in aeronautical engineering has been in technology and not in basic design. To back this up they point to large and successful aircraft companies that have survived by becoming very set in their ways. Ways differ slightly from company to company. There is the Boeing way, the Lockheed way, the Douglas way. The "way" is really a kind of philosophy, an orthodoxy about how one builds an airplane. Change doesn't come easily to aircraft companies. If there was one thing Canadair did not suffer from, it was an overbearing corporate orthodoxy about how to build airplanes. Canadair's reputation for designing and building "Canadair" airplanes was modest compared to its history of building airplanes developed by others.

If Halton got his chance to design a new airplane for Canadair, then Andy Throner, the company's vice president in charge of manufacturing, would be the man to build it. In 1975 Throner was a 25-year veteran of the company who had started as a preflight mechanic. Throner was responsible for all the tradespeople who would be called upon to build the new jet, and he was convinced that Canadair had accumulated enough manufacturing experience to build whatever Halton wanted to design. That experience came from building other people's products and learning their philosophies about tooling and manufacturing.

Throner had learned his trade in his native Germany during a four-year apprenticeship at Messerschmitt-Bolkow-Blohm, and when he came to Canadair he joined a number of highly skilled tradespeople from Italy and France. During the fifties Canadair developed a formidable manufacturing capability through the use of in-house apprentice programs and the acquisition of high-precision tools. By the time Throner took charge of manufacturing, Canadair had the largest machine shop in Canada and a reputation for producing quality products.

The more complex projects always provided Throner with the greatest challenges and opportunities for learning. One of them was the CF-5 fighter airplane built under license from Northrop for the Canadian government. For Canadair the aircraft proved to be a major challenge to build, partly because it had a completely machined wing. That meant the wing was not made by bending pieces of sheet metal and joining them with rivets; rather it was made from solid blocks of metal that had been precisely sculpted by drills and chemical processes. Such precision required tools and processes that could meet very high degrees of accuracy and tolerance. Northrop showed Canadair how to make parts with lower degrees of tolerance that would still fit together by adjusting the manufacturing process. This tactic became part of the Canadair repertoire of manufacturing capabilities.

Canadair had other jobs that called for complex machining and manufacture. On the Lockheed C-5A program it made big and small machined parts working in titanium. On General Dynamic's F-111 project, the division learned to make the wing box and pivots for the variable-geometry wing, a job with very precise requirements. And on the ill-fated Dassault Mercure project, which stopped production after 16 aircraft, Canadair was exposed to a whole new philosophy of precision tooling. The North American philosophy of designing and building precision parts dictated that a female part and a male part were each made with high tolerances so that the two would faultlessly join together in assembly. The French, on the other hand, believed it was futile to try to get both parts to high degrees of tolerance since the assembly process could easily be stalled by two parts that didn't fit. Better to design the parts with varying tolerances and let the assembly person make the adjustments for a final fit. This difference in philosophy reflected the lower degree of skill of the North American tradesperson compared to a European counterpart, and the belief that machines, not people, build airplanes. The European idea fascinated Throner, although it was clearly more suited to a company like Dassault than to Canadair. North American companies, including Canadair, hired their tradespeople pretty much off the street, gave on average no more than six weeks of training, then put them back on the street when times got bad. Dassault gave employees jobs for life and put them through many months of apprenticeship. A Dassault worker assembling parts could be trusted to bring the tolerance of the assembled parts into line. In North America this was not expected of the worker, and the two parts had to be tooled to exact tolerances. Nevertheless, Throner applied the French approach on occasion when the right people were behind the tools. Another trick of the trade for Canadair.

Canadair's factory had its share of horror stories. The first airplane it ever designed and built entirely in-house, the CL-41 Tutor, had a peculiar stalling problem that was caused by an error in manufacturing. One day in 1964 an RCAF pilot in training was approaching the wrong runway at a military airfield outside Edmonton. The tower ordered him to divert to another runway. As the pilot entered a high-speed turn the airplane stalled and crashed. The Canadair accident-investigation team discovered that, to fit the leading edge on some of the airplanes, workers had been using baseball gloves filled with sand. This installation process made each leading edge different and made the stall characteristic of each airplane different.

For the most part, however, in terms of meeting the schedule with a quality product, Canadair had a solid reputation in the industry. Canadair did a good job on the F-111 swing wing box, and General Dynamics rewarded the company by making it sole supplier. Boeing, one of the most demanding companies, gave Canadair more quality awards than any other airframe component subcontractor. If there was one thing that bothered Throner about the launch of a new airplane program it was that he could no longer expect the technical support he had received from General Dynamics, because Canadair was being sold to the government. Still, Andy Throner could build just about anything Harry Halton wanted.

The new year of 1976 heralded the beginning of a new life for Canadair. The company had been sliding perilously close to oblivion only a year earlier. Now it had a new owner, the Canadian government, it had a design on the boards for a new airplane, and its top engineer, Harry Halton, was recovering nicely, albeit paralyzed from the waist down. To ice the cake, Ottawa's order for CL-215 water bombers had doubled, resulting in the largest production run for the aircraft since its launch. Fate, it seemed, was smiling on Canadair, considering the company nearly lost the LearStar to another company.

Halton knew of Bill Lear only by reputation and had never dealt with him personally or professionally. During one of Kearns's numerous visits to Halton's bedside—he visited Harry nearly every day—Halton said he would like a team of Canadair engineers to go down to Stead, Lear's facility outside Reno, and have a look around.

"It'll give me an idea of what sort of person we're dealing with here," Halton told Kearns.

In January 1976, a team of Canadair engineers flew to Stead. What they found was a Nevada ghost town. The hangars were empty. Blueprints and reports no one read were scattered everywhere. Lear was involved in numerous development and production programs that seemed strangely inactive. There was Lear Avia, Lear Motors, Leareno and Lear Enterprises. Yet the companies had only a handful of employees. Lear's new baby, the LearStar, had only one employee, Larry Heuberger, the aeronautical engineer who had been with Lear since 1964 and who had collaborated with Lear and Ally to come up with the early LearStar specifications.

Carl Ally met Canadair's engineers at the Stead facility. Speaking for Lear, who was not present for most of the visit, Ally explained that Canadair would purchase the LearStar program for a fixed sum plus royalties on each aircraft sold. Lear would work as a consultant on engineering and business matters, but he would not have any decision-making authority.

As part of his negotiating strategy, Ally pulled out a file, which he said showed ongoing negotiations with other interested parties. One of Canadair's engineers took a look, and sure enough there were references to financing and shared production proposals with governments in Taiwan, Italy, Kuwait and Saudi Arabia. How serious these other parties were, Canadair's engineers couldn't guess. But it was clear that others had their eye on the LearStar.

The only technical work available to the engineers was the very preliminary design work done by Ben Aziz, the California aeronautical consultant Lear had contracted to come up with an airplane design using the new wing and engines. Not much work had been done because Lear was broke. Lear also had a certification proposal for the LearStar, but a meeting with the Federal Aviation Administration scheduled for the previous November had never taken place. There were wing and fuselage designs, but no load data to support the designs. An engine had been selected—the Avco Lycoming

ALF-502—but it hadn't been certified for flight yet. From what Canadair's engineers could see, the LearStar was still not much more than an idea in the mind of Bill Lear.

Later Lear invited the Canadair engineers to meet him in his office. One of those engineers, Canadair's flight sciences chief, George Turek, was amazed by Lear's attitude toward building the new airplane. From his drawer Lear pulled out a sample of lightweight Plexiglas and tossed it on the table. "There's the windshield for the airplane," Lear said. Turek was confused. What did he mean? Didn't Lear know the windshield was a minor concern compared to the other design challenges of building a lighter airplane? It soon dawned on Turek what Lear was saying. The piece of plastic was a symbol of Lear's idea for a lighter airplane, and all he had to offer was the idea.

The idea certainly appealed to the Canadair engineers who saw a golden opportunity. Lear may have had nothing more to offer than an idea, but Canadair's engineers felt confident they could make something out of it. With what in retrospect was stunning naïveté, the engineers reported to Halton that, from what they saw, the LearStar would be less difficult to manufacture than any of Canadair's other aircraft products with the possible exception of the CL-215. However, they did think Lear's schedule, 24 months from design to certification, was too optimistic. At least they got that right.

In Montreal the engineers delivered their report. Kearns asked Halton if it was worth going any further. Halton said yes. "Then," said Kearns, "I guess it's time to meet the man himself."

Bill Lear came up to Montreal at the end of January 1976. All the negotiations were kept secret and only a handful of employees knew about them, although rumors had begun to float through the company. Halton was still in rehabilitation, the sole patient of world-renowned rehabilitation specialist Dr. Gustave Gingras, and was undergoing an intense program. When Lear came to town Halton got out of the office he had set up at the clinic for the first time since his illness.

Lear was unlike anyone Canadair had experienced. Visitors to Mahogany Row were usually high-ranking generals or foreign diplomats. Low-key stuff. Lear was the complete opposite. His massive body and booming voice, his impressive name dropping, his irresistible charm and boyish playfulness, all these things dazzled Canadair executives. Kearns, a gregarious fellow, took to Lear immediately.

With almost no props, Lear put on a compelling show laying out an aircraft program that would be easy to do and not cost a lot of money and that was sure to sweep the general aviation market off its feet. It was an impressive act. The only one who wasn't impressed was Harry Halton.

"I looked at the drawings Lear brought with him and I listened to what he was saying and the two things were not consistent," Halton would recall later. "He didn't have an expert grasp of aeronautical engineering so some of the terms he bandied about in the meeting didn't make a whole lot of sense. He wasn't offering to sell us a design, he was selling an idea."

When it came to the question period, Halton asked Lear how he could be so sure the aircraft would perform as specified without wind-tunnel test data. Lear stunned Halton with his answer.

"Wind-tunnel tests are only for engineers who have little confidence in their own ability," Lear said, adding that the Douglas Company had spent a fortune on wind-tunnel testing for the DC-9 only to redesign the aircraft during flight testing of the prototype. This was a gross exaggeration of what had happened.

"With today's computer methods you can design an airplane on a computer without having to go into a wind tunnel," Lear said.

That was the most absurd thing Halton had heard. He knew the state of the art, and he knew no manufacturer would dare to go from the computer screen to the shop floor without wind-tunnel data to back up the design. Halton looked at Lear's schedule and realized that if Lear included wind-tunnel testing in his schedule, the schedule would fall apart. Wind-tunnel testing takes time to process and extends the schedule by as much 40 percent.

Halton thought Lear was dreaming. "I recognized pretty soon that Bill Lear is perhaps more an entrepreneur than a designer of aircraft and I have some very great reservations about some of the things he is putting forward," Halton wrote in his diary.

After the meeting, Kearns asked Halton what he thought about the proposal. Halton said he had a lot of reservations but, if Kearns wanted it, he would do some preliminary studies to establish the worthiness of the project. Underneath Halton was not entirely convinced that Canadair needed Bill Lear to design a new corporate jet.

"How involved would Lear be with the project if we decide it's a go?" Halton asked.

Kearns, who knew that he would have quite a sales job on his hands to get his new board's approval for the project, put it bluntly to Halton. "We need this guy, Harry. The Lear name will be vital to selling the project. But don't worry about that now. Let's just find out if we've got something here or not."

The more Halton found out about Lear's proposal, the less he thought Lear had anything to offer. He was particularly concerned by Lear's weight figures. Weight is the great leveler in all aircraft programs. If an aircraft was heavier than planned, then the ratio of the aircraft weight to the thrust of its engines (the thrust-to-weight ratio) was also skewed, and the aircraft wouldn't perform as promised. When Halton and his engineers picked Lear's specifications apart, they found that Lear's weight estimates for an empty airplane (the manufacturer's empty weight) were off by about 50 percent. The plane Lear had in mind would weigh 18,000 pounds instead of 12,000 pounds. By the time the aircraft arrived at a completion center where the customized interior would be built, the weight would be more than 20,000 pounds. The underestimation would haunt the program.

"In retrospect, perhaps Lear's low weight estimates led us to our own relatively low weight estimate of 14,885 pounds," Halton would say later with a great deal of understatement.

Halton needed more data, so he sent three of his top engineers to see Ben Aziz of Aeronautics R&D in California. It was there, Lear had said, that he had all his data on the supercritical wing. While the engineering team found Aziz's outfit to be very capable, there was no sign of the data. On the contrary, when the engineers showed Aziz what data Lear had given them in Montreal, Aziz dismissed it as "exaggerated."

With almost nothing to work with except some dubious Lear inputs on weight, engine type and cruising altitude, Halton set up a LearStar program plan. When a preliminary costing of production, engineering and materiel was completed, Halton was staring at a $500 million program. It dwarfed anything Canadair had risked before on a single program.

By March 1976, Fred Kearns had decided it was time to get a decision. With Halton's program plan for the LearStar in hand Kearns went to his board of directors, a newly constituted government-appointed board that consisted of people who knew very little about Canadair or the business. He convinced them that Canadair had very little to lose by taking an option and everything to lose if it was a good project and someone else got it. After the board approved the motion, Kearns called Bob Wohl, Canadair's vice president of contracts and legal affairs, into his office and asked him to look over Halton's program plan. Then Kearns said, "Let's go to Reno and get an option on this."

Wohl at first didn't know what to make of it all. Wohl, who worked for General Dynamics, had helped with Ottawa's acquisition of Canadair from General Dynamics, and he and his wife were making plans to leave Montreal. She had quit her job and he had called GD's human resources division and asked for a transfer. Wohl was the last original GD executive at Canadair and, as he would say later, he saw the writing on the wall: the glory days were over.

"There were no new defense programs coming down the road and we had just lost a bid to do the final test and assembly on the Lockheed Aurora program," Wohl would later recall. "As far as I could make out, the Canadian government's interest in Canadair was to supply the company with offsets. That is, Canada would buy off the shelf from a foreign company and Canadair would get some of the subcontract work as part of the acquisition deal. Indeed, it appeared to me that Canada was getting farther and farther away from ever developing its own aircraft because of the tremendous costs involved at the time."

Wohl was no stranger to new programs. Born in Chicago to Central European immigrant parents who moved to California, Wohl attended the prestigious University of California law school. But hard times hit his family and he was forced to quit school and take a job reading contracts for the Convair Division of General Dynamics while he continued to study law at a recently founded law school at the Catholic University of San Diego.

Things were positively popping at Convair when Wohl joined in 1956. Sputnik had been launched by the Russians, and it struck fear into the hearts of America's defense policy thinkers, who immediately decided that the Russians were capable of lobbing a deadly missile clear around the globe. Sputnik triggered a tremendous buildup in missile and rocket technology, and in 1956 the Atlas rocket program, launched by Convair the previous year, was in the thick of it. Overnight Convair's missile group went from 500 to

40,000 people and became a separate operating division of GD. Employees worked six days a week for three years.

It was a crash program in more than one sense. The first three missiles launched all crashed, and nobody understood why. The technology was very new and not fully appreciated. The Atlas rocket is really like an inflated balloon—it doesn't have an internal structure. An airplane does. Charlie Ames, the young chief product engineer on the program, asked every engineer what he thought the problem was. Then Ames took all the solutions and, with the okay from the U.S. Air Force, the program's customer, carried out every single recommended change. It worked. The fourth flight was a success, and to this day nobody really knows why.

Wohl enjoyed a fascinating career at GD. After the military program he went on to be GD's Atlas project manager for the Mercury civilian space program and was there when John Glenn rode into space. Recognizing his ability to manage programs effectively, GD transferred Wohl to its headquarters in New York and for several years Wohl flew all over GD's far-flung empire putting out fires that erupted because of poor program management. One of those fires was Canadair's contract for the Lockheed Galaxy program.

In early 1969 Wohl took a call from Montreal. It was Fred Kearns. Wohl had met Kearns on two occasions and knew Canadair was having problems with the Galaxy program. It came as no surprise when Kearns said that the Galaxy was rocking the company to the core and he, Kearns, needed help right away. Wohl went to Montreal and with Kearns began preparing what would be a compelling case against Lockheed, one that would see Canadair win back in damage claims nearly all it had lost in the program. Kearns was so impressed with Wohl's effort that later that year Kearns flew to New York to make Wohl an offer.

"I've just spoken with your boss and he says it's all right if I talk to you," Kearns said. "How'd you like to come to Montreal and be my vice president?" In March 1970 Wohl moved to Montreal.

Six years later, Wohl figured his stint with Canadair was over. Then he went into Fred Kearns's office and found out he was going to Reno, Nevada, to see the famous Bill Lear.

Wohl was impressed with what he saw in Reno. As soon as he entered the office he noticed the prestigious Collier Trophy for excellence in aviation and the pictures of Lear with presidents and movie stars. He was in the presence of a living legend.

The conversation soon turned to business, and that is when Wohl met Mrs. Bill Lear, Moya, for the first time. Her role in the discussions soon became apparent. Lear was having second thoughts. Despite earlier claims that he didn't want any decision-making authority, Lear was asking for that authority, and Wohl and Kearns were refusing to include it in the option. Moya sat through all this silently knitting until Lear's voice reached a certain pitch of anger and frustration. Then in a soft voice she said, "Why don't you and I go out for a minute and talk about this, dear?"

"Yes, Mommy," Lear replied.

Wohl reflected on the fact that he was being asked to negotiate a deal that contained a singular lack of engineering and design contributions from Lear. What is it we're actually buying here? Wohl thought. Lear wanted a lot of money, a guarantee that he would manage the project and a short option period. Canadair had offered $400,000 for the LearStar concept up front, but withheld promises of program management pending board approval, something they knew they would certainly not get. Lear returned with Moya and verbally accepted Canadair's offer. They agreed to meet at the lawyer's office early the next morning to close the deal.

Everything seemed to be going great. Before leaving Reno, Carl Ally gave Kearns and Wohl a little thrill ride. Ally was great friends with an airplane designer named Ted Smith and had bought one of Smith's airplanes, called an Aerostar. It was a remarkable little propeller plane that was capable of great speed and performance. Both Wohl and Kearns had heard of the Aerostar, and when Ally offered to give them a ride Kearns at least jumped at the chance. With Kearns in front beside Ally and Wohl in the back, Ally buzzed a local ski resort, going up the ski runs and over the top of the mountain. Kearns had a ball, Wohl got queasy.

Then Ally gave the controls over to Kearns saying, "I know you're an old fighter pilot, Fred, so take her in and land her." Kearns hadn't flown for more than a decade, and Wohl knew it. But the old instincts were there, and Kearns brought the Aerostar in without a hitch. It sure beat dealing with army generals.

Kearns left the wrap-up to Wohl and happily departed for Florida.

The next day Wohl got up bright and early and went to the lawyer's office. Lear didn't show.

"Where's Bill?" Wohl asked the lawyer, but he didn't know, either.

Lear breezed in shortly before lunchtime and said casually, "I've decided not to go with you guys. I'm going with somebody else."

Wohl was floored. He had no idea that Lear was dealing with anyone else. But he could see there was no changing Lear's mind. He politely said good-bye and left to catch a flight for San Francisco. Perhaps it's a good thing I'm leaving Canadair, he thought, because I really dropped the ball on this one. When he got to San Francisco he called Kearns and broke the bad news. Kearns took it philosophically.

"Well, Bob, if that's the way it is, that's the way it is. We'll just have to wait and see what happens next." Obviously Kearns knew Lear well enough to suspect anything was possible.

Wohl didn't learn until much later what had gone on while he waited for Lear at the lawyer's office. Lear had been dealing with another interested party, Ling-Temco-Vought Corporation (LTV), on the other side of town. LTV's aircraft division had lately become very interested in the LearStar 600, and Lear, who wasn't very happy with Canadair's unwillingness to promise him a major role in the program, tried to get such a promise from LTV. LTV was willing to make more of a commitment than Canadair, although they said they would have to have it approved by higher-ups. That was good enough for Lear, and he said he was prepared to sign the option over to them.

But soon after Wohl returned to Montreal, the LTV offer began to unravel. When LTV's top management looked at what the program was going to cost, a cold wave of reality set in and negotiations with Lear were halted. It devastated the management, who saw the LearStar 600 as a golden opportunity. And it left Lear in the lurch.

A week later a humbled Lear called Kearns and said he was willing to do a deal. There was no more discussion of Bill Lear having a major management role in the program. It was agreed that the deal would be signed in New York in early April.

4

Gentleman Jim

Carl Ally, Lear's front man, was doing a brilliant job of pulling together people who needed each other at just the right moment. He knew Kearns didn't have anyone to market the airplane should Canadair decide to build it. Canadair's marketing department was nothing to speak of apart from staff for the CL-215 water bomber; for the most part the company had only one customer, the Canadian government. If Canadair took up the option to build, Kearns and the other top executives would be expected to round up the launch orders. That, Ally knew, would be an uphill battle, to say the least. These guys didn't know the "bizjet" market at all. But Ally knew someone who did, and it just so happened that someone was looking for a job.

A few days before Kearns left for the New York signing he got a call from Ally. "There's a fellow I think you should meet as soon as possible," Ally told Kearns. "His name is Jim Taylor." Taylor, Ally went on to say, was a marketing genius, the man behind the launch of the industry's fastest-selling bizjet, the Cessna Citation; the man who had sold more than a hundred Falcons, the French business jet, in the United States; the man with a personal telephone directory worth its weight in gold. Ally heard that Taylor had been recently fired from Cessna, and he told Kearns that if Kearns could get Taylor on board he would have the business aircraft industry's number-one salesman.

On the flight to New York to sign the option deal with Lear, Kearns told Halton about Ally's call. It certainly sounded interesting. The program could really use the skills of such a bizjet marketing specialist. "The question is," Halton pointed out, "why did Cessna fire the industry's number-one marketing genius?"

James Blackstone Taylor, the third of six children, took his name and his passion for airplanes from his father, James Blackstone Taylor the elder, known as Jimmie. Jimmie was a dashing figure. Born to affluent Park Avenue parents, he looked more like a bond salesman than a test pilot. Yet for a time—1917 to 1942—the Princeton University dropout was regarded by the U.S. Navy and the aviation industry in general as the most competent, if not the most daring, test pilot who ever took to the air. It was Jimmie who made the first takeoff from and landing on the U.S. Navy's first aircraft carrier, the *U.S.S. Langley*. When he tested civilian aircraft, his violent, unrestricted aerobatic shakedown maneuvers were, according to one witness, "a sight to see." In all Jimmie tested more than 450 military and civilian aircraft and had flown faster and higher than any other human. Eventually the risks of the job caught up with him and he was killed in 1942 at the end of a flight test. Ironically, he died not during a daring maneuver; a new electric control mechanism failed as he was trying to land, and the airplane crashed. Two years before his death Jimmie Taylor had written, "The future of aviation is probably locked up in the dreams of the younger generation and it is impossible to predict what the next few years will bring to the industry. Planes that were marvels a decade ago are regarded as old fashioned and obsolete today . . . Of such things has aviation been made and by our own mistakes we have profited."

One mistake Jimmie Taylor felt he had made was not finishing university. He didn't want his son to make the same mistake and forbade the boy from following in his father's footsteps until he finished university. It was not to be. Jim, blessed with his father's good looks and charming ways, waited until the afternoon following his father's funeral before rushing to join the U.S. Navy. The ever-impatient son felt pretty smart getting in as the first naval cadet without a college education, although as son of ace pilot Jimmie Taylor such things could be conveniently overlooked. Later he would confess that even his high-school diploma was something of a fraud. "The headmaster at my prep school was a good friend of the family, and he sent a letter to go with my application. It said I had graduated when in fact I hadn't. When the Navy found out later they would have booted me out if it weren't for my excellent record."

Taylor stayed with the Navy for four years before he discovered that the regimented life wasn't for him—he was a free spirit. He thought it would be far more interesting to work in civilian aviation. The surfeit of DC-3 aircraft after World War Two gave Taylor his opportunity. Hundreds of the aircraft were being used by small-time operators hoping to cash in on the new boom in commercial air transport. Everybody was using wartime aircraft like DC-3s to make a business flying everything and anything they could get onto a waybill. Taylor hitched up with one of these operators, a company that flew lobsters one way and passengers the other. There was cutthroat competition, and Taylor's company failed after only six months. His last act was to help sell off the company's DC-3. That's when he found his calling: he made his first airplane sale. It was also his last sale for some time because the customer, television personality Arthur Godfrey, hired Taylor to be his personal pilot.

After a two-year stint as Godfrey's aerial chauffeur Taylor left to become sales manager for a small one-product manufacturer of metal caps. The company was sinking swiftly when Taylor joined, and he soon realized why. Nobody had been out selling the product. The company, Upressit Metal Cap Corporation of California, manufactured patented closures for containers that sealed the contents until pressed, hence the name. The company sold its product through distributors who hadn't seen anyone from Upressit in years. Taylor convinced the board to buy a company airplane he could use to tour the country in order to pump up sales. When he discovered that the distributors were carrying many other products and couldn't be persuaded to mount any special sales efforts for the little caps, he decided to cancel all Upressit's distributorship agreements and turn sales over to the company's small sales staff. They were, of course, expected to start flying all over their sales territories.

"Go out there and sell these damn things yourselves, for God's sake!" Taylor told the stunned salespeople at Upressit. "Doesn't anybody around here realize that we'll get bigger margins and we'll get richer faster if we do it this way?"

Taylor's direct marketing gambit worked. Upressit's sales turned around, and Taylor was made president after only two years with the

company. Ten years later, Taylor lobbied the company's shareholders to sell Upressit to its largest competitor, American Flange &
Mfg. Co. It was quite a sales job. The preferred stock was heavily in
arrears, and nothing was offered to the common stockholders for
their vote. Upressit's New York law firm said it couldn't be done.
Taylor had, however, tripled sales and diversified the product line,
and he made shareholders believe that he had the company's best
interests at heart. Unfortunately for Taylor, American Flange, a
family-owned company, did not have Taylor's best interests at heart.
It rewarded Taylor by making him vice president of wining and
dining. "Some vice president," he would later recall. "They wouldn't
even let me see the numbers of my own division." Not only that, the
new owners didn't share Taylor's enthusiasm for business aviation.
The last straw came when American Flange sold Upressit's airplane
and told Taylor to fly commercial. Fed up, Taylor quit and picked up
where he had left off fourteen years earlier: he joined an aircraft
brokerage firm and began selling used airplanes.

Taylor focused his attention on a niche market, and in this he was
ahead of his time. The sibyls of the airplane industry had boldly
predicted phenomenal growth in hobby aviation—a helicopter in
every backyard, thousands of monoplanes parked like Chevys in
huge new urban airports built to meet the demand. It never happened. Taylor knew enough about the business to guess that a good
niche market was the best bet, and he recognized a steady and reliable
source of real profit: rich people, powerful people. Taylor was getting
to meet many of them in his new role as aircraft salesman. The son of
Jimmie Taylor, ace pilot, got on well with the captains of industry
who could afford to buy and sell airplanes for their company or even
for themselves in the same way someone else might buy a car. Taylor
was a good salesman, had ideas about how a corporate airplane could
be used to a company's advantage, and was very well connected.
However, he was selling used propeller aircraft, which paid him
rather modest commissions. He hungered for an opportunity to get
involved with the emerging small jet business, where a fortune could
be made. Moreover, he felt that the newly developing business jet
had more potential than as just a shuttle service for company presidents. It could be a tool for the broader community called corporate
America, a tool to improve business much in the same way Taylor
had done while at Upressit. For Taylor, this was the future; it was

only a matter of time before the small jet took its place in business aviation. In this, Taylor was correct.

In the late fifties the U.S. military told the industry it would buy a small jet "off the shelf", developed with private funds, that could carry eight to twelve people. At the time one didn't exist. North American Rockwell and Lockheed each designed and built the first small passenger jets: the Sabreliner T-39 and the JetStar C-140 respectively. After the military had bought their share, the two aircraft became popular in corporate aviation, particularly the larger JetStar, and it wasn't long before other companies came out with small passenger jets.

Grumman followed a few years afterward with the Gulfstream II, an airplane designed specifically for the top of the corporate aircraft market. Unlike the Sabreliner and the JetStar, the Gulfstream II was designed to provide what the market wanted in a business jet. It would be as fast as the JetStars, which were increasing in number. But its ability to fly higher than airline traffic, to use short fields, to fly coast to coast and to carry a generous payload such as fine mahogany or hand-tooled leather made it an aircraft that would provide the airliner-like service demanded by the chief executive officers of major international companies.

In 1963 Taylor heard that Pan American Airlines' Business Jet Division was looking for a salesperson to market a French-built business jet in the American market. He saw his opportunity to put his belief in corporate aviation into practice.

Since the early fifties Pan Am's legendary chairman, Juan Trippe, had been one of the pioneers in corporate aviation. Pan Am had become involved in corporate aviation out of corporate necessity. Pan Am operated a money-losing network of 88 airports it had acquired after the war and had always sought ways to increase their utilization. Utilization meant landing fees, the lifeblood of a commercially operated airport. One way to increase revenue from airport fees, Trippe realized, was to place more aircraft in the hands of people who could afford them. In 1950 Trippe did just that: he bought 16 surplus Douglas B23 bombers, converted them for executive transport and sold them all to top executives he knew personally.

When business travel entered the jet age Trippe considered acquiring JetStars and Sabreliners and selling them to the business market through Pan Am's newly created Business Jets Division. (He didn't consider the Learjet because it was in the class of small jets and the people he dealt with preferred to fly in larger aircraft.) Then he heard about Avions Marcel Dassault of France, which was trying to interest people in a new small passenger jet it wanted to develop, the Mystere. Trippe told Dassault that if they put fan-jet engines on it, he'd back the program. He placed an order for 40 Mystere business jets with an option for 120 more and took a major equity stake in the program. The airplane was still on the drawing board when Pan Am began casting around for someone with experience selling aircraft to the corporate market.

Taylor heard about this and saw it as his golden opportunity. He had little difficulty convincing Trippe to hire him as a salesman in Pan Am's Business Jets Division. Taylor told Trippe the time had come to change the way jet airplanes were being marketed. Until then jet airplanes had been marketed and sold over lunch; the example of Trippe selling to his friends was typical. Other planes were sold through brokers or distributors. However, if something went wrong with the airplane, the customer and not the broker or distributor had to get it fixed. Customers were at a disadvantage because they had little or no contact with the factory. In fact, Taylor argued, it was probably the whole complex process of owning a jet that was preventing an aircraft company from making major inroads into the marketplace. Taylor wanted to convert the wider corporate world to the religion of business aviation, and he would do it with a promise that the customer was boss. The key would be to give the market what it wanted, just like in the automobile industry, then make it easy for the market to keep and operate the product.

Selling the Mystere in a market that was unfriendly to foreign products, in particular products that came from a country with a special anti-American bent such as France—these were the days of President Charles De Gaulle's anti-American ranting—required nothing less than an aggressive marketing strategy. The first thing Taylor did was give the airplane a name change. He knew he would have to anglicize the name one way or another, and Mystery just didn't cut it. He came up with a list of names for Trippe, who never got back with an answer. Finally Taylor cornered Trippe after Trippe had had lunch with Ford Chairman Henry Ford II, who was marketing the new Ford Falcon. "Look, Jim, let's just call the thing the Falcon." Trippe kept the name even after his French colleagues refused to adopt it because Falcon pronounced in French had a rather vulgar meaning. (In France it is still known as the Mystere.)

Taylor's next step was innovative and no less controversial for the French manufacturer. He tried to involve marketing in the aircraft design process. If marketing was going to stand behind the product, then it would have to know everything about the airplane, and it would have to insure that the airplane being designed met the requirements of its prospective market. The few existing models of business jets that had been built so far were designed first and sold into the market later. The military, for instance, required only that the Jet Stars and Sabreliners accommodate a certain number of people. Lear sold the jet he wanted to build, the fastest small civilian jet in existence. Only the Gulfstream, Taylor's number-one competition, could claim to be a jet designed for the corporate market. The usual practice was to design for pilots and engineers, since the engineers had to build it and the pilots had to fly it. It didn't matter much what the passenger thought about it. Both Grumman and Taylor knew that CEOs decided whether an airplane would get bought, and Taylor wanted the primary aim to be to build an aircraft that satisfied the CEOs.

Taylor wooed this market of CEOs and other high-ranking corporate executives with promises that their corporate needs could be met by an airplane designed with them in mind. Taylor sent dozens of prospective customers, many of whom had never seen the inside of an airplane factory before, on expenses-paid trips to Dassault's factory in France. However, Taylor's plan for a market-driven product was grounded by the French. Henri de Plante, Dassault's chief engineer, was a formidable character with an ego to match, and even the company's president, Claude Vallieres, didn't dare cross him. The only person de Plante listened to was the man himself, Marcel Dassault. In the end, the market was told what kind of airplane it would be receiving.

Taylor made better progress with his notion of "concept selling." Since captains of industry with private airplanes already knew the virtues of having one, and probably owned more than one, Taylor pursued companies that didn't own an airplane and sold these customers on the idea that a flight department could work as a management tool. Taylor was selling more than an airplane, he was selling a concept.

His message appealed more to the entrepreneurial types than to the staid and solid bank presidents who were unconcerned with such things. Entrepreneurship was certainly important to many companies in the 1960s. Corporate America was changing. The proliferation of large conglomerations, products of mergers and acquisitions with powerful boards and rotating leadership, meant the decision to acquire an airplane would be made by a board, not a single person. These boards tried to fight organizational stagnation by promoting entrepreneurial initiative, and for Taylor that meant getting the salespeople, the customers, the deal makers on the company jet and zipping across the country before the competition could get there. It was a persuasive argument, and it helped Taylor to sell a lot of jets.

In the years Taylor worked at Pan Am, from 1963 to 1969, only Learjet sold more aircraft (267) than Pan Am (184). The Falcon became the aircraft of choice of corporate America, and dozens of companies began to operate their own flight departments. By 1969 Taylor had become the guru of selling jet aircraft to the corporate market.

Three years later Dwayne L. Wallace was depending on Jim Taylor to save his program. The lean and leathery Wallace, chairman of a company with one of the best-known names in aviation, Cessna, was in desperate need of a marketing miracle. In the past four years the Cessna company had spent more than $35 million, more than it had spent before on a single airplane program, developing its first business jet, which in 1972 was just beginning to come off the production line. Wallace had predicted that within the decade the company would sell a thousand of these new little jets, a number roughly equal to the total number of all corporate jets ever sold in the United States. It was a bold prediction, and so far only one jet had been sold, to Cessna's engine supplier, Pratt & Whitney of Canada. To make matters worse, general aviation was still mired in a recession; Cessna was taking a beating. Sales were down forty percent; profits were down fifty percent. An old barnstorming pilot, Wallace was again flying by the seat of his pants, but this time the optimistic fly-boy was flying nose down. In 1972 he was depending mightily on Taylor to help him pull his little corporate jet program out of its dive.

The world's largest maker of light airplanes, Cessna was founded at the turn of the century by Clyde Cessna, an aviation designer who had been lured, along with scores of other aviation designers, to Wichita, Kansas, by a rich oil baron who held a competition to design an aircraft for his own use. Many designers remained, and since then some 30 aircraft manufacturers had ridden the aviation-business-cycle roller coaster through Wichita. Beech and Cessna were the only ones from those early days to have survived the ups and downs. Cessna survived thanks to the relentless optimism and salesmanship of one man, Dwayne Wallace, Clyde's nephew. In the depths of the Depression Clyde Cessna had closed his aircraft factory; Wallace, then 22, convinced his uncle to reopen his aircraft factory and let him build airplanes. About the only thing Wallace had at the time was optimism. He sometimes had to meet the payroll by scraping together money gathered from his winnings as an ace weekend racing pilot. Wallace eventually got the company on its feet in the 1940s with some big contracts to provide multi-engine trainers for the army. Under Wallace's stewardship, Cessna became a maker of 44 different types of airplanes with 53 percent of the light-plane market. Lear, another alumnus of Wichita, is remembered as the upstart of general aviation in Wichita. (Unmatched in the industry for his ego and bravado, Lear was circumspect while in Wichita, and viewed the aviation clique there with a mixture of fear and awe.) Wallace is remembered as its blue-blood member.

For many years Cessna's board considered but turned down plans to get into the business jet market. Perhaps rightly for the time, the question always seemed to be, Who needs another business jet? Few in the 1960s could have imagined that the business jet market would take off the way it did a decade later, and the Learjet, which surprised everyone with its success, had a solid grip on the class of small business jets Cessna wanted to enter. A maker of piston-powered aircraft, Cessna was also constrained by its experience with jet technology, which was limited to the AT-37 trainer, which competed with Canadair's CL-41 Tutor. Cessna hadn't developed a turboprop product. The cost of developing new engine technology and a new airframe would have been tremendous, certainly more than Cessna's board was willing to gamble at the time. One proposal, to convert the AT-37 into a two-passenger business jet, was correctly deemed not what the market had in mind.

By the late sixties, new developments in turbofan engine technology and new restrictions on aircraft-generated noise—a bad blow to aircraft operators with older engines—made Cessna think once again that maybe there was a need for a new small business jet. Furthermore, if it were a small enough business jet, it could get businesspeople into small airports until then used almost exclusively by propeller-driven aircraft. In 1967 Pratt & Whitney of Canada (which for a brief time was called United Aircraft of Canada Limited) approached Cessna with a design for a new turbofan engine, and Wallace knew he had found his engine. Pratt & Whitney and Cessna signed a joint deal to develop the new turbofan to go with a new airframe. It was an investment with tremendous risk for both sides.

Deliveries of the new jet, smaller and less expensive than a Learjet, came on stream just as a recession hit, and again the question was asked, Who needs another business jet? Especially now? *Forbes* magazine wrote that year, "The longer sales stay down, the more he [Wallace] sounds like an old-time Wichita barnstormer flying by the seat of his pants." At this point it was all up to Taylor. It was his program to make or break.

Taylor joined Cessna in 1969 with all the subtlety of an invading force of tanks. At first the five-passenger Fanjet 500 was going to cost $590,000. When Taylor got there, he changed the name to Citation (after Triple Crown winner Citation) and boosted the price to nearly $700,000. The price included a complete ready-to-go package designed for the concept market, that is, for customers who had never owned an airplane before. He invited pilots and their bosses to the Wichita factory and went on the road with an innovation in jet-plane marketing—a full-scale mobile mock-up of the Citation's interior. He launched the broadest marketing studies ever undertaken of the business aircraft market and began identifying a host of business operator requirements rarely if ever considered during a business jet development program. But perhaps his most controversial marketing technique, at least for Cessna, had been to shut out Cessna's vast network of dealerships, the backbone of the company's success until that time, from the program. It was a bold move that ultimately helped the Citation achieve success in the market, but it also may have cost both Wallace and Taylor their jobs.

As Taylor saw it, Cessna had to overcome an image problem before it could go out into the world and sell jets. People thought Cessna made little propeller airplanes, not jets. He said the best way to beat that image was to sell directly from the factory, not through distributors, who were used to selling the little airplanes. The factory would support and service the aircraft. The decision angered many of the board members who felt that the company owed a great deal to the 600 or so distributorships who sold Cessna products. Taylor had a certain view of these distributorships: he saw them as cluttered hangars run by people who knew a great deal about handling an airplane and little or nothing about handling customers. For many of the distributors, the only sales tool was price cutting, paring their gross margin on planes to sometimes five percent. Taylor wanted something completely different. Instead of selling a stripped airplane and letting the customer select the options, Taylor wanted a total package that included avionics, training of pilots and mechanics and a service and maintenance program. He wanted to make acquisition and maintenance of an airplane easy, not complicated. And he would offer all this right from the factory. Taylor didn't want to compete on price, he wanted to compete on the overall product.

Wallace backed Taylor and gave him carte blanche to set up an independent factory-based marketing organization, and Taylor started looking for salespeople. Cessna didn't have much of a marketing department, given the system of distributorships in place, and what salespeople Cessna did have Wallace didn't want working for Taylor, since he thought they should continue selling what they knew how to sell, small propeller airplanes. In the end, the Citation marketing organization bore the indelible stamp of Jim Taylor. He began picking his crack team of salespeople by placing an advertisement in the *Wall Street Journal*, and more than 350 individuals showed up for interviews. These were no ordinary interviews: they lasted eight hours and involved knowledge, logic and character testing. One participant said it was like a screening program for NASA, not an application for a sales job in the aviation business. The field was extremely competitive because a job selling airplanes could make someone very rich, and because the recession had created a bumper crop of unemployed professionals looking for work. One of the people who responded to the *Journal* ad wrote: "Mr. Taylor, you can take your ad out. I'm your man." That man was David Hurley, a 28-year-old college dropout who joined Taylor and became one of the industry's most successful business-jet salesmen in the United States.

With Bill Juvonen, another successful airplane salesman Taylor had recruited when he was still at Pan Am, Taylor and Hurley crisscrossed the country marketing the new Citation. The start of this enterprise proved difficult for a number of reasons, not the least of which was the airplane's rather bland performance specifications. Simply put, the Citation was a slowpoke. Learjet people called it the Nearjet; other critics said the Citation was the only business jet that ran the risk of being struck by birds from the rear. Another problem was the increasing competition from used business jets, a new phenomenon in an industry where jets had hardly been around long enough to be considered used. Given the legislated requirements of keeping an airplane in a near-new state for safety reasons, prices for used but top-condition aircraft were on average 25 percent less than the cost of a new airplane and offered a tremendously competitive option for a company looking for a business jet. Were it not for the U.S. government's 10% investment tax credit on new capital acquisitions, which lowered the spread between new and used aircraft prices to 15%, the Citation might never have been sold.

Taylor's marketing style was comprehensive. He launched one of the first mass-market campaigns for the industry. The names of 55,000 "prospects" around the globe were put in a computer and became part of Taylor's promotional pipeline. A typically bizarre Taylor marketing gimmick that got the customers' attention occurred when he planned a demonstration flight and sent invitations—by carrier pigeons! A more risky gimmick that was scoffed at by the critics was Taylor's leasing plan, which offered a lease on a Citation for six months to a year for a $50,000 refundable deposit. The thinking was, once leased, later sold. Mitsubishi, another small aircraft manufacturer, had tried the same strategy several years earlier with disastrous results, leasing many of the MU-2 turboprop corporate planes it had assembled in Texas. Mitsubishi ended up with a lot of planes when customers decided not to buy.

Fortunately, Taylor's schemes worked in Cessna's favor. In 1969,

Taylor had boldly predicted that Cessna would deliver a thousand Citations within a decade. In 1972, during the recession, *Forbes* pooh-poohed that prediction. A decade later, a contrite *Forbes* magazine reported on the one thousandth delivery of a Citation and mentioned with good grace its erroneous prediction in 1972. There are more Citations than any other business jet in the world today.

But many on Cessna's board never forgave Taylor for shutting out the dealer networks. Longtime dealers felt betrayed, and some urged customers not to buy Cessna jets. "I'll be damned if I'll help 'em," one of them was quoted in an industry magazine. Taylor also opposed the plan of the company, backed by the dealers, to have the Citation certificated for single-pilot operation. The dealers supported this because they wanted to tap into the single-pilot market, the one they knew best, but Taylor continued to oppose anything that had to do with the dealers. The board had to be concerned by this. They had approved the decision because Wallace had insisted it be done his way, but it had been a hard decision to live with, and despite all his marketing successes, Taylor, who had already sold 300 aircraft by 1976, was never embraced by the board as a member of the Cessna family.

Taylor had also alienated a number of Cessna's engineers with his incessant meddling. He still believed the business jet should be a market-driven product, and he drove engineers to the brink with a flurry of market-based design requests. A former Cessna engineer recalled the end of Taylor's tenure at Cessna: "We heaved a collective sigh of relief and went home to celebrate."

So why was Jim Taylor fired? "A change in management," Taylor said later. In fact, Taylor got caught in a palace coup that saw Cessna's heir apparent, Delbert Roskam, suddenly retired, and Dwayne Wallace was suddenly kicked off Cessna's board of directors in a purge widely believed to have been directed by Wallace's own protégé, Russ Meyer. Meyer was an Ivy League lawyer with wealthy connections (his wife was a Kodak heir) who had left a successful law practice as an associate to a celebrity defense lawyer to become the president of Beaby Aircraft Co., a maker of small recreational airplanes. He later negotiated the company's sale to Grumman, then became president of Grumman's Gulfstream American Division. Wallace discovered Meyer while the latter was at Grumman and offered Meyer a vice president's job at Cessna. Sometime after

Meyer's arrival, the board rebelled against Wallace. Meyer was made chairman and Wallace, the man who took a bankrupt company and made it a household name, was removed from the board. Wichita buzzed with gossip over the bizarre corporate maneuver. Meyer and Wallace apparently never spoke to each other again, though both sat on the board of Wichita's largest bank and a number of society committees. What was behind the board revolt has never been made public, but many believe it was Wallace's decision to shut the powerful dealer network out of Cessna's most profitable aircraft program.

When Meyer took over Cessna in 1975 Taylor had built himself a nice little empire with the Citation program. The Citations sold into the market were being serviced after sale by Taylor's group, which included scores of Cessna employees. Meyer wanted control of the Citation program; he wanted to launch a family of Citation aircraft. It was obvious both couldn't control the program.

If Taylor was conspicuous by his success within the company he was also conspicuous by his consumption of company money in the name of marketing. Before his departure from Cessna, Wallace once complained to Taylor about his extraordinary lunch bills at New York's posh 21 Club, to which Taylor replied, "You know, Dwayne, you can't sell Citations at the YMCA." Meyer was also concerned by this, but he was more upset with Taylor's riding roughshod over the dealers. Meyer had supported the dealership method at Grumman and wanted to restore good relations with the dealers at Cessna. He also had a department of engineers who felt harassed by Taylor. One way to appease those people and gain their support and confidence after the purging of Wallace would be to ditch Taylor. It happened at the end of March 1976, a week before Canadair signed the option with Lear.

After a routine sales meeting Meyer asked Taylor to stay behind. Meyer closed the door then sat down. "I've decided, Jim, that our philosophies are not compatible and that one of us has to go and it certainly isn't going to be me." Bang. It was all over for Taylor at Cessna. Meyer wasn't ruthless. Although Taylor had been with Cessna only seven years, he did get a "vested interest," a sort of capital annuity paid to executives who stay at least ten years, pro rated to seven years. But Meyer was petty. Taylor lost his club privileges and the company car even though he would be living in Wichita until he got his family settled elsewhere.

By the time Taylor left Cessna he could name every CEO who operated a business aircraft or should operate one. (Taylor had taken a memory training course while at Cessna.) He believed his concept marketing, selling to the successful entrepreneur who had a small executive aircraft or who was interested in acquiring the first executive aircraft, was the key to market growth, and that the successful business jet would be one designed with the market in mind. With his list of Falcon and Cessna customers, he knew the business like nobody else and was a hot property. Rockwell was spending a small fortune on a re-engined version of the Sabreliner jet and quickly made Taylor an offer. Carl Ally heard about Taylor's firing, too, and immediately called Kearns.

"He's expensive," Ally told Kearns of Taylor. "But he's worth it."

A few days later Taylor was in Montreal meeting with Kearns. A deal was worked out, and afterward Taylor called his two top salesmen, Dave Hurley and Bill Juvonen.

"Come to Montreal right away," Taylor told them. "I've found us another airplane to sell."

Getting Taylor on board the proposed program would prove much easier than getting Bill Lear to sign on the dotted line.

5

Opening skirmishes

With tears streaming down her face Steffi Halton struggled with the wheelchair, trying to get her husband to perhaps the most important meeting of his career. She wasn't used to this at all. Steffi was a compact woman with blond hair and generous curves whose life as her husband's "little girl" had been turned upside down by his paralyzing illness. A leading member of Montreal's Jewish community, Steffi was no wallflower. She was smart, determined and successful. But this was almost too much.

It was April in New York, and Steffi had decided she was going to wheel her husband to his meeting. It was only eight blocks from the hotel to Carl Ally's Park Avenue office where Canadair would finally take an option on Bill Lear's design, and Steffi, who was still adjusting to the fact that her husband would be confined to a wheelchair for the rest of his life, thought it would be nice to wheel Harry there on such a glorious spring day. Little did she know that New York didn't have curb ramps on its eight-inch-high sidewalks. With every ounce of strength her little body could muster, she bumped and pushed her way down the seemingly endless eight blocks. Nobody helped her. She cried at the cruelty of her fate. She cried for her husband who could not help her. She cried for herself. But when she finally arrived at Carl Ally's office, Steffi was changed by the experience. Never, she vowed, would this happen again. At Canadair, Steffi soon became recognized as the protector of the man who was going to lead the company's greatest airplane adventure.

There was little Harry could do. He braced and shifted himself in the wheelchair as Steffi faced each curb. Less than one week out of the clinic, Halton was exhausted and more than slightly irritable. He had been woken up very early that morning by a telephone call from Lear. "Your figures for today's announcement are unacceptable, Harry," Lear had said. "We can't release them like this." Before the New York signing, Halton had called up some of his industry pals to check out Lear. "You're getting a handful with Lear, Harry," one of them had warned Halton.

The option signing in New York was going to be very much a Lear affair, certainly an event more grand than the signing that didn't happen when Bob Wohl had been left cooling his heels in Reno three months earlier. Had the Reno signing taken place there would have been a press release, nothing more. Now they were in New York, a city where the aviation media and the largest population of executive aircraft owners were located. Lear had decided to make the most of it. Everybody was going to hear about his comeback. To begin with, Lear didn't like what Canadair was about to announce: an airplane some two thousand pounds heavier than the one he had imagined. As far as he was concerned, the LearStar was still his airplane.

In a last-minute attempt to change the numbers, Lear sent his engineer, Larry Heuberger, to Halton's hotel room. With Lear on the telephone, the three of them wrestled with the numbers.

"That plane's too heavy, Harry," Lear said. "I want at least two thousand pounds taken off it."

For three hours Heuberger and Lear pressured Halton to drop the weight. Halton knew Lear's figures were already too low. He also suspected, from what he understood of the man, that Lear would almost certainly change his mind later.

Lear was unhappy with more than just the weight specifications of the airplane. He realized Halton was going to make his comeback less than he had hoped for, and that he really wasn't going to have much control over the program. Kearns couldn't afford to discourage Lear from thinking he would have a significant role to play in the engineering and certification of the airplane, but he did make it clear to Lear that Halton, as Canadair's chief engineer, would have the final say. In the dispute over the weight figures, Halton had shown that he wasn't about to roll over for Lear.

As everyone gathered in Carl Ally's Park Avenue office a truculent Bill Lear began stalling again. Shades of the Reno incident. Ally saw this and quietly ushered Moya Lear into an outer office, where he told her it was time for her to pull in the leash on her husband. It was certainly Lear's last chance to leave more than just his name behind — the contract called for royalties which, if the program was launched and was a success, would pay the Lear family a generous sum for years to come. (Ally would also receive a portion.) Moya understood the gravity of the situation. Ally left her in the outer office and went to Lear. "Look, Moya's not well. She's in the back room. You better go see her, Bill." Lear disappeared into the outer office. It didn't take long. The royalty agreement was a powerful argument for Moya; she told Lear he should think of his children, who would benefit from it. A few minutes later Lear came back.

"OK, let's get it over with."

At a Society of Automotive Engineers technical meeting in Wichita a week after the signing, attended by Lear and Halton, Lear gave an address on the LearStar 600. Halton listened as Lear presented aircraft specifications completely different from those announced in New York. Lear mentioned only in passing that he had sold the design to Canadair. Halton shook his head.

"So it's going to be like this," he told Steffi.

In Montreal, Kearns could barely contain his excitement. The critical elements were coming together very nicely. He had on the program the designer of the world's most successful business jet, Bill Lear, and he had the industry's top salesmen with Jim Taylor and his group, who had sold hundreds of Citations, another very successful business jet. If the magic of these men could be captured for Canadair's benefit, then the LearStar could become the next Learjet or Citation.

What he really had was a potent blend of personalities and egos, one that would prove to be very difficult to manage.

As spring turned into summer in 1976 a powerless Bill Lear raged against his fate from a room high up in the Château Champlain in downtown Montreal. Slowly but surely his LearStar 600 was turning into something quite different from what he had in mind. Harry Halton and Fred Kearns were designing a monstrosity, and Jim Taylor planned to make it even more monstrous. And they were doing it without Lear's help. That was what bothered him the most.

It didn't start out that way. After the April signing in New York

Halton had two months to come up with a final workable configuration of the LearStar. A maximum gross takeoff weight had to be calculated, then they had to select an engine, determine a range and arrive at a price, all before June. In June Taylor would invite potential customers to Montreal to show them the final picture of the airplane. The configuration wouldn't be frozen. Taylor had convinced Kearns and Halton that Canadair had to listen to the wishes of the marketplace before freezing the design. This would be a market-driven product, unlike previous Canadair offerings. Once Canadair had a configured airplane, orders in hand and an idea of the total development cost, Kearns would seek the go-ahead from the Canadian government in September, the month the Lear option was set to expire. The schedule was extremely tight and at the outset depended on the fullest cooperation of the man who had designed the LearStar 600, Bill Lear. The first thing to go in this tight schedule was Lear's cooperation. Within a short time he had alienated himself from the program.

Lear was disappointed over who would build the first version of the LearStar. After the April signing he had reason to hope he would build the prototype of the LearStar in Reno. Informally, this is what Canadair had in mind. This would have given him considerable influence over the design of the airplane. Then he would handle the certification by U.S. aviation authorities. He had good credentials in this field, given his fortuitous experience certifying the Learjet 23. But when Halton made his first visit to Reno shortly after the New York signing, his interest in seeing Lear build the prototype declined precipitously.

Halton was disappointed by what he saw. The reports from his engineers seemed to differ from the reality. Lear had offered his Stead facility for the flight testing and certification program, but since Stead was surrounded by a tight ring of mountains, a flight-test program was out of the question. Halton wasn't impressed with the people or the facilities, either, and decided that his engineers' glowing reports of Lear had been based on their enthusiasm to see the program proceed.

Back at Canadair, Halton asked Jim Taylor, who was now working in Montreal, if Taylor knew someone who could give him an honest assessment of Lear's strengths and weaknesses. Taylor recommended a former U.S. Defense Department researcher called Albert

W. Blackburn, known in aviation circles for his ability to spot the flaws in unsound airplane programs. Blackburn's report didn't have much to say in Lear's favor. Lear, he said, went bankrupt with the early Learjet models because of terrible drawings, poor quality, poor systems design and cosmetic gimmickry instead of sound engineering. Blackburn's report confirmed Halton's suspicions.

Lear continued to press Halton to let him build the prototype. He said he personally knew of aircraft parts suppliers and vendors from the west coast who were competent but hungry and who would do the prototype work cheaply and quickly in exchange for some promise that they would supply the program with parts. Halton had Lear's West Coast suppliers checked out by his own people. Most of the suppliers were in no position to do the work at the schedule and cost predicted by Lear. Lear had also promised supercritical wing data, but his contractor, aerodynamicist Ben Aziz, said there was no data beyond the preliminary work because Lear had run out of money. Finally, inquiries to Canada's Department of Transport (DoT) confirmed that the DoT would not accept an FAA-approved prototype of the LearStar without checking it. After only one month into the option period, Halton decided that Lear would not build the prototype.

With nothing to do in Reno, Lear came to Montreal at the end of May. For the first few months he lived at the Château Champlain and visited Canadair's offices daily. Canadair had its LearStar 600 design engineering works in a specially set up room in the middle of the Canadair factory, and Lear wandered from table to table telling engineers to change this or to add that. Canadair's engineers thought Lear and his airplane had come right out of left field. Except for George Turek and the people who had gone to see Lear in Reno, the engineers hadn't been informed that the negotiations had taken place. When Lear and his LearStar were sprung on them, there was some confusion. Lear acted like a chief designer when it was known by all the engineers that there was only one chief designer at Canadair, Harry Halton.

The engineers soon realized that Lear had nothing to offer, and they did everything they could to avoid him. When Lear wanted his way, however, there was no avoiding him. Odd Michaelson, the bookish and gentle Canadair chief aerodynamicist responsible for the airplane's aerodynamic design, sustained Lear's wrath after telling him that a 90-inch fuselage diameter and a 20-passenger payload wouldn't work aerodynamically. To carry that many passengers the fuselage would have to be wider. "What do you mean?" Lear shouted. "You don't know what you're talking about!" Michaelson knew exactly what he was talking about. This exchange took place in front of a dozen engineers and sowed antipathy toward Lear. He could not have failed to notice the patronizing attitude of many of Canadair's engineers, who wished only that he would stop disrupting their work. Angry exchanges became more frequent, and soon the engineers were ready to revolt. Halton, recalling Kearns's desire to keep Lear on, reluctantly asked one of his top engineers to "look after that man."

About the only useful thing Halton received from Lear was a back-door delivery of some wind-tunnel test data on the supercritical wing from the Gates Learjet wing study. Such transference of proprietary data is illegal, though not uncommon, in the industry, and it made Canadair paranoid about even using the word *supercritical*. The cost of not being able to promote the supercritical wing directly perhaps outweighed the benefits of the data. Indeed, the supercritical wing was one of the most important features of the new airplane, yet Canadair could only whisper it in the ear of a customer. Canadair did not design a "supercritical wing," but a wing that had a supercritical aspect for about three-quarters of its length; the last quarter had a "modified" aspect. Even though Canadair had experience with transonic designs, in particular on the Sabre warplane program, the wing was still a considerable challenge for Canadair from a design point of view.

The development of the supercritical wing was a big step in the evolution of the jet airplane wing. For many years a constant in aerodynamics was that once an object reached a certain air speed—close to the speed of sound, or transonic speed—drag increased sharply and a large burst of energy was required to accelerate the aircraft past the speed of sound. This issue remained academic until the jet engine made higher cruise speeds possible and aerodynamicists began designing aircraft to fly at supersonic speeds. Many supersonic military aircraft were built in the 1950s, but they could exceed Mach 1—the speed of sound—only by using an enormous amount of fuel to get through the transonic stage.

The Area Rule changed all that. With the development of sophisticated supersonic wind tunnels, which could replicate the environment of an object flying at supersonic speeds, and with the application of computers to the wind-tunnel data, aeronautical engineers could experiment with transonic airplane designs. In the early 1950s, at the National Aeronautics and Space Administration research facility, an aeronautical engineer named Richard Whitcomb made a breakthrough discovery. Using the new experimenting tools he was able to analyse the effect of the distribution of air over the exposed surfaces of the airplane and the resistance it encountered. By redistributing the air over the exposed areas causing resistance, Whitcomb could minimize the fierce turbulence at speeds approaching the speed of sound. The result of Whitcomb's research was a table of coefficients, called the Area Rule, that allowed airplane designers to reduce transonic drag by controlling the distribution of air. Designers worked to design an airplane that would fly more efficiently and at greater speeds.

The development of transonic airframe and airfoil (wing) design distinguished the new aerodynamically advanced airplanes from the merely conventional. The French designers of the Falcon/Mystere business jet gave the airframe a bump around the engine area near the rear of the plane—much like the shape of a cola bottle—which reduced the amount of surface area exposed to drag. This came to be known as the Coke bottle design. Transonic aerodynamics also led to radically new designs for the airfoil. One such design was the supercritical wing, and this is what would make the LearStar different from any other business jet at the time.

To a large extent the concept of a new airplane stands or falls on the aerodynamic design of the wing and its ability to function properly at takeoff, landing and high subsonic speeds. The wing must support the weight of the aircraft structure and its payload; it must store fuel and develop sufficient lift for the airplane as it moves forward through the air. The task of designing a wing involves both the aerodynamicists and the structural designers; each often has to trade off his or her desire to meet the requirement of the other. The objective of both is to have a wing that maximizes lift and minimizes drag. One way to do this is to reduce the exposed area of the wing by reducing the size of the wing. This reduction in size is a planform change to the wing area. Every square inch of the wing surface must work harder to develop more lift. The smaller wing can be made thicker in profile. The two changes, planform and profile, can give the airplane greater fuel efficiency at high cruise speeds. With the use of computer models and wind-tunnel testing, these design changes could be simulated.

Computer simulation helped solve one drag problem in particular: *supercritical airflow.* As the aircraft approaches transonic speed, airflow over the wing passes at supersonic — or supercritical — speeds, even though the aircraft is still traveling at subsonic speed. The supersonic airflow that passes over the wing then decelerates to a lower velocity through a shock wave. This creates a suction and increases drag. Whitcomb and other aerodynamicists used the newly gained knowledge in transonic aerodynamics to examine supersonic airflow. They discovered that the area of supersonic flow produced almost no lift. If the supersonic flow could be defeated, drag would be reduced and the lift capability of the wing would not be affected. British designers were the first to come up with solutions to controlling the peaky sections in the supersonic zone while at the same time greatly enhancing the lift capabilities of the wing. In the late 1950s the first of the supercritical wings began showing up in the design of the airfoils for the British Trident and VC-10 passenger aircraft. The revolution in digital computing power in the 1970s made greater advances possible. The supercritical wing soon promised even better low-drag, high-lift characteristics.

These improvements gave aerodynamicists something to work with. They could make the wing thicker without losing lift capabilities. As well, they could store more fuel in the thicker wing, so the plane could fly farther. Structural designers, however, viewed the improvements with some trepidation. By making the wing thicker, aerodynamicists were making the overall structure of the wing more complicated, in particular where the wing joined the fuselage. The thicker wing caused complications for the structural designer. It wasn't impossible to trade lift for wing thickness; it was just more complicated.

Lear's constant interference and lack of solid contributions made him largely expendable in Halton's vision of the program, but not in Kearns's. Kearns expected Halton to be the chief engineer, but he also expected Halton to use Lear as much as possible. This made things complicated for Halton. Lear often misled and sidetracked the designers, sending Canadair in the wrong direction and wasting valuable time.

Halton knew Lear's weight figures were unrealistically low. The weight estimates determine a host of other design factors, principally how strong the wings should be, how powerful the engines should be and how much it will cost to build the airplane. The weight also determines the performance of the airplane—the heavier the airplane, the more fuel it requires. If the weight estimates are wrong, the whole airplane has to be redesigned to compensate. A variance of a few hundred pounds can have a tremendous impact on the final design.

The retired president of a company that competed in the business jet market did Halton a favor and compared Halton's and Lear's estimates with his experience on his company's program. Both sets of weight limits seemed out. Lear's were off by about 50 percent. The retired president told Halton he was looking at an 18,000-pound airplane. He also told Halton that Lear's cost estimates were way too low, largely because he had underestimated the engineering work-hours required to develop the plane. Halton was jittery over Lear's low cost estimates. He had heard that Dassault, whom he considered the world's best makers of prototypes, had spent $150 million building the first new Falcon 50 prototype. And the Falcon 50 was essentially a derivative of the Falcon 20. Then Halton discovered that the 50,000-foot altitude suggested by Lear, the altitude necessary to achieve the range and performance Lear promised in his LearStar, was not certifiable. Lear failed to mention that in the United States the flight rule stated that only Learjets could fly this altitude. So Halton had to lower the altitude, and that shortened the airplane's range. Ultimately the range was scaled down from Lear's 4,000 nautical miles (NM) to a more realizable 3,600 NM. The size of Lear's wing, 350 square feet, was, according to Halton's chief aerodynamicist, not feasible. It would have to be enlarged, particularly if the weight figures were going to increase. Less and less was this looking like Bill Lear's plane.

Lear and Halton also disagreed over the use of power controls on the aircraft. There are three ways to control the moving surfaces — the rudder and ailerons — that allow the pilot to direct movement of the airplane in the air: manual controls, power-assisted controls or fully powered controls. The Learjet was a small, relatively simple airplane designed to use simple manual control mechanisms. Lear swore by them. But Halton wasn't going to build another Learjet. He wanted a different class of airplane. In Halton's view, the LearStar would be closer in design to the Grumman Gulfstream and Dassault Falcon — roomy, airline-style comfort with all the systems and safety features of a jet airliner. The LearStar was not going to be another hot rod, not even a hot-rod Lincoln. Halton knew pilots would prefer fully powered controls for the aircraft he had in mind. He also knew, from experience on the Sabre program, that designing an airplane's aerodynamic shape is a lot easier if there are power-driven control mechanisms, which give the pilot a larger margin of aerodynamic control over the airplane. Without them, aerodynamicists have to be more careful about the aerodynamics of the airplane. Indeed, the Learjet is a difficult airplane to fly precisely because of the unforgiving aerodynamics of its manual controls. There was no question in Halton's mind: the LearStar would have the power controls or there would not be a LearStar at all. Lear didn't agree.

Halton called in Frank Davis. He had been the boss at General Dynamics' Fort Worth facility during the days of the F-111 and was a highly respected engineer always willing to lend a hand if Halton asked for it. Halton asked Davis if he could prepare a report on the use of power controls for the LearStar program. Davis agreed that power controls were absolutely essential. With report in hand and chin out, Halton confronted Lear.

Lear raved and threatened to disassociate himself from the program. His only power over Halton was the threat of withdrawal of his name from the program, which would have upset Kearns. But if he withdrew his name he would forfeit his royalties, and Halton doubted he would do that.

Lear continued to shout, and Halton lost his patience. He remembered reading about a comment Lear had used to wither a bold engineer. "Listen, Lear, when you put up half the money, you can make half the decisions!"

Lear fell silent. He recognized the comment. When the next

dispute arose, Lear went over Halton's head to Kearns. There wasn't much comfort there for him. Kearns told him, "Bill, I don't know what the heck you're talking about. I'm not the engineer. Go back and discuss it with Harry." With no one to talk to at Canadair, Lear began to make his criticisms public.

Lear was not the only person whose career comeback with the LearStar was being frustrated. Jim Taylor, super salesman, also had some things to prove, and he was on the team pending a final go-ahead. After his experiences with Dassault and Cessna, Taylor was convinced of the necessity of a market-driven product. Since Canadair had no experience in this field, Taylor felt his contribution could make or break the program. He had started Canadair on its way to the promised land of riches by making the company listen to the market. But keeping Canadair on the road would prove to be difficult.

Taylor felt the LearStar could easily be the ticket to taking a big piece of the top-of-the-line corporate jet market then dominated by Grumman and Dassault. Two groups were targeted: those with Gulfstreams and Dassault Falcons who were looking for a replacement, and those with smaller aircraft who were looking to move up to a bigger jet. If Canadair couldn't build an airplane that was better than the Gulfstream and the Falcon, the whole effort would be a waste of time.

To fly bigger, faster and farther than a Gulfstream or Falcon, the LearStar would have to be designed to meet the requirements of one class of corporate jets, with intercontinental range and airliner-type systems and safety features. But in the interest of maximizing the potential market, Fred Kearns had decided, over Taylor's fierce objections, that Canadair couldn't afford to cater strictly to the corporate user. The company would also offer a cargo version of the airplane. Taylor knew enough about the aviation business to recognize the contrary. Diluting the design effort would not be cheap—it would be costly, and it would compromise the features that would compete with Grumman and Dassault. On this issue, Taylor and Kearns had their first conflict. At the center of the issue was a man named Fred Smith and his company, Federal Express.

In 1976 Fred Smith, founder and chairman of Federal Express, was hailed as an innovator who had challenged conventional wisdom about air transport, and in particular the air cargo business. He had had the idea at Yale as an honor student in economics and political science when he wrote a paper about a transportation system that would send goods by air around the country. The goods would be delivered within 24 hours anywhere in the country. Airplanes would all fly from a central airport along spokes to hundreds of airports, return the same day loaded with goods, then the goods would be sorted at the central airport and flown to their destinations the next day on another airplane. It was an early example of the hub-and-spoke system that dominates airline planning today, and the first "just-in-time" system of transporting goods for industry. Smith was a visionary, but the world was not ready: the paper earned a C.

After returning from a tour as a Marine pilot in some of the hottest combat areas in Vietnam, Smith resurrected his dream of an express delivery network. With $5 million of inheritance as his contribution, he managed to raise $72 million to launch Federal Express in 1973. He bought 33 used Falcon jets (it was just after the 1972 recession and there was a surplus of used business jets on the market) and had them converted to cargo haulers to serve the 33 airports for which he had managed to secure landing rights. On April 13, 1973, his first Falcon took off with 18 packages. Volume picked up quickly and FedEx looked like an overnight success until the 1973 OPEC oil embargo. Fuel prices suddenly went up, and FedEx began losing $1 million a month. Smith was forced to find another $11 million, $5 million of which came from Canadair's owners, General Dynamics. (GD was later forced to unload its FedEx interest when it was decided that an aircraft manufacturer could not own part of an airline.)

In a tapped-out and depressed venture capital market, the amounts of money being consumed by FedEx were enough to make the company a metaphor for an industry that was teetering. In its first two years, FedEx lost $27 million. But by 1976, the year Canadair met Fred Smith, FedEx was back in the black, making nearly $4 million on revenues of $75 million, thanks in part to a strike at a major competitor, United Parcel Service Inc. Smith had confounded the critics and looked every bit a winner.

After the OPEC crisis, Smith was determined to replace his Falcons with airplanes that were more efficient to operate. He couldn't reduce his operating costs by using larger aircraft because, in those days before deregulation, his Civil Aeronautics Board operating certificate limited him to using aircraft certificated to carry no more than 7,500 pounds of cargo. He had to find a more efficient small airplane. Enter Lear in 1975 with his LearStar 600. Smith was interested and signed a letter of intent to buy 25 of them if they were produced; however, the letter wasn't binding in any way. A year later Lear hadn't found a backer, and it seemed matters would be left at that. Smith was considering other planes, but then Canadair entered the picture and FedEx found itself being asked again to buy 25 LearStars. This would have made FedEx the most important customer, what the aviation trade would refer to as the launch customer or launch order.

Kearns liked the idea of FedEx as a potential launch customer because it would give the program a broader market base, cargo as well as executive. It was that kind of thinking that would lead Kearns to support Halton's decision to go with the 106-inch diameter fuselage. Halton thought the size was essential to configure an airplane with the flat floor necessary for moving cargo containers. Kearns could see that it would also be big enough for four-abreast airliner-type seating. Indeed, what Kearns saw right from the start was a basic aircraft design that could be modified for use in diverse roles with the minimum amount of design change and cost.

FedEx was Kearns's biggest hope for the success of the program. Kearns saw the future when he flew down to Memphis to meet Fred Smith and saw FedEx's huge automated sorting center, a gigantic hangar where Falcons rolled in and out continuously all through the night, swallowing and disgorging thousands of parcels. But instead of Falcons, Kearns saw LearStars. And not just 25 LearStars but 300 when FedEx expanded into hundreds of other cities. Right from the start Kearns pinned his hopes for success on the success of FedEx.

Naturally, Jim Taylor was far from happy about having FedEx as a potential launch customer. Taylor wasn't pleased with the idea that FedEx, an in-house account he had no claim to, could tie up 25 early delivery positions and the sales commissions they represented. More important, the idea appeared to undermine his understanding with Kearns at the time he came on board: that he would get 50 orders in time for go-ahead if he had complete control of global marketing.

With the FedEx deal underway, it was clear that Taylor's control would be quite limited.

There was one solution to the conflict over delivery positions: a much shorter development schedule. If Canadair could deliver the airplanes sooner, then Taylor would have less to complain about. Indeed, from the start Taylor had put considerable pressure on Kearns to set a short development schedule. Taylor warned that the competition was going to be intense and timing would mean everything. Grumman, Canadair's principal competitor, announced that it was on the verge of launching the G-III, an aircraft that would make it very difficult to sell LearStars to Gulfstream owners. Everyone was talking about building jets with supercritical wings and fuel-efficient high-bypass ratio engines. Even Beech and Mitsubishi, two makers of propeller-driven airplanes, had started thinking of building business jets. The prospect of these manufacturers coming out with competitive business jets all at the same time was a source of considerable concern for Taylor. Canadair had to deliver its product as quickly as possible.

After the New York signing, Harry Halton had come up with a rough schedule to build the first airplane in three years and certified and delivered a year and a half later. The 54-month schedule was 18 months shorter than the norm for launching a completely new airplane. With the FedEx positions taking up a large part of the order book, Taylor said he'd rather scrap the program than wait four and a half years to deliver the first corporate jet. Kearns went along with Taylor's view because the longer the program took the more costly it would be. "This has got to be a cheap program," Kearns reminded Halton. Bill Lear was beside himself with Halton's schedule. "I want to see this aircraft leave the ground before I'm six feet under it, Harry!" Halton slashed the schedule and fixed the first flight for just over two years, instead of three, with first delivery one year later. During informal reviews of the LearStar program by Halton's engineering cronies at Douglas and Boeing, the technical aspects would be generally praised, in particular the airliner-like systems and certification, which would make the LearStar the most sophisticated business jet in the industry, but the critics reminded Halton that his schedule was at best unattainable, at worst crazy.

Taylor continued to be concerned about the possible dilution of the design in the effort to meet FedEx's requirements, which were many. Even before the FedEx order had been signed, it was setting the agenda for a number of issues that Taylor felt compromised his vision of the corporate jet. Taylor's fear (later realized) was that the cargo version would siphon off a significant part of the engineering effort, and that the FedEx cargo requirements would make the airplane heavier. But Harry Halton wasn't about to let marketing tell him what his priorities were. They were set by Kearns and no one else, not even FedEx. Taylor warned Kearns repeatedly that FedEx was a big mistake. He had serious doubts that FedEx was worth all the effort, because he didn't trust Fred Smith. FedEx planned to give only a $250,000 deposit for an order worth more than $100 million, contingent on financing from Ottawa. In terms of overall risk, FedEx was putting very little on the table. It was a problem Taylor could do little about, except complain.

Despite Taylor's misgivings, one of FedEx's requirements helped to make the executive jet a much more reliable airplane and gave Canadair experience in a strategic area of knowledge. The cargo LearStar would have to meet the most demanding of aircraft requirements: dispatch reliability. Essentially, "dispatch reliability" means that the manufacturer guarantees in writing the airplane will be reliable, say, nine times out of ten when it goes to work. This was a novel concept not only for Canadair but for the airline industry. Air Canada, for instance, was negotiating with Boeing over the same requirements, and the Crown airline was finding it tough sledding. Negotiations were no less difficult between Canadair and FedEx. Halton and his team worked closely with Jim Riedmeyer, FedEx's vice president of engineering and operations, to meet the demanding requirements of the FedEx order. Negotiations over these guarantees were long and arduous and ate up a significant amount of time during those critical months before go-ahead. The negotiations ended up delaying the go-ahead by three months. But the effort proved invaluable in later years when Canadair wanted to convince customers of the airplane's operating reliability.

The final and most bitterly contested design issue was the choice of engine to power the airplane. In May 1976, before Canadair's negotiations with FedEx got underway, the biggest fear in Taylor's mind was that Canadair would choose the wrong engine. Taylor wanted General Electric engines for the LearStar. As far as Taylor was concerned, the selection of the engines was really the selection of the soul of the airplane: airplane programs were made or broken on the selection of the engine. It was bad enough to have a cargo-executive hybrid; if Taylor didn't at least get the engines he wanted then he wouldn't have the right airplane to sell to the corporate market. For Taylor the issue was most important. When he found out that FedEx didn't want the General Electric engines, Taylor was on a collision course with Canadair's management.

The basic jet engine seems like magic but is really an example of magnificent simplicity. The engine operates like a kind of boiler. Air drawn into the engine is squeezed by a series of compressor blades until it is at a very high pressure. Fuel is injected into the air, then ignited. Like a boiler, the engine creates hot gas, which produces thrust when it is forced out the rear of the engine. On the way out the rapidly expanding air turns the blades of a turbine, which in turn drives the compressor blades that compress the air pouring in from the front. Thus air is going out the back faster than it is going in the front.

We have here the basic operating principle of the engine, the third law of motion laid down by Sir Issaac Newton in the seventeenth century: for every action there is a reaction, equal in force and opposite in direction. You push the air back, you push yourself forward. The French had perhaps the most appropriate name for this machine: *une reaction.*

For more than 30 years this was the state of the jet engine industry. Then engine designers began to experiment with fan engines. The idea of the fan engine had been around nearly as long as the jet engine itself. The fan is placed at the front of the engine and acts as a bypass mechanism: it sucks air in the front then shoves it into a duct that bypasses the combustion or boiler section of the engine. The by-passed air meets up with the hot exhaust air, with the result that the bypassed air also expands, creating more thrust. The additional thrust is created without the use of additional fuel. The higher the amount of air bypassing the combustion chamber, the greater the efficiency in terms of thrust per fuel unit consumed—called the bypass ratio. Furthermore, the additional thrust is created without a commensurate increase in noise. The result is a quieter, more fuel efficient but still powerful engine.

In the fan jet, the turbine drives the fan as well as the compressor blades. The fan jet engine creates considerably more heat than a standard jet engine. Dealing with the heat stress on more than a hundred turbine blades is a formidable challenge from design and manufacturing points of view. How to design a turbine that won't self-destruct under the stress? There are two ways: improved cooling systems or stronger, more heat-resistant blades in the turbine.

Engine manufacturers began to come out with low-bypass fan engines, but high-bypass fan engines remained a dream since the complications were more than a match for the manufacturers. Then, in the mid-sixties, the U.S. military put out a request for proposals to build a leviathan of an airplane called the Lockheed C-5A Galaxy. Breakthroughs were made in the development of high-bypass fan engines. The Galaxy would require an engine with enormous amounts of thrust, more thrust than existing engines could deliver. A new engine would have to be built. To develop a high-bypass engine required more than the addition of a fan to the front of an engine. That's what General Electric discovered after it won the bid to develop the high-bypass ratio engines for the Galaxy. The GE engine was expensive, leading-edge technology built from the core of the engine up, and the program was one of the most difficult and expensive in the engine-maker's history.

Not every company had the resources to build a new high-bypass engine from scratch, and engine manufacturers without the resources started putting high-bypass fans on existing engine cores using cooling systems or heat-resistant blades or both. One such company was Avco Lycoming, a Connecticut maker of military helicopter, jet-turbine and piston engines. Avco Lycoming claimed it was close to certifying a relatively inexpensive high-bypass engine for civilian use. When Bill Lear heard this, he knew he had found the engine for his LearStar.

Taylor mistakenly assumed that the Lycoming ALF-502 engine was in the preliminary design proposal because Lear said it should be. FedEx hadn't expressed an interest in which engine was selected, so long as the airplane met FedEx's specifications. Taylor was shocked when he heard that FedEx wanted their LearStars powered by the Lycoming engine. Just after the April signing between Lear and Canadair, Taylor had been assured by his old friend, FedEx President Art Bass, that FedEx would support Taylor's choice of engine, the

General Electric TF-34. Unfortunately for Taylor, Bass was on his way out of FedEx and was no longer in Smith's inner circle. A visit to the GE and Avco Lycoming factories by Smith and Riedmeyer had caused Smith to prefer the Lycoming engine, which included an easy-to-service modular design of the major components. (Taylor did not know that Smith was unhappy with the way he had been treated by GE, the maker of the engines on his Falcon jets, in the past. FedEx and GE had been having a difficult relationship, and Smith wasn't interested in a repeat performance if he could avoid it.)

Taylor sent two of his people to Memphis to put a little persuasive pressure on FedEx's chief engineer, Jim Riedmeyer, to get Smith to change his mind. Taylor picked the wrong man. An angry Riedmeyer immediately called Halton and said, "I didn't appreciate having those guys here." Riedmeyer didn't mind being consulted on which engine might go into the program, but it was up to Canadair, not FedEx, to make that decision. He thought lobbying a customer on the engine selection lacked class.

In mid-May 1976, it became apparent to Taylor that Halton also was beginning to favor the Lycoming engine, mainly because it was nearly certified for flight and fitted into Canadair's schedule. GE was not even close to certification. With Lear, FedEx and Halton lined up in favor of the Lycoming, Taylor began to fear that Kearns might concur. The engine selection was expected to be made in time for the first customer seminar at the end of June. That left Taylor about six weeks. He was no airplane engineer but he was ready to tangle with Halton over this complex engineering question, using a compelling amount of data and arguments put together by his friend Albert Blackburn. Together the two launched a barrage of memoranda at Kearns and anyone else who would listen.

Taylor and Blackburn favored a derivative of the GE TF-34 military engine, which was used to power some 200 S-3A carrier-based airplanes and which had been selected to power the Fairchild A-10. They liked the model because it offered more power than the Lycoming engine and had a remarkably good operating history. Blackburn pointed out to Taylor that Halton's weight figures would surely rise as development progressed, and the added power of the GE engines would give Halton more margin for weight growth, in retrospect an accurate prediction. Blackburn supported GE because the company had first-class credentials and was the acknowledged leader in the development of high-bypass ratio engines. GE had tracked the technology then found its opportunity to develop it in the complicated Lockheed C-5A Galaxy heavy transport program. Avco Lycoming had come up with a less expensive derivative of the core of the T-55 helicopter turbine engine, and the company had a less than sterling reputation for quality and innovation. Taylor and Blackburn were far more enthusiastic about having GE involved in the LearStar program than GE was itself.

GE's engine division was known in the industry as a conservative rather than a sporty player. Jack S. Parker, GE's long-time head of the aircraft engine group, said in a *New Yorker* magazine article in 1982: "This is a sporty game. Both airframe people and engine people will very frequently represent something that turns out to be somewhat beyond their reach in order to get a job." GE wasn't interested in competing with little guys like Avco Lycoming for what was clearly a big gamble and a very sporty program. Canadair was making bold claims, and many of those claims depended on the engine. Converting and certifying a GE military engine for civilian use was not something to be taken lightly; it involved risking millions of dollars in development for a single airplane program that had no guarantee of succeeding. GE had taken part in the Dassault Mystere/Falcon business jet program, and they were not keen to try another one. GE had converted a military engine for the Falcon and nearly took a bath when the airplane came in way over weight. Customers could have demanded penalties from GE and Dassault. GE rushed through an engine modification for more thrust and saved the program, but it made the company keenly aware of the risks involved in the business jet game. They also remembered the run-ins with Fred Smith, and the antipathy was mutual.

Avco Lycoming, on the other hand, badly wanted to become a player. For years Avco Lycoming had been trying to get its ALF-502 engine into the civilian and military turbofan engine business. Their version wasn't as elegant as the GE turbofans because it needed a geared fan, but it did the job—it generated more power with less noise. Avco Lycoming had developed the engine to go in the Northrop A-9 attack aircraft for a major Air Force order. Northrop lost to the GE-powered A-10 Fairchild. A few years later Avco Lycoming thought it had a buyer when Dassault chose the engine to power the 30-passenger Falcon 30, but the program was canceled. Then the engine was selected for the Hawker-Siddeley 146 short-haul passenger aircraft, but the program was postponed in 1975 because of uncertainties in the market. By the time Canadair came on the scene, Avco Lycoming was desperate for a program, any program, that wouldn't die on them.

For a year before go-ahead, Bill Lear had worked closely with Ned Dobak, Avco Lycoming's top marketing man and general manager for the engine program. Lear prepared him to sell the Lycoming engine to the company that would build the LearStar. It was going to be a class act with all the stops pulled out.

Canadair's engine selection process began in earnest in May 1976 when Avco Lycoming, General Electric and Rolls-Royce were invited to make their engine presentations. Since no engine manufacturer produced the kind of engine Canadair was looking for—a 7,500-pound thrust high-bypass fan engine—Canadair's selection process was primarily a matter of choosing the engine that could be developed at the cheapest price in the shortest time. Rolls-Royce, whose offices were just a few miles away, was the first to make its presentation. Rolls-Royce didn't have a great deal to offer, since its engine, the RB-401-07, had only a theoretical schedule and was still waiting for corporate go-ahead. Rolls-Royce had been given the invite out of consideration as a past vendor to Canadair on the CL-44-6 program and the Silver Star T-33 trainer.

GE's presentation was barely more impressive. Gherhard Neuman, who made the GE presentation, and Harry Halton had known each other since the early sixties when Neuman was GE's chief engineer. He had worked with Halton on the CF-104 program, which used the GE J-79 engine. It was a dry and technical presentation that made the nontechnical people in the room start to look at their shoelaces and their watches. There was a slight stir when, in response to a question from Taylor, Neuman dwelled at length on the potential problems with the Lycoming engine, in particular a possible fan gearing problem. But on the whole the presentation lacked enthusiasm, since Neuman knew of Halton's tight schedule and of GE's diffidence about getting involved. Taylor tried to convince Halton afterward that GE would throw its weight into meeting the schedule, but Halton wasn't hearing the same words from GE: he was told by GE people that they wouldn't even try to meet the LearStar schedule. Taylor's campaign to move GE and Canadair closer together fell flat.

By contrast, the Avco Lycoming presentation was emotional. Canadair executives remember more than anything else the good feelings of the first meetings. Indeed, there was no problem too difficult and no request too unreasonable for Avco Lycoming. It could meet the schedule and it could uprate the engine to higher thrust levels with little difficulty. The engine would not be expensive, it would be developed quickly, and it would meet customer requirements, specifically the dispatch reliability of the FedEx order.

After the presentations Kearns asked Halton to make his recommendation. Halton tallied up the three engines and placed them in a preliminary order. Rolls-Royce was at the bottom because of their schedule. The GE engine looked good, but it was very big and heavy, it was expensive and it wasn't near certification for civilian use. It went in the middle. That left Avco Lycoming, and they looked good.

In the weeks at the end of the engine selection process Lear and Taylor bombarded Halton and Kearns with memos, trade reports, consultants' reports, comparative studies and telephone calls. Near the end nerves got frayed. "The reason you want this engine so badly, Taylor, is that you're in GE's pocket!" Lear once shouted in Mahogany Row after Taylor had shown up Lear's lack of understanding about engines. Lear's comment was a dangerous and actionable statement in an industry paranoid about its integrity. It looked fairly obvious to everyone that Avco Lycoming was far and away the front runner. To everyone, that is, except the engineers.

Halton's engineers saw the weight targets of the LearStar going up, and they knew that the more powerful GE engine offered a tempting solution to beat the weight problem. But the larger, more powerful engine presented the airframe designers with two problems: greater weight and greater aerodynamic interference caused by having a large object close to the main fuselage. The most difficult area for Halton's engineers at the time was the rear part of the airplane, right where the engines were supposed to go. They knew very little about the airflow patterns in that area, and there wasn't time for wind tunnel testing. Both the Lycoming and GE engines presented a challenge to the aerodynamicists, but the GE engine was the larger, more difficult challenge. All aircraft with engines mounted on the back have problems with the center of gravity (CG), and an airplane with a poorly

located CG will not fly efficiently, if it flies at all. The heavier the
engines the more severe the problem. Given a choice, Canadair's
engineers would have chosen the Lycoming engine.

On the Sunday afternoon before Halton was to give Kearns his
recommendation for the engine, two of Halton's top aerodynamic
engineers, Odd Michaelson and George Turek, called Halton and
asked if they could come by and see him. When they arrived they said
the engineering department was worried he might go for the GE
engine. If Halton selected the GE, he could count on trouble in the
department. Things were complicated enough, and they didn't need
the GE engine on top of it. Halton was taken aback. The last thing he
wanted was dissent in his engineering department, and he understood the significance of this visit by Turek and Michaelson. The visit
convinced him that he had no choice.

The decision was Kearns's to make, and despite the difference in
the presentations it was an extremely difficult one. Halton's recommendation was very important. Ignoring the advice of the top engineer was something the CEO of a large technical enterprise did at
great peril. But following such advice when instinct says that the
advice is wrong could be just as dangerous. Kearns believed that the
success of the program depended on selecting winners to take part.
Bill Lear was a winner with the Learjet, Jim Taylor was a winner in
marketing, FedEx was a winner in the cargo business. Avco Lycoming was not a winner. It was a wanna-be. As Kearns's top finance man,
Peter Aird, asked, "Fred, do you want to buy an engine from a $600-
million company or a $6 billion company?" Halton's recommenda-
tion put Kearns on the spot, because he really would have preferred
doing business with GE.

Just what happened next is still a matter of some dispute. According to Jim Taylor, on June 22, 1976, a Friday, Kearns called Taylor
into his office and in front of salesmen Hurley and Juvonen said, "Go
ahead and call Jack Parker [vice chairman of GE] and tell him he's got
our business." The unusual thing about this is that Kearns did not
also inform Halton and finance VP Peter Aird, his two most senior
managers in the company. Then, again according to Taylor, the
following Monday, Federal Express chairman Fred Smith let Canadair know that it would reconsider its position in the program if
Canadair went ahead with the GE engine. How FedEx found out
before Halton or Aird is also a mystery, unless Kearns informed

FedEx of his decision. Taylor says Kearns called him into his office that Monday and said, "I'm sorry, Jim, but we can't go with the GE now." While this series of events is backed up by other Canadair vice presidents, only two men, Fred Kearns and Fred Smith, would know the truth, and neither of them ever clarified the matter. Smith bristles at the suggestion that he blackmailed Canadair. GE's vice chairman, Jack Parker, says that some years later Kearns said he regretted having reversed his original decision in favor of the GE engine. Kearns did not explain to Parker what motivated him, and the truth will never be known.

What is known is that on the same Monday Kearns sent a memo to Halton and Taylor telling them he had decided on the Lycoming engine. He concluded the memo with a paragraph directed specifically at Taylor: "All activity with General Electric shall cease immediately and full attention is to be diverted to getting on with the marketing of our Lycoming-powered airplane."

By selecting the Lycoming engine, Kearns gained one important thing: he had for once made Bill Lear happy. The next day, Lear's seventy-fourth birthday, Lear picked up the telephone in his Reno home and called Fred Kearns. He wanted to know if Kearns had made up his mind yet on the engine selection. "Bill, I've got a birthday present for you," Kearns said. "We selected the Lycoming yesterday."

In June 1976, Canadair presented its plans for the Lycoming-powered LearStar in the first customer seminars in Montreal. The presentation took the industry by surprise. As one U.S. player later pointed out, "The Canadians seem to know something the rest of the industry doesn't." No one was more surprised, however, than the Grumman Aircraft Company, makers of the Gulfstream II executive jet. The LearStar provoked disbelief and concern among Grumman's people. Its G-II was no match for the LearStar, and the G-III, an on-again off-again program, would have a low-bypass turbofan engine. The G-III would also be heavier and cost more to operate. The potential was there for Canadair to do serious harm to Grumman's position as the premier executive jet builder in the world.

That Canadair was capable of making Grumman nervous says something about Halton's design. Grumman was a veteran player with a secure hold on a niche in the aviation market. While the upstart Learjet appealed to the nouveau riche, the expensive Grumman Gulfstream jet planes were reserved for the truly rich and powerful, the Establishment, who had been the pioneers in business aviation long before Lear's time. These were the owners of flying mahogany-and-satin private rail cars. Gulfstream knew the market was ready for a new model business jet. Gulfstream operators indicated they wanted an aircraft with more range. On transAtlantic runs, the heavy, gas-guzzling G-II had to stop at Shannon or Gander, both if the winds were wrong. Grumman's new jet, the G-III, would use a supercritical wing, but if the LearStar was what it was cracked up to be, the G-III might never see the light of day.

For the first seminars in the summer of 1976 it was standing room only in the poorly ventilated Canadair lecture theater. Hundreds of pilots, airplane owners, trade media and curious people wanted to hear Canadair's plans for the LearStar program. Harry Halton gave a two-hour presentation on the configuration, a design based on sound logic without cosmetics or design whims. Using currently available technology, Canadair would build a more sophisticated business jet than already existed, outfit it with advanced systems and certify it to the highest standards. It would fly farther and faster and cost less than the competition. The airplane program was made to sound sensible, practical, desirable and eminently possible. People couldn't believe Canadair intended to do all this in 36 months. Nevertheless, the presentations impressed nearly everyone. There were two important exceptions: Bill Lear and Jim Taylor.

Shut out from the design process almost completely, Lear made a great fuss over Halton's decision to give the airplane a fuselage that was 106 inches in diameter. That was much wider than Lear had imagined. He told everyone who would listen that the larger, heavier airplane designed by Halton wouldn't fly as promised. He called it "Fat Albert," a devastating moniker for an airplane program betting on an extremely low weight target. He said it was no longer a Lear airplane. Not everyone at the seminars was displeased with this last possibility. Many of the customers were looking for a real jet, not a "Mickey Mouse Learjet," as the aircraft had come to be known among certain pilots.

As for Jim Taylor, he resigned himself to the fact that the airplane in its final configuration was not what he wanted to see and told prospective customers that while the Lycoming was a good engine, Canadair could have had a better airplane with the GE engines.

Taylor fought successfully to keep one thing as part of the sales presentations: the notion of selling airplane "packages." A major tenet of Taylor's concept marketing philosophy was not to complicate the situation by giving customers all sorts of options they didn't really understand. Instead, Taylor wanted to do what he had done at Cessna—offer a complete package with few options. Halton vigorously objected to this. He wanted to offer various items as options because that would mean any resulting weight increases and additional costs would be the responsibility of the customer, and Halton would have an easier time of meeting his weight and cost targets for the airplane. In this matter Halton lost. Kearns agreed with Taylor's plan, and in the end the airplane became heavier and more expensive to build. Several hundred pounds in weight and hundreds of thousands of dollars in production costs were added. Ironically, Taylor would practically disown the airplane later on because of the excess weight, even though he was partly responsible for it.

The hundreds of pilots and professional business aviation people who showed up for the seminars, albeit with free hotel accommodations and a sumptuous meal at the Ritz Carlton Hotel, walked away mightily impressed with Canadair. The seminars took a company that was virtually unknown to the business jet industry and made it the talk of the town. But despite Taylor's claim that the real benefit of the seminars was the opportunity to listen to the needs of the market, Halton found the seminars useless in this regard. The pilots and owners couldn't agree on what should be in the airplane, and for that reason Halton opposed the idea of a complete package. There was no way Canadair could hope to please everybody with a single package. Still, for perhaps the first time, Canadair was winning kudos for listening to the needs and requests of the customer. In one meeting with the chief pilot and aviation department manager of Sheffield Oil, a $4 billion company, Kearns, Halton and Aird personally gave a presentation at Taylor's request. The Sheffield people were very impressed. They were about to make a new acquisition, and the Gulfstream II had been at the top of their list. The presentation changed their thinking. When they returned to their head office, they recommended the LearStar.

After the seminars, Halton wanted Lear out of the program. The design engineering was in top gear and Lear was driving the engineers crazy. Kearns had told Halton that Lear had to be associated with the program. The politics of Lear's name could not be ignored, regardless of the difficulties.

"Our customers are going to be paying Lear a royalty and they want to see that it's a Lear airplane or they're going to ask us why they have to pay royalties to him," Kearns explained to Halton. Kearns feared that Lear would lash out in public and say that Canadair couldn't do the job. But a worse prospect for Kearns was the loss of Lear from the program before it got the go-ahead from the government-controlled board. Kearns took Lear's threat to leave seriously and didn't presume he would stay with the program for the royalties. Halton had to put up with Lear, bad mouth and all, and that was that.

"How you prevent Lear from bugging your engineers or doing public harm to the program, Harry, that's up to you," Kearns told Halton. "But Lear has got to stay on the program."

Halton felt estranged from his boss. "I don't think Fred appreciated just how difficult it was for me to handle Lear while at the same time trying to get the program moving," he would later say.

The end of Lear's active participation at Canadair was coming. During a board luncheon with all of Canadair's directors present Lear burst into the room clutching a wooden mock-up he had made of the LearStar. "Ya wanna see Fat Albert with a nose job?" Lear was clearly getting out of hand, yet nobody knew how to control him. Some quietly suspected he was losing his mind. In fact, Lear was not well. He had leukemia. He also had a worsening condition of water on the brain that was becoming severe. When Lear packed his things at the Château Champlain and prepared to fly to Reno to visit his doctor, Kearns made his move.

"Moya, please don't bring Bill back until we're ready for him," Kearns asked her before the Lears left Montreal. "He's not helping us by being here." Kearns would still need Lear, particularly when Canadair made its pitch to the government. Until that time, Lear was persona non grata at Canadair.

Halton reflected much on this falling out with Lear. He was convinced that Lear gave Canadair so much trouble because he still believed he was entitled to certain decision-making rights, the rights of a living legend, and that he really didn't object to the decisions themselves. Lear wanted to appear to be close to the heart of the program, to be seen as its leader and champion. This was supposed to have been a Lear comeback, but it wasn't working out that way. Instead, Lear began to distance himself from Canadair's design of the LearStar 600, saying the company had turned his original sleek design into a "Fat Albert."

Kearns became very concerned about Lear's rages. The loud whisper campaign continued, this time through the media, and it was making him very nervous. As Canadair prepared for the day it would approach the Canadian government for a decision, Kearns told Halton to come up with some sort of solution, and fast.

Halton decided to give Lear what he had wanted in the first place, control over the prototype development program. Halton set up a second design team in Reno with Lear at the head. It was a sop to Lear that would cost the company several hundred thousand dollars, but it worked. Halton said Lear's design team had to work with the same fuselage as the one Canadair had been working with, so Halton got the satisfaction of seeing Lear eat his comments about "Fat Albert."

Lear stayed at his Reno facility with his design team. He called his design the Allegro. Lear didn't have any employees in Reno, and he contracted the design work to a new firm called Astec Aviation set up by several young ex-Boeing engineers in Seattle. The design Astec came up with had Lear stamped all over it. It had an unusual feature: the engines were buried in the fuselage. While civilian aircraft usually have engines that hang like appendages from the rear fuselage or the wings, Lear opted for a design more commonly used in military aircraft. This was a controversial element for a civilian aircraft, one that promised less drag and better range but raised difficulties for production and certification. Such a design had never been certified for civilian flight. The world's first civilian jet, the British Comet, had a similar design. The Comet's engines, which were buried in the inboard portion of the wing, had on occasion stalled on takeoff. There was speculation from aerodynamicists that the Allegro's buried engine intakes would also be susceptible to engine stall when the airplane yawed or rolled from side to side. Despite Lear's statement that only engineers with little faith go into wind-tunnel testing, he put the Allegro into the wind tunnel at Canadair's expense. A month later the Allegro design was dead. Lear suddenly threw away the concept and came up with a new design that looked very much like the LearStar. Indeed, except for the buried engines, which Lear held on to, it *was* the LearStar. The little boy Lear was having fun, but Canadair was making things happen. That was the way things stood until program go-ahead.

Kearns had more than Lear to deal with. Jim Taylor, his top salesman for the airplane, continued to moan about FedEx as a customer. Taylor painted the FedEx deal in very dire financial terms: for next to nothing Smith got a fleet of LearStars at a bargain launch price and, if the aircraft become a success, the value would go up even before he received them. Smith couldn't lose. If he decided not to take delivery of the aircraft he wouldn't have to sacrifice his deposit, miserly as it was. He could sell the airplane delivery positions for a tidy profit to somebody else, not an uncommon practice in the industry. Meanwhile, Canadair was taking all the risk. To satisfy FedEx, Canadair committed itself to a more complicated airplane for a cargo market it had no certainty of succeeding in. Why was Kearns hoping that a state-of-the-art executive jet could bring Canadair riches by hauling small packages? The idea was wrongheaded, and Taylor repeatedly said this to Kearns.

Kearns did not share Taylor's enthusiasm for the business jet market. While Kearns had picked small jet aviation because there weren't very many alternatives, it was only a small niche in the larger aviation market, and he believed that by itself it would not yield Canadair a future. Business aviation grew from modest beginnings to become a worldwide fleet of nearly five thousand aircraft of fifty-two types manufactured by seventeen companies in nine countries. But people who got enthusiastic about corporate aviation knew that the market was inconstant. The reasons for operating a corporate jet were not always evident, and it was certainly not an indispensable tool for corporate America. America had, after all, the largest network of commercial airline transport in the world. Kearns recognized corporate aviation for what it was, a jittery market that was vulnerable in bad economic times. It was a fickle and risky market, one where a multimillion-dollar jet could win a sale because of the size of its toilet.

Taylor believed the LearStar program had the potential to be a one-thousand-airplane success story if Kearns would focus Canadair's efforts on the corporate market and leave the cargo market for later. Despite visible reminders of the 1972 recession, more corporate jets were being delivered in 1976 than before (283), and very few of them were being used as cargo haulers. Business aircraft of all types were coming on to the market and forming a transportation system that rivaled the commercial airlines. According to an upbeat *Business Week* report, the U.S. fleet of corporate aircraft was flying several times as many hours as all domestic airlines combined. And still there was room for growth. The report went on to say that of the largest one thousand companies, only 502 operated their own airplanes. "That leaves a sizeable virgin market which salespeople from a dozen U.S. and foreign builders are tripping over each other to develop," *Business Week* said. A Harvard professor was quoted as predicting that business airplanes might eventually become to the airlines what private autos were to public transit.

Heady stuff. The truth was that the dozen manufacturers were tripping over themselves because there were too many companies working a relatively small piece of real estate. Notwithstanding the Harvard professor, it wasn't at all like the automobile industry with its mass-market consumer base. This was a market with paying customers numbering in the low thousands, not millions. Rockwell, Cessna, Gates Learjet, Dassault and Grumman were all planning to offer new models, updated models or plans for a new model to meet the growing demand for corporate aircraft. In the same year Kearns considered launching Canadair into the corporate jet business, a director of North American Rockwell, a billion-dollar defense contractor with only $200 million in general aviation sales at the time, was asking his board the question, "Why are we even in this business?" It was too small and difficult a market to work successfully.

The LearStar existed only on paper, but selling it to the corporate market was not difficult at the start. For a modest deposit, a customer got a position to own an aircraft that, even if it didn't do everything promised, would almost certainly appreciate in value before delivery. It was like a penny-ante gamble on whether Canadair could pull it off. One group of pilots was so enthused with the LearStar it approached Taylor through a leasing company, Polaris Aviation in San Francisco, to see if the group could form a limited partnership and buy a LearStar. Taylor didn't like the idea of people speculating on the product, but his salesmen, Dave Hurley and Bill Juvonen, saw the group as a way to sell more aircraft. It was agreed that Polaris could buy an aircraft if the pilots got approval from their respective company boards indicating the purchase would not be a conflict of interest. Neal Fulton, one of the pilots, went to his board at Olin Corporation and asked for the okay. Before the meeting was over, Olin agreed to buy a LearStar for itself. The same thing happened at Federated Department Stores. Juvonen's and Hurley's ploy was a stroke of genius.

Shortly after the first two seminars, the orders started to come in. Taylor's dynamic sales team, Hurley and Juvonen, had been focusing on the pilots and operations managers of their old customers from the Falcon and Citation days and had been pulling in all the IOUs and favors they could muster to get people to look at the program. They got a call from one of those pilots, Charlie Morris of Mobil Corporation, when they were fishing together in New Hampshire. "Why don't you guys come by and pick up the cheque?" Charlie said. Hurley and Juvonen had made their first sale. This was a key sale because Mobil's flight operation was run by one of the most respected individuals in the industry, and his nod in favor of the LearStar gave the airplane a valuable stamp of approval. After that the orders came in at a steady rate. By the end of October more than 25 orders were completed.

It was during Taylor's initial marketing foray that summer that he scored an important hit against the LearStar's main competitor, Grumman. Taylor's group snagged an order from a long-time Grumman customer, Xerox, which shuttled 15,000 employees a year on five corporate airplanes between its Stamford headquarters and its Rochester plant. Its flight operations department, run by veteran pilot Dick Van Gemert, was considered one of the best. The Xerox deal gave the LearStar credibility and raised the profile of the airplane within the business jet market.

Despite Taylor's success, Kearns was uncomfortable with his top LearStar salesman. Kearns found Taylor's marketing style and methods not to his liking. He didn't understand the necessity of the marketing gimmickry or the aggressive advertising. The advertising bothered him considerably. Taylor's blasts at the competition in the pages of the *Wall Street Journal* were unnerving to Kearns, and he worried about the reaction they would cause.

Kearns also didn't understand why Taylor couldn't get an international marketing effort going, in particular why Taylor couldn't sign on Alexander Couvelaire, the president of Euralair, a successful European operator of executive transport. Couvelaire was a friend of Lear's, and he thought the LearStar would have a lot of success in Europe. Couvelaire had a LearStar salesman in mind for Europe, another friend of Lear's, Alex Kvassy. But when Couvelaire and Kvassy met Taylor, negotiations stalled. Kearns approached Taylor and asked why Couvelaire and Kvassy were not getting any satisfaction. Taylor replied that the two wanted all sorts of Lear-inspired features on the LearStar that no one in their right mind would agree to provide. Taylor had had enough of watching FedEx dilute the design effort with noncorporate aviation requirements; he didn't want Couvelaire doing the same.

It's not clear if Couvelaire wanted Lear-inspired features, but one thing was certain: he wanted to run his own European marketing arm with airplanes purchased from Canadair. To Taylor, this represented another shoestring order for a fleet of LearStars from a customer who could possibly turn around and dump them on the market for a profit. Kearns didn't see it that way. He believed that Couvelaire, with his well-established operations, could have been Canadair's launch pad into the European market. Taylor didn't agree, and thus began Kearns's and Taylor's long-running dispute over foreign sales. In the end Couvelaire and Kvassy walked away from the program.

"The facts clearly show that North American business jets have never had effective overseas marketing," Taylor wrote Kearns in a memo designed to justify his refusal to court Couvelaire. "There are very few effective people around with successful records of selling internationally . . . a single-point program management concept [that is, Taylor's group] is the only way to assure a successful and profitable program." Kearns would hear a lot more about this single-point marketing concept.

At the end of September 1976 the Lear option was about to expire, but after five months of grueling and complex negotiations Canadair was still a long way from closing the deal with FedEx. And as far as Kearns was concerned, no deal with FedEx, no program. Lear agreed to extend the option for another month, and Canadair returned to the table with FedEx.

The slow pace of negotiations between Canadair and FedEx was in part due to the fact that neither party had much experience with many of the design issues, specifically the dispatch reliability of the airplane. This one request determined hundreds of other engineering and contractual issues relating to engine and airframe reliability. The thousands of specifications and piles of detail were mind-boggling, considering that the whole process of arriving at set numbers and fixed configurations was done through negotiation between supplier and customer. There were revisions, revisions and more revisions. The process dragged on all through the summer and autumn, and as the end of the option extension approached Kearns began putting the screws to Halton: if there was no satisfactory conclusion to FedEx's demands for dispatch reliability by the end of the month, there would be no program. Kearns would not seek the go-ahead on the basis of Taylor's orders, which amounted to 25 and were climbing.

By the end of October it appeared Canadair and FedEx were close to a deal. When Kearns arrived in the last days of negotiations, all Canadair's top people were busy trying to wrap things up and all were exhausted. Halton, Wohl and Peter Aird were anxious to close the deal although not all were satisfied with it. Finance VP Aird, echoing Taylor, expressed his unhappiness with FedEx's deposit of only $250,000, but there was little he could do about it. It was all FedEx could muster at the time, and Kearns had said it was okay. Financing was another question. FedEx was already servicing a huge debt, and finding $100 million in the finance market for the deal was impossible for them, so Aird had brought down the people from Canada's Export Development Corporation (EDC) whose mandate was to help finance Canadian exports. They were impressed with FedEx, but there were no commitments. In the end, Canadair accepted that the deal would have to be subject to FedEx getting EDC financing.

Finally it seemed it might all come down to price. Despite reports to the contrary, FedEx's price for the aircraft was not discounted, but it almost happened that way. The cost price per unit for the first 200 aircraft had been figured at a little more than $4 million, and Canadair's price to FedEx was $4.75 million. At one point near the end of negotiations Jim Riedmeyer, FedEx's vice president, took the offer into a meeting with his top people. Time passed and Kearns started to worry. When Riedmeyer came out of the meeting, Kearns was ready to go down on price. He wanted FedEx badly and was willing to pay for it. "We've got a deal!" Riedmeyer said. Kearns breathed a sigh of relief. He'd done it without slashing the price. The deal was closed with a handshake, and on the way down in the elevator Kearns let out another big sigh of relief.

"Thank God we got that out of the way," he said.

But it wasn't quite over. In the conference room, Halton was still negotiating numbers with FedEx on the dispatch reliability issue. At a quarter to three in the morning Halton wheeled himself to the bathroom and told Steffi, "I just can't agree on some of the reliability numbers FedEx wants from us. I won't go any higher. I can't justify the higher numbers." Five minutes later Halton went back into the conference room and put some numbers on the blackboard. They could take it or leave it, Halton had decided. By three o'clock, FedEx had agreed to Halton's numbers.

The sun was shining brightly on Canadair on a crisp autumn morning as a Learjet made its final approach on its flight from Memphis. Inside the jet was Fred Kearns, and he was anxious to get to his office to start making telephone calls. Exactly one year after he had given Harry Halton the drawing for a new airplane at his bedside, Kearns was about to launch the program that would turn that drawing into a reality. The FedEx deal for 25 airplanes was in the bag and, with Taylor's 25-plus orders, the program go-ahead was a mere formality. Kearns knew he couldn't make money on 50 orders, but at least the program had momentum, and a cascade of orders seemed possible if not inevitable.

Kearns got out of the Learjet and drove to the executive office. There was a Cabinet session that morning in Ottawa, and Kearns called Memphis to make sure the signatures were on paper in time for the meeting. Then he called Antoine Guerin, Industry Trade and Commerce's assistant deputy minister, who was standing outside the Cabinet room waiting for the news.

"We got it, Tony."

Next Kearns pulled out a resolution he had drafted for his board of directors: that the board approve the exercise of an option to purchase the LearStar 600 name and original design and to commit to the production of the aircraft.

Canadair received the go-ahead from the government and its own board of directors on the last day of the Lear option. Kearns knew it was now up to Harry Halton to make the program successful. Halton had a major task ahead of him. Within a short period of time, Halton was expected to deliver both a business jet and a cargo airplane, powered by an unproven engine, fitted with state-of-the-art systems and a high-technology wing, and certified to the latest safety standards.

Experienced observers were amazed by Fred Kearns's daring and could not help but think that the whole enterprise was a gigantic gamble. If everything went right, Kearns might, just might, pull it off. Nobody imagined that Fred Kearns would deliver an airplane close to what had been promised in what still stands as one of the shortest development schedules on record. Nor did they foresee that nearly everything would go wrong.

Shortly after program go-ahead, Jim Taylor wrote Canadair's legal counsel Bob Wohl to say for the record, "Personally, I feel that Fred Kearns could have sold the Canadian government on going ahead without Federal. We had enough orders without Federal by program go-ahead and we would now have an even better airplane than we do because of the bending of many executive version requirements to meet the cargo requirements and demands." Taylor continued to object to the FedEx deal, and he continued his campaign to get the GE engine into the program. His efforts would undermine Kearns's leadership in the difficult days ahead.

6

Building the dream machine

T he LearStar program turned the mood at Canadair completely
around. The 1976 employee Christmas party was a celebration.
Employees came forward to shake hands with Kearns and Halton
and to thank them. The company's future had been restored, and the
employees were ready to work hard to make the program a success.
Indeed, they were going to have to work very hard. The LearStar
program was going to be the biggest undertaking in the company's
history.

With the nod from government to go ahead with the LearStar
program, Canadair flung itself into action with vigor and tremendous
self-confidence. The critics were right, the challenge was immense—
to design, develop and certify a completely new airplane in just 36
months. To meet the tight schedule Harry Halton had to roll into the
program at high speed, a classic seat-of-the-pants try at beating the
clock. He immediately commenced the preparation of the manufacturing tooling that would be required to build the airplane, even
though he still wasn't sure what it was he would actually be building.
This commencement of detail design work before concept definition
had been verified by test data was like starting to build a house before
the blueprints were complete. Halton's modus operandi was simple:
"We keep moving forward until we realize we are on the wrong path
and then we change our path." Boeing and others warned Halton
that he was taking a big risk, but Halton had no choice. He had to
keep moving, making design decisions sometimes without a shred of
data to back him up.

Halton had the Herculean task of pulling all the elements of this aircraft program together. During the next 14 months, 220,000 pounds of raw material had to be milled; 5,000 engineering drawings were required; work had to be certified at 1,200 stages; 7,000 production orders had to be completed; 15,000 parts had to be assembled; 15,000 wire segments, about 60 miles of wire per airplane, had to be installed. The torrent of people and goods that flowed through the company to meet the next deadline was massive and unceasing. The factory floor was like a spinning top. High-priced talent rode around on company bicycles getting "urgent rush" items to their destination. Purchasing people begged and pleaded for early deliveries. Milling machines were operating 24 hours a day with no provision for breakdowns. People working 80-hour weeks month after month were having heart attacks and physical breakdowns on the job. One employee, a retired engineer brought in during the development phase, dropped dead of a heart attack where he worked. The pace was frenetic, and the employees loved it.

Rolling through this maelstrom, with his scraps of paper, his formidable memory, his high intelligence and his limitless energy, Halton directed the program from his custom-designed powered wheelchair. There was no other way to do it. He knew right from the very start that if he was to pull this off, he would have to manage the program single-handedly. No decision could be made without Harry. This wasn't the time for bureaucratic management with committees, processes and controls, and endless meetings. Decisions had to be made quickly. Reflexes had to be sharp. The program demanded an entrepreneurial style, with the boss involved at every step of the way, being everywhere, talking to everyone. There remained one problem. Despite the talent in the company, no one in Canadair engineering had ever designed and built a commercial jet airplane, and Halton needed a top engineer who had that kind of experience.

Selling the new airplane to the general aviation market also involved selling Canadair's engineering abilities. To give Canadair's engineering increased credibility, Kearns and Halton decided to hire a senior engineer with general aviation background. Through a New York head-hunting agency Halton found Ron Neal, a 42-year-old program engineer from Beech Aircraft in the United States. As Halton's new chief of engineering, Neal was Halton's right hand. But where there should have been a fist in a velvet glove, a man to ride herd on this frenetically paced enterprise, there was instead a friendly handshake. Neal was unanimously declared a nice guy by the engineering group, then largely ignored. He should have been a tough manager, the type to lean on the engineers, someone to make sure all the tasks were being completed correctly and on time. Instead, Neal was a fairly passive manager who didn't upset anyone. That pleased engineering, since they wanted to continue dealing with Harry, not with an outsider, particularly one from the United States who would try to tell the Canadians how to do their jobs. The problem was that since Harry had global responsibility for the program he no longer had much time to spare for his engineers. One day George Turek, the flight sciences section chief and one of Halton's most senior engineers, asked Halton why he had hired Neal.

"He's a U.S. engineer from general aviation and that helps us sell the program in the United States," Halton told Turek. "Besides, we're getting old, you know, and we need some younger talent around here." Since Turek was but a few years older than Neal, he didn't know whether to laugh or get angry. It didn't matter. Halton had already sped away in his wheelchair.

After program go-ahead it was decided that the time had come to deal with Bill Lear. The final selection in the "design competition" between Canadair's staff and Lear's Astec group took place in Lear's Reno office in January 1977. Kearns, Wohl and Halton went down for what was expected to be the painful moment of reckoning. Even though it was meant to be a design review of the two configurations with a selection afterward, everyone knew the fix was in for Lear. No one thought Canadair would drop its design for Lear's. Avco Lycoming, Canadair's engine supplier, warned Canadair that they wouldn't associate themselves with Lear's design, which still called for the buried engine intakes. Instead of a design review, the meeting was Lear's last attempt to control the airplane program he helped to launch.

Halton chaired the meeting. Canadair made its presentation of the LearStar 600 then turned the floor over to the design team from Astec. The Astec engineers took the offensive, perhaps knowing that Lear didn't stand a chance. They said Canadair's LearStar design was unacceptable and was based on insufficient data. It wouldn't fly. Boeing had told them that Whitcomb's version of the supercritical wing that would be on the LearStar was too theoretical and would not work, and if Boeing didn't think it was worth pursuing then who was Canadair to say otherwise? Indeed, Boeing believed that there wasn't enough test data on the design, making it risky, at best. Halton listened patiently to the litany of criticisms and nodded now and then in agreement with the Astec engineers, particularly when they said that the airplane's tail would have to be changed to a T-tail because of the location of the engines. (The LearStar 600 would have had a T-tail but for the fact that the tail had been designed by Lear, and Kearns didn't want to delete Lear's only visible contribution to the design effort.) The Astec engineers did everything they could to discredit the Canadair design. The Canadair engineers responded in kind, and the meeting degenerated into a shouting match with abuses and accusations hurled across the table. Then Fred Kearns said, "Enough!"

Kearns wasted little time in announcing his decision to go with the Canadair design, and the meeting ended on a somber note. However, Kearns didn't want to alienate Lear entirely. Lear's name had given Canadair credibility when it came to selling the program to people like Jean Chrétien, one of the ministers who had recommended the program go-ahead to Cabinet, in part on the strength of Lear's enthusiasm for the airplane. While Lear's value to the program was now marginal, his potential for doing harm was very real in Kearns's mind. So Kearns invited Lear to submit another design.

Lear was pacified by this invitation, although the design would be paid for with advances on Lear's future royalties. He drafted another design, again very similar to the LearStar 600, and some months later submitted it to Canadair, who neither accepted nor rejected the design until Lear pressed Kearns to give him an answer.

"Please understand, Bill, we can't have you coming up with a design that will compete with the LearStar," Kearns told him, adding that his design had been rejected. By this time, with development of the LearStar in full swing and orders approaching 80 airplanes, Kearns had decided that Lear's name was no longer needed for the program.

"By the way, Bill, we're renaming the airplane."

The name Challenger came from a list of 250 names submitted by a New York advertising agency. Canadair's executives liked the name because it symbolized the effort that was being undertaken: to challenge the business jet market with a superior new product that would cost much less than the competition. It wouldn't be the first

Canadian Challenger, either. A company in Sudbury, Ontario, marketed a two-seater propeller monoplane called the Challenger in the early sixties. After the name was chosen, Kearns put the rights to the LearStar name into an envelope and sent it to Lear in exchange for a reduced royalty. Even though Lear's contribution to the final product was insignificant, to say the least, Kearns didn't dare to challenge Lear's right to a royalty. He was confident that Canadair could build the Challenger without Lear's help, but he wasn't confident enough to enter into a legal tangle with the business aircraft industry's man of the year. Kearns accepted the royalty agreement as the price that had to be paid to get the LearStar, now called the Challenger, launched.

Forbes magazine reported that February, "The Canadians are now calling the shots, leaving Bill Lear in an unaccustomed position of relative powerlessness and, like Shakespeare's King Lear, raging against his fate."

When it had reacquired Canadair in 1976, the Canadian government did not make the company a Crown corporation but decided to hold it in trust through the Minister of Industry Trade and Commerce (ITC). ITC was a ministry of national economic development that doled out hundreds of millions of dollars in development money. The ministry had eclipsed External Affairs and its system of foreign trade commissions to become the most powerful source of economic development in government. In the past Canada had sought investment from foreign sources through External Affairs, but policy in the 1970s was focused on generating investment and development from within the country, with the public purse taking the lead. It was the heyday of economic nationalism.

Big as ITC was, however, it had neither the resources nor the desire to provide Canadair with sufficient equity to fund the huge lines of credit an aircraft manufacturer required. Although Canadair did not have any equity, it did not have any debt, either, so the bureaucrats at the Ministry of Finance came up with a solution that was majestic in its simplicity: debt financing.

ITC's usual practice was to provide development money in the form of grants. The grants involved a complex process of monitoring and reporting, and the amount of work that would be necessary for a new aircraft program was daunting for the government. Debt financing was a much tidier arrangement. All the government would have to provide would be guarantees to Canadair's lenders. The grant process could be avoided, the program would get launched, and the government would not have the public's money directly at risk. There would be a review process, but the government and the company would not be required to provide the degree of reporting typical of the grant system. For the most part Canadair could decide how it used the debt financing.

In 1976 the government provided Canadair its first support, a letter of comfort signed by the ITC minister to cover the $20 million line of credit inherited from General Dynamics. Peter Aird, Canadair finance VP, was anxious to get away from such letters, but he couldn't. He raised about $60 million without any government letters, but his bankers, the Canadian Imperial Bank of Commerce and the Provincial Bank (later the National Bank), told Aird they would only satisfy additional requests for money if they received a letter from the government. Legally the letters were dubious, and Aird preferred a more conventional tool for raising money—pledging the assets of the company. Yet after the first letter of comfort had been issued, lenders demanded one as a condition of lending. Most lenders treated the letters exactly like a government guarantee; according to the letters, the lenders would be consulted fully if the government sold the company, and so long as the government owned the company the debts were safe. As Aird soon found out, no letter, no credit.

He realized this when he prepared to raise the first issue to underwrite the program in 1978. Early that year Merrill Lynch visited Canadair to discuss the possibility of setting up a Eurobond issue. The cheaper interest rates in the European market would save some money, and Aird wanted to issue $70 million in bonds without any letters or guarantees from the government. Merrill Lynch said no: the European buyers wouldn't get involved in such a large financial undertaking without some sort of government support. Canadair had no choice but to get another letter of comfort. The letters of comfort didn't matter too much to Aird after the Eurobond issue closed successfully, however. He felt he had secured the program's complete financing with some money left over and that he wouldn't need any more letters of comfort. The program's peak cash requirement, some $150 million, had been met. But before the year was out Aird realized that Canadair was going to need more money, and when he tried to raise it, potential lenders asked for a government letter of comfort.

With the program riding on the letters, the disappearance of Lear from the scene raised some eyebrows in ITC. As far as Kearns was concerned, Lear had served his purpose. But the Canadian government had expected that Lear and his company would be providing considerable technical expertise and support for the project. With Lear out of the picture, it was obvious Canadair was going to go it alone. The Canadian government had always been concerned over the size of the risk and insisted that Canadair make an effort to find another partner. Canadair, after all, was coming out of a low period in terms of activity, and it seemed logical that a partner who could provide access to additional technical expertise and reduce the financial risk should be involved. Both Kearns and Halton objected to this idea. They were quite confident Canadair had the capabilities to do the job, and they believed a partner would complicate a program that had to move at breakneck speed. Still, they had no choice but to at least go through the motions.

A number of potential partners presented themselves within the first few months of program go-ahead. SAAB-Scania, the Swedish maker of automobiles and fighter jets, expressed a desire to take a 10 to 15 percent interest in the program. SAAB reviewed Canadair's data and said that although the schedule was demanding they saw no problems meeting Canadair's delivery requirements. There was just one hitch: SAAB didn't have a lot of excess capacity at the time and so postponed a final decision. As well, Swedish employment law made changes in workers a cumbersome and costly exercise. Layoffs were virtually unheard of during down cycles in Sweden, and SAAB was concerned about expanding too quickly. When they finally called Canadair back, it was to say their participation wouldn't be possible.

Aeritalia, the primary Italian state-owned aircraft manufacturer, had lots of excess capacity and was very keen on becoming a risk-sharing partner. Renato Bonifaccio, Aeritalia's chairman, had visited Canadair in June 1976. After looking over the Challenger designs, Aeritalia said they wanted to supply major structural components

and some instrumentation, a significant part of the production program. Aeritalia's engineers wanted the engineering work. The company had just been left at the altar by Boeing when the latter put the
new 7X7 program on ice. Two dozen Aeritalia engineers at Boeing
suddenly found themselves with nothing to do. Instead of sending
the engineers home, Aeritalia sent them to Canadair so they could
familiarize themselves with the Challenger. The Italian engineers
liked what they saw and told head office the project was a winner.
They said Aeritalia should become partners as soon as possible.
Instead Aeritalia postponed its decision. Halton meanwhile quietly
hoped that the Aeritalia engineers would disappear. While Halton
was prepared to have Aeritalia in the program, his engineers didn't
like the Italians' haughtiness and didn't give them much work to do.
The Italians stayed for the better part of a year at Canadair at
Aeritalia's expense and did practically nothing while the rest of the
company slaved away on the program.

The pressure to find a risk-sharing partner increased when the
Challenger's launch customer, Federal Express, suddenly backed out
of the program in the fall of 1977, one year into development. That
year the U.S. Congress stunned the aviation world by tabling sweep-
ing changes that deregulated the aviation industry in the United
States. FedEx Chairman Fred Smith had been lobbying federal aviation authorities since the OPEC crisis for an amendment that would
allow him to operate larger aircraft. Because of the small jets Smith
was using, people joked that he had to fly them in formation to get all
his parcels to their destinations, which was close to the truth. Larger
airplanes were the obvious solution. When Washington tabled its
deregulation bills for the aviation industry, among the new amend-
ments was something informally called the Federal Express Bill. It
created a new class of all-cargo air carrier, and gave FedEx and other
cargo carriers wide latitude in their choice of airplanes. While Canadair's executives knew that deregulation was coming, the extent of
the changes floored them. In about the time it took FedEx to deliver
a package, Fred Smith's reason for buying the Challenger had disappeared. FedEx could now buy bigger second-hand Boeing 727s for
not much more than a new Challenger and have triple the operating
capacity. Jim Taylor's warning to Kearns that Fred Smith was playing
many options appeared to have been correct.

Kearns was disappointed. He feared negative reaction to the loss of

FedEx as a launch customer, particularly from Ottawa. To deflect the damage of the cancellation, Kearns thought of ways to get FedEx back. One way was a new, longer Challenger model he planned to develop. Suddenly the notion of launching a second model before the first one had been delivered to customers became a distinct possibility. To keep FedEx in the program, Kearns promised Smith that Canadair would develop a stretched version of the Challenger sooner rather than later.

FedEx converted its deposit for the stretched version and agreed to be a potential launch customer. By the time Kearns decided to proceed, relations between Canadair and FedEx weren't as close as they had been. When FedEx had dropped out, they had threatened to sell their Challengers for a tidy profit. Canadair had had to pay them $8 million as a settlement to prevent this, and the dispute had left a bitter taste in the mouths of many of Canadair's senior officers. They felt FedEx should not have received a cent. It was, after all, FedEx who had bailed out of their program. They weren't happy to have customers speculating on the value of the aircraft, and they were particularly distressed when their launch customer and closest ally in the development of the airplane threatened to do just that.

The collapse of the FedEx deal came as a major disappointment to Kearns, but it made engineering and marketing extremely happy. When FedEx announced its intentions to withdraw from the program, engineering was still struggling with one of FedEx's requirements, the aircraft cargo door near the most critical point of the aircraft, the area joining the wing to the body. There was a sigh of relief in the engineering offices the day FedEx dropped out. Unfortunately, it was too late to take out the extra weight that had been built into the airplane to meet other FedEx requirements, and to this day the Challenger carries that extra weight. Taylor was also delighted because FedEx's positions on the production line became available and could be sold at a much higher price than FedEx, as the favored launch customer had paid. It was a boon to the salespeople, who took in hundreds of thousands of dollars more commission than would otherwise have come to them.

Then two things happened. Grumman, makers of the Gulfstream business jet, delayed plans to go ahead with development of the G-III, which would have been a direct competitor. And Fred Kearns met Akram Ojjeh.

In the annals of the Challenger program no customer provoked as much argument and passion as Techniques Avant Guarde (TAG). TAG was a business concern owned and run by Akram Ojjeh, a high-rolling Saudi trader who made his fortune dealing in small arms and high technology for his oil-rich friends in much the same way as another Saudi trader, Adnan Khashoggi. TAG came to Canadair through Challenger salesman Bill Juvonen, vice-president of U.S. western sales under Jim Taylor.

When Juvonen worked for Taylor at Cessna, he met Akram Ojjeh's son Aziz, a fellow Stanford University alumnus who wanted to learn how to fly so he could buy himself a business jet. Juvonen was unsuccessful in selling Aziz a Cessna Citation at the time—Aziz bought a Falcon 20—but he remained in Juvonen's book as a potential customer, and when Juvonen began working for Canadair he looked up Aziz.

There were two positions, or unsold planes, on the production line, left out of the original production order of 56 aircraft when Juvonen reached Aziz in Chicago in the fall of 1976. Juvonen gave Aziz the Challenger pitch, and soon the two of them were jetting across the country to Aziz's California home. Aziz was powerfully impressed with Canadair and the Challenger, particularly the price, and he placed an order for one aircraft. Juvonen left, pleased with himself, but the next day things got even better. Aziz called back to buy another Challenger. He wanted aircraft number 21 for his father, and he said his father wanted to talk to Juvonen at the Paris Air Show about a possible distributorship. He wanted to sell airplanes to his rich Arab friends.

This was great news. Canadair was planning to have its interior mock-up of the Challenger ready for the Spring 1977 air show; it was a perfect time to meet a wealthy Arab trader. The Arab world was rich, following the oil crisis of the early 1970s, but difficult to sell to directly; business aircraft manufacturers had tried direct selling without success. The Ojjehs could provide Canadair with a different approach, someone inside the Arab community trading its product.

Kearns wasn't aware of Juvonen's contact when he flew to the Paris Air Show to unveil the Challenger mock-up. He wasn't planning to meet with Akram Ojjeh. Akram showed up at Canadair's chalet at the end of the last day of the show, after Kearns had left, and had a look at the mock-up. It was the first time Juvonen had met Akram, and he was surprised. Aziz was tall and blond, Akram short and swarthy. Juvonen shook hands with Akram and they went inside the mock-up.

Akram was impressed. As he sat with Juvonen and Aziz, Akram turned to his son and said to him in French, "Aziz, you have done an excellent job. This is a wonderful aircraft for our nouveau riche friends." Then he turned to Juvonen and asked in English, "How do you say nouveau riche in English, Mr. Juvonen?" Juvonen laughed but stopped when Akram turned to his son and, in English, said, "I want ten more aircraft and I want to meet this Mr. Kearns and Mr. Taylor right away."

Juvonen shot out of the mock-up like a bullet and went looking for Kearns and Taylor but, as he had suspected, they had left for London to meet one of Canadair's financial backers. Juvonen sent a message to their hotel, and he and Aziz flew to London in the Ojjehs' Falcon 20 to pick them up. In Paris, the four of them piled into the backseat of Ojjehs' Rolls-Royce and went looking for Akram. He was at home, at the Château Le Forget.

The château, one of 52 homes Akram owned in Europe, was a national monument, which he had spent four years and millions of francs restoring, making it fit for a prince of the modern age. From the French doors of a large salon, Kearns looked out over what he thought was a greenhouse.

"I guess he must be growing tomatoes there," Kearns said innocently.

Juvonen and Kearns went to look at the greenhouse; it was a covered, heated pool with a discotheque. Kearns was amazed at the opulence. Juvonen told him the story Aziz had told about how, when Akram bought a large home in Cannes, he also acquired a Ferrari and a Maserati.

"They bought the house and didn't know the cars were there," Juvonen recounted. "When they opened the garage doors and found the cars, they were taken completely by surprise." Such wealth was amazing to Kearns.

Returning to the main salon, Kearns met Akram. Beside him was a beautiful young woman Kearns took for Akram's daughter, but she was introduced as his girlfriend. (The woman, a daughter of a Syrian defense minister, married Akram soon after.) Everyone went into the dining room. Over lunch, the charming began in earnest.

"Fred, what year is your birthday?" Akram asked. When told it was 1924, he said, "Then we shall drink champagne from 1924." And from the basement, one that Akram had never visited, since it was his first meal in the house, a servant brought a 1924 Lafitte Rothschild. Akram's glamorous villas, beautiful women, wine cellars, lavish parties and connections with rich and powerful people swept Kearns, the son of a feed-mill operator from the Ottawa Valley, off his feet. Kearns, ever the gregarious fellow, came to love TAG's parties, and he delighted in the glittering lives of the Ojjehs.

They quickly became friends. Akram, the arms dealer, found a kindred spirit in Kearns, the president of what had been a military contractor. Akram was attracted to things technological. TAG owned precision engineering and manufacturing companies, including the makers of the TAG Huer watch, and supported a car on the Grand Prix circuit. Kearns lit Akram's enthusiasm with talk of his technologically advanced business jet. They could see mutual benefits. Kearns saw the potential of selling jets to rich Arabs, and Akram saw the Challenger jet, and even Canadair, as a new jewel in his collection of high-technology enterprises.

"We would like to become a partner in this program," Akram told Kearns. Kearns resisted, with Taylor in full agreement, arguing that his government likely wouldn't allow it. But they agreed that TAG would have an exclusive distributorship to the Arab nations. When Kearns returned from the Paris Air Show he had an order for ten more Challengers, the biggest single order since Federal Express, and a new distributor for Challenger aircraft. He also had a new friend. Akram was different from other customers: he took an interest in the company and the people who ran it.

Bob Wohl, Canadair's legal counsel, was negotiating the TAG contract. He called Kearns.

"I've got some good news for you, Fred, they've raised their order to nineteen aircraft."

"That's great! But why nineteen? That seems an odd number."

"Nineteen plus the two already sold adds up to twenty-one, Akram's birthday."

"Oh, of course."

Not surprisingly, Jim Taylor objected to Canadair's relationship with TAG. By agreeing to Akram's plan to buy the airplanes and then resell them in the Arab world, Canadair was setting itself up for trouble. For Taylor the TAG deal was shaping up to be a carbon copy of the FedEx deal: it would take up a number of positions on the production line and it posed the threat of competition with Taylor's marketing efforts should TAG try to resell its airplanes in Taylor's domain. The deal violated what Taylor considered the basis of his coming aboard the program, that he, and only he, would have global control of marketing, the single-point marketing strategy. Taylor did everything he could to discourage Kearns from selling TAG any more airplanes. Kearns ignored Taylor and embraced TAG as the company's single most important customer.

With TAG on board, it was time to deal with Aeritalia. Canadair's would-be risk-sharing partner continued to talk a good game, but it still hadn't come up with a financial commitment from its owners, the Italian government. Finally Ottawa agreed to let Kearns suspend negotiations with Aeritalia and suspend the search for a risk-sharing partner.

Throughout the development phase, which ran from program go-ahead in November 1976 to certification in November 1980, Harry Halton controlled every aspect of the Challenger program. He also consulted extensively with outsiders. He had, after all, been in the industry for nearly forty years and knew a lot of people. Years of cocktail parties, dinners, conferences, favors and business cards had given Halton the connections he needed to call on the best and the most experienced to help him out. His list included K. Van Every at General Dynamics, a well-known aerodynamicist and friend of Canadair who helped Halton find six experts in the field of aerodynamics, and Halton's old friend Frank Davis, who provided professional analysis at a moment's notice.

From Boeing he got help from the director of preliminary design, Lloyd Goodmanson. From Lockheed came Bob Howard, who, with a group of retired Lockheed engineers who had worked on the L-1011 jumbo aircraft program, defined the Challenger's powered flight control system, one of the most complex aspects of the program. Halton had a mole at Lockheed who provided cost and engineering data from the JetStar program. He called Fred Ades, an Air Canada vice president of engineering, who helped out with the

FedEx requirements, and Thor Stephenson, former president of Pratt & Whitney. And he called dozens of consultants. Canadair paid handsomely for these services. Without them, the program would likely never have started.

These people supported Halton in a lot of the conceptual work. A greater challenge was finding the engineering work force needed for the massive amount of detail work that had to be done, and quickly. Like other North American aircraft manufacturers, Canadair had routinely gone to England to recruit aeronautical engineering talent during program buildups, and over the years had hired some three thousand British aircraft engineers. But by the mid-1970s, there were immigration quotas from Ottawa, and the British government was attempting to stem the brain drain. On a number of occasions Kearns and his vice president of personnel, Jacques Ouellet, went to Ottawa to plead with immigration officials to let British engineers into the country. Then they had to deal with Quebec City, which also had a say in immigration. The Parti Québecois had come to power, and the massive influx of highly skilled English-speaking people raised a few eyebrows. There was, however, little choice but to give Canadair what it wanted. Quebec's education system offered few courses in aeronautical sciences, and the pool of local talent was very shallow. Quebec knew this. When Halton needed more than eight hundred engineers to get the program rolling, the province made an exception in its restrictive immigration policy

To find British workers Halton used contract agencies, known as job shops. The British government helped develop the engineering contract agencies to loan engineers to offshore companies, in the hopes the engineers would stay in their native country. Canadair obtained nearly half its peak engineering requirement from these contractors. The engineers were more expensive—they earned about a third more than a comparable staff engineer—and the level of engineering talent was mixed. The mixed quality of talent and higher pay caused some tension among the Canadair engineers. But when the development phase was over, Canadair could send the British engineers home.

The amount of detailed design work was so enormous, however, Halton needed to go outside the company for help. He decided to set up a design office in the Los Angeles area, as there was a large pool of aeronautical talent there. Halton incorporated the office as a U.S.

subsidiary of Canadair, to preclude any export restrictions, and employed about forty engineers and staff. But the L.A. office soon fell twelve weeks behind schedule, and it never caught up. Design changes in the program in Montreal were coming at such a rate that the L.A. office couldn't keep up with the flow. When the completed designs finally arrived from L.A., the Montreal engineers said they were not acceptable: many of the most recent changes hadn't been incorporated. Eighteen months into the program, Halton closed the L.A. office,which had incurred costs of $5 million.

Another outside source that caused some trouble was Aeronautics R&D, the California company Lear introduced to Canadair. Aeronautics was contracted to come up with comprehensive aerodynamic load data, which were needed to begin the structural design of the airplane. These data would reveal how strong the structure should be to withstand stresses of external loads and other factors. The information was a long time coming and was an early cause of both the schedule problem and the weight problem. When the data finally arrived they were deemed unacceptable, largely because the contractor had not kept up with the changes in design. Halton abruptly canceled Aeronautics' contract and gave it to a major aerospace company.

Before long, both by design and by circumstance, Halton and his people were alone in running the program. Lear was gone. The outside design offices were gone. The risk-sharing partners were gone. Akram Ojjeh very much wanted to become a partner but Kearns wouldn't hear of it. The Canadian military contractor that had never designed and built a commercial jet airplane before had the program all to itself. It was all up to Harry and his Canadair engineers.

A conceit in the industry is that a new airplane is an airframe built around a new engine, that the airplane is as good as its engine. The reality is that while developing an engine takes much longer than developing an airframe, the risks are much higher for an airframe because there are many more unknowns and unknown unknowns, what the airframe industry calls "unk unks." The British-built BAC One-Eleven was the first civilian airplane to have its engines mounted on the rear of the fuselage with a T-tail horizontal stabilizer. This aircraft had a fatal design flaw that wasn't recognized until after a prototype crashed, killing half a dozen test pilots and certification officials. After the crash BAC and Douglas Company, which was designing a similar aircraft, redesigned the tail portion of the aircraft. The T-tail-induced deep stall remains one of the industry's most famous unk unks.

In his dash to keep to the schedule, Halton ran into numerous design unknowns. They came from many sources: a lack of confirmed data to tell how strong and how heavy the airframe structure would have to be to support itself; a lack of experience in designing an airframe to meet airline-type certification requirements; a lack of experience in designing a supercritical wing; and a lack of understanding of how difficult it would be to build an airplane with the kind of weight and range specifications announced at the first customer seminar in June 1976.

Dealing with all these unknowns would affect one crucial area: weight. Accurate and realistic prediction and control of the manufactured weight of an aircraft is always the biggest challenge facing an aircraft designer. Few aircraft have been developed without some increase in weight over initial predictions. Too much weight growth, and basic assumptions such as fuel capacity and engine thrust must be adjusted—causing increases in weight. Canadair underestimated the weight of the Challenger because they lacked load data—the information a designer needs when figuring the structural weight of the airplane. This was the start of Halton's chronic weight and schedule problems. When the test data finally came in, Halton was forced to change the initial design. He wrote in his diary: "I now believe that the conventional wisdom of not starting detail design without having *confirmed* detail [test data] is good wisdom and should not be tampered with. Alas, schedule pressures did not permit us to follow it."

Six months into the development schedule, increased weight figures came in for nearly every part of the airplane: pylon increased by 50 pounds; avionics up 27 pounds; engine mounts up 90 pounds; baggage door up 40 pounds; fuel system up 70 pounds; tail plane up 80 pounds; fuselage up 40 pounds; flight controls up 20 pounds; and so on. These seemingly modest increases were significant. The Challenger was a relatively small aircraft designed to fly long distances and was sensitive to the smallest increases in weight. The way things were going, it looked like the Challenger would be thousands of pounds overweight. The choices: to redesign major components; to select a new engine with more power to compensate; or to admit that the airplane wouldn't perform as promised. Halton decided he had to take some action.

At the April 1977 customer seminar, he announced a weight-reduction program intended to shave 2,000 pounds off the airplane by using nonmetallic composite materials of carbon, Kevlar and glass fibers set in a resin. These materials were to replace aluminum in secondary structural components. The industry, including Canadair, had used the new materials in less critical areas, but the extensive application announced by Halton was unprecedented. No one knew how the new materials would stand up to the stresses and temperatures of an airplane in flight at 36,000 feet and flying near the speed of sound.

But the composites program was flawed from the start. The engineer who headed the program tried to build a composite replica of the metal part. There wasn't time to implement a full development program: parts had already been designed, many of them were already in production, and nobody was willing to go back and redesign the parts. The quick composites were not good enough for the design engineers, who rejected them out of hand. Prototype components sat on shelves collecting dust, and Halton's weight-saving program, which never got past the first of five phases, died on the vine.

Halton had a difficult time getting his engineers to deal with the weight problem seriously. He kept challenging them to reduce each part by an ounce. They would have reduced the weight of the aircraft by more than a thousand pounds this way. He had more success with the companies that supplied Canadair with the manufactured components. He threatened them with terrible retributions if they didn't meet his strict weight limitations. But he never succeeded in persuading his own Weights Group to toe the line. The group had the power to reject any drawing if it didn't meet Halton's increasingly strict weight limitations, but they rarely used the veto. They were, to use Halton's words, "a too-nice set of guys" who didn't want to put pressure on design engineers who were already sweating to make the crazy schedule. Halton wanted the group to be weight controllers, but they were really weight accountants.

Near the end of 1977 Halton asked two outside consultants to carry out a weight reduction study. One was Ed Heinemann, the renowned chief designer of the lightweight U.S. Navy A-4 attack aircraft; the other was K. Van Every, Halton's contact at General Dynamics. The study recommended substantial changes to the airplane's systems and structural design. But the engineers complained that changes could not be incorporated if Halton wanted to meet his schedule. Changes to drawings were taking place at a high rate—in one month there were 1,500 changes—and many of them were being made to parts that were already in production. Halton's engineers balked at the notion of adding more changes for the sake of a weight program. Halton wrote in his diary: "All in all, during 1977, weight was the subject of innumerable memos and notes on my part to all concerned. Alas, with little success." As one engineer put it, "Sometimes Harry Halton just wouldn't face the facts, and one fact was we just couldn't meet the weight estimates he had predicted."

Every month thousands of design changes came from engineering. The detailed design process was falling apart, because each change caused other changes, and the designers simply couldn't keep up. The changes sometimes came about because Canadair's engineers were not yet fully familiar with an innovative system or new component they were designing. The main entry door, for example, generated hundreds of design changes because of problems incurred at altitude. There were problems with the landing gear doors, the fairings, the steering system, the power controls and the Branson fuel tanks. The flight test, static test and certification program generated thousands of changes. Material problems caused changes. Each day the company faced material availability problems, and each one generated more engineering changes to accommodate a substitute. But by far the most critical design change problem was weight growth. This was the predominant factor in making the airplane less than what had been promised to the customers.

Under Halton's direction, a group of engineers formed the Performance Improvement Program and struggled to trim the airplane one ounce at a time. They went all over the aircraft looking for items to change to make it lighter. After Halton had finally given up on shedding any more weight he initiated an increase in the maximum certificated takeoff weight of the airplane from 34,000 pounds to 36,500, then to 38,500 and finally to 40,100 pounds. The design changes were so numerous that the manufacturing people joked they were working on a new airplane every day.

There was one fact Halton was coming to terms with, one that was as serious as the weight problem: it now appeared certain he was going to have real problems with the airplane's engine, the Lycoming ALF-502.

Years later Fred Kearns would confess to Harry Halton that if he, Kearns, had gone to Avco Lycoming's engine facility in Stratford, Connecticut, and seen it for himself, it is quite possible he would not have considered the Lycoming engine. Canadair had signed the engine contract before anyone visited the facility. Those who went down all came back with the same impression: the place was a dump. Before the signing Fred Kearns had said repeatedly, on the subject of suppliers, "We don't need to see them because they are the experts and they know what they are doing." Early in the program Halton began to worry that perhaps these experts did not know what they were doing.

Harry Halton was the first Canadair person to view Avco Lycoming's facility. Decrepit as it was, the Avco Lycoming factory hummed with activity. Like Canadair, Avco Lycoming was a military contractor coming out of a major downturn when the Challenger program came along. The year Canadair signed with Avco Lycoming, the company received a long-awaited $40-million military contract to develop an engine for the Abrams XM-1 tank. The ALF-502 found another customer in the British Aerospace 146 small airliner program, and the company's LTS 101 turboshaft helicopter engine was a large-volume product. The increased level of activity made Halton optimistic. It showed that other clients had confidence in Avco Lycoming's capabilities. He was, however, concerned that too much activity might make Canadair just another customer to Avco Lycoming, and not a very important one, at that. It soon became apparent that's exactly what was going to happen.

If there was one thing that had impressed Canadair about the Connecticut engine manufacturer during the first negotiations, it was their commitment to support the Challenger program. Jim Kerr, Avco Lycoming's chairman, was an engine man who knew what things to say and how to say them. In airplane programs, the engine supplier and airframe maker often treat each other more like partners, since they both have their share of risk to assume, although the engine maker's is usually much less. In retrospect, this impression showed Canadair's naïveté.

Avco Lycoming's experience in turbine equipment was predominantly in the military, where the customer pays the cost of engineering and modifications and even buys many of the expensive machines to do the work. Avco Lycoming was used to paying partners, not risk-sharing partners. Even though Canadair had similar experience dealing with the military, it didn't occur to Kearns and the others that Avco Lycoming's commitment was anything less than a major risk-sharing partnership. All Canadair had to offer, in reality, was a purchase order and a lot of trust. In the end they got what they paid for.

Halton was disappointed by Avco Lycoming's lack of engineering depth when the two companies got their engineers together to start working on details. Soon after program go-ahead, Ned Dobak, the ALF-502 program manager, brought Avco Lycoming engineers and thermodynamic specialists up to Montreal to work with Halton's engineers on the engine intake and exhaust nozzle design. In Halton's eyes they were a lot less than he had expected from a committed engine supplier. They were few in number, only about half a dozen, and short on experience.

The Canadair-Avco Lycoming relationship proved difficult right from the start. Avco Lycoming moved the size of the engine nozzle up and down, which drove Canadair engineers crazy — the nozzle size helped determine the engine's performance on the airplane. Two Avco Lycoming performance computer decks — computer data cards that predict engine performance and are inserted into the computer program containing airframe design — proved to be invalid because they didn't have the correct airframe design data. Each side blamed the other for the inaccuracies, and this was the beginning of a long and frustrating process of trying to determine the specific range of the airplane.

Canadair and Avco Lycoming argued over thrust control and the necessity for engine synchronization. They argued over the methods of measuring installed engine thrust. Idle thrust, the amount of thrust coming out of the engines when the airplane is parked on the ground, became the next issue. Canadair requested that idle thrust be reduced in order to lessen wear and tear on the carbon brakes, installed to replace the steel brakes in order to save weight. Avco Lycoming said they couldn't lower the idle. To complicate matters, a feud broke out between Avco Lycoming and Rohr, the maker of the engine nacelles—the body that covers the engine—as to who would be responsible for the brackets that would attach the nacelles to the engine. Halton wasn't too concerned with the details of such disputes—but he was upset that the disputes arose at all.

The problems made Halton begin to suspect the worst, that Avco Lycoming's people didn't have an accurate understanding of the engine's thermodynamics, that is, how the air and fuel combined to create engine thrust under various conditions. They didn't know because they hadn't completed testing and development. The engine was not as advanced in development as Avco Lycoming claimed at the contract signing. One reason Canadair had selected Avco Lycoming had been that the engine appeared ready to go, with only certification left to be completed. Now the engine showed signs of needing development. Halton's suspicions were reinforced every time Avco Lycoming recalled its computer cards. Halton asked Thor Stephenson, former president of Pratt & Whitney, to carry out a thorough inspection at Avco Lycoming. Stephenson came back with a lot of warnings.

He said they didn't have a dedicated test bed for the engine. (The test bed was used to test thermodynamics.) He found this surprising, since every other manufacturer had one. Stephenson told Halton: "It's obvious that Avco Lycoming has some development work to do on your engine. Don't let them develop the engine by testing it on your airplane because that's what's going to happen unless you stop them."

Halton didn't let this warning distract him from his task, which was proceeding relatively smoothly, given the apparent chaos of the whole process. By early 1978 the Challenger was beginning to take shape on the factory floor, and it was an incredible sight to behold. In just 14 months the plane had gone from a drawing on a sheet of paper to an airframe on the shop floor, and Halton felt a tremendous sense of pride in his people and in himself. He was going to meet that crazy schedule after all. That is, if Avco Lycoming didn't screw things up.

But there were serious problems on the horizon. Halton was losing the battle against the airplane's weight, which was now nearly 2,000 pounds over the 15,000-pound Manufacturer's Weight Empty estimate. It was almost certain the airplane would be overweight. But a far more serious threat to Halton's development program was also apparent: the people who were going to certify the airplane were making some very scary noises.

The flight test and certification program for a new airplane usually accounts for about a third of total development costs. It is an extremely complex and detailed process of evaluation that involves millions of work hours and thousands of hours of flight time. The certification requirements for the Challenger were tough: it was to be the first commercial jet aircraft in North America to be certified under a new set of airworthiness rules recently established by the U.S. Federal Aviation Administration, the FAA. The new regulations were in a revised version of a document known as Federal Air Regulation (FAR) Part 25, the best known and most widely applied safety standard in the world.

But they were U.S. safety standards. Canadian authorities adopted FAR 25 as a standard, but Canada's Department of Transport (DoT) had a right to interpret that standard, and DoT didn't agree with the FAA on a number of issues. The man who exercised the right of interpretation was Ken Owen, a former RCAF test pilot who was director of airworthiness for DoT. It was Owen's boss, Walter McLeish, who had given Canadair such a tough time with the CL-215 water bomber. The Challenger flight test and certification program was going to be the biggest thing Owen and his people had ever seen, much bigger than the CL-215 program. For the first time they were going to certify a high-speed commercial turbofan airplane from scratch. It was a major task for a bureaucracy with limited resources and personnel. Owen often complained to Canadair and de Havilland in the hope that they would put pressure on Ottawa to beef up DoT. But there was little either company could do for him. And the lack of resources did not stop Owen from challenging one of the most respected aviation authorities in the world, the FAA.

Early in the development program Canadair found itself in the middle of a petty intergovernmental feud between the DoT and the FAA. The origins of the feud went back to an aircraft crash on July 5, 1970. On a beautiful Sunday morning an Air Canada DC-8 with 136 passengers was approaching Toronto International Airport. Everything was routine until the airplane was about 50 feet over the runway. For some reason still not explained, the second officer deployed the ground spoilers, which forced the airplane to drop like a rock onto the runway, shearing off one of the engines. The captain, unaware that he had lost an engine and struggling to control the airplane, tried to get airborne again for another approach. He made only a partial ascent. The wing that had lost the engine began to disintegrate. The leaking fuel exploded, and the airplane came crashing down from an altitude of 2,000 feet. Everyone on board was killed. It was Canada's worst aircraft accident. In the crash inquiry that followed, Justice Gibson ruled that the Canadian government had a responsibility to make a "reasonable inspection" of all types of foreign-built aircraft before they were certificated for airworthiness in Canada.

The Department of Transport, feeling itself the target of blame to a degree, interpreted the judge's "reasonable inspection" to mean that the 32-year-old bilateral agreement between the United States and Canada, under which they accepted each other's standards for airworthiness, no longer applied. No longer would aircraft approved by the FAA be accepted automatically for certification in Canada. More foreign-designed planes were seeking certification—even a Russian-built Yak-40 that was to be sold to a Canadian operator—when the DoT decided it would no longer rubber-stamp foreign designs. The lack of a bilateral understanding was further demonstrated in 1971 when the U.S. government sought to develop a multilateral accord with the world's aerospace industries. Under the accord, it would be easier for all countries to certify their aircraft abroad. In the end, Canada was the only country not to sign. Instead the DoT would conduct complex inspections of every new aircraft seeking certification in Canada, including airplanes from the United States.

The change was accompanied by another shift in DoT policy regarding the process of certification. In the civil aviation world there were two basic approaches to certification. In Britain, the chief engineer of an airplane program was given the responsibility of making sure the design conformed to airworthiness rules. In the United States, a program engineer had that responsibility. The engineer, called the Designated Engineering Representative (DER), prepared an outline describing how the aircraft manufacturer conformed to airworthiness rules *before* certification began. This approach appealed to the DoT, which was beginning to develop airworthiness requirements and a philosophy of certification. But the

DoT decided the manufacturers could not be trusted, as they were under the U.S. approach. The DoT decided to put DoT test pilots into the aircraft certification program from the start, rather than let the manufacturer use a DER. This was decided about the time of the CL-215 program, and it was when Canadair discovered that certification was a problematic process.

For one thing, Canadair's test pilots didn't like having DoT pilots looking over their shoulders all the time. Canadair wasn't alone in feeling harassed by the DoT. Its determination to set its own standards and validate FAA-approved aircraft for certification in Canada drove U.S. airplane manufacturers crazy. In the early 1970s, the DoT sent a team of 18 technicians to the United States to validate all the data of a helicopter destined for Canada. The validation cost the helicopter manufacturer a small fortune. The DoT got the FAA's back up when its pilots put a DC-10 into a high-speed dive that resulted in millions of dollars in damage to the horizontal tail. McDonnell Douglas, the manufacturer, said they would use their leverage through Canadian production agreements to get the DoT off their backs. It worked, although a Canadian carrier received its order of DC-10s months behind schedule.

High-ranking FAA officials remained deeply upset with the DoT after the DC-10 incident. The director of FAA's flight standard service, Dick Skully, cornered a senior DoT official at a Canadian embassy reception in Washington and said, "We're going to get even with you guys." He kept his word. A letter to the DoT in February 1978 said that the FAA intended to validate all the DoT's certification efforts for Canadian-built aircraft seeking certification with the FAA. The Challenger was the only Canadian-built aircraft seeking certification in the United States at the time; it might be the victim in the dispute between FAA and DoT. Canadair could see it coming, but was helpless.

The DoT never acknowledged the FAA letter. Since the Air Canada crash, the small and admittedly understaffed DoT had effectively isolated itself from the FAA. And, as Canadair found out when it tried to elicit some sympathy for its plight, few people would believe there was a dispute going on between the two agencies. Nobody could imagine the two agencies playing politics when the safety of thousands of flying passengers was at stake.

By 1978 Halton felt he had to do something. He managed to

convince the DoT that it would be a good idea to establish a liaison with the FAA for Challenger certification. Ed Bridgeland, Owen's predecessor and a diplomatic sort, was sent to talk to the FAA. It didn't help much. He met John Shaffer, the FAA's top safety administrator, and Al Blackburn, the Canadair consultant working for Jim Taylor. They had lunch in Washington, D.C., and it became apparent Canadair was headed for trouble.

Blackburn asked Bridgeland why the DoT never responded to the FAA letter. He said that if the FAA decided to validate the DoT's certification procedures, the Challenger program would be delayed. Bridgeland replied that the FAA should abide by the treaty. The fact that Canada did not abide by the treaty didn't seem to matter. But how could the Department of Transport expect the FAA to accept their certification of the Challenger if they still intended to make difficulties for airplanes built in the United States?

A month later a team of DoT officials descended on an aircraft manufacturer in the United States, Sikorsky helicopter. Ray Borowski, a regional FAA director, was furious. "This is a blatant derogation of our technical competence," Borowski told Blackburn. "I suspect there is some empire building going on here. I don't want to make the Challenger a pawn in this battle of the bureaucrats, but it soon may be out of my control."

These were the noises that were making Halton very uneasy as he proceeded with the final design and development stages of the first Challenger airplane. Then he had his first disagreement with the Department of Transport, over the stall issue.

Stall speed is a vital reference point for designers and airworthiness regulators. For the airplane designer, it's the speed upon which certain minimum operating speeds are based, a reference point to determine landing speed, which then determines the length of runway needed to land the airplane. The lower the stall speed, the better the takeoff and landing performance. With a good stall speed, an airplane can get into and out of small airports, which is of vital importance to business jet operators. They want to be able to fly into any airport, particularly when major airports are overflowing with traffic. Often just a few knots of stall speed can have a profound effect on the acceptability of the aircraft to the market. For airplane safety regulators, the stall speed establishes the airplane's lower speed boundaries—the envelope—for safe flight. For the Challenger, the stall speed should have been a fairly routine flight certification issue. It wasn't.

From their first meeting in July 1977, Halton had been telling Owen that the Challenger's inherent stall characteristics were probably not going to meet FAR Part 25 requirements and that an artificial stall barrier system would be necessary. Such a system would prevent the aircraft from going into a stall either by warning the pilot or by forcing the airplane out of the stall condition. This could be done with a stick shaker and stick pusher. When an airplane approached stall, the stick would shake and, if the airplane continued toward the stall, the stick automatically pushed forward to get the nose of the airplane down so the airplane could pick up speed and avoid the stall. The mechanism was called an artificial stall barrier.

Most conventional airplanes have a controllable natural stall— when the airplane reaches its stall speed, the pilot gets a warning. The airplane may shake, which is called a buffet. The nose may go down. Or the wing may drop to a small degree. These are small changes, and the pilot can execute an easy recovery. The FAA recognizes a wing drop of 20 degrees as the safe limit for a controllable stall. The Challenger's engineers suspected the airplane would have a wing drop much greater than 20 degrees. That would mean the airplane would have an *uncontrollable* natural stall—the pilot would *not* be able to recover once the plane went into the stall.

The Challenger's wing would drop more than 20 degrees because of the supercritical wing design. The wing was designed for high speeds, which results in a diminished performance at low speeds. It was also subject to a higher degree of pressure at low speeds than were other wing profiles; that pressure would cause the wing to drop at low speeds.The pressure gathered at the wing tip and made the wing drop severely. One possible solution was the use of high-lift devices, such as movable flaps installed on the leading edges of the wing. The devices would improve lift performance at low speeds and help reduce the drop. Halton did not give the high-lift devices serious consideration because his version of the supercritical wing was extremely lightweight and would not have supported the high-lift devices. He also suspected the devices would not withstand high-speed impacts with birds. Halton could use artificial stall warning mechanisms, which would prevent the pilot from going into a stall; or he could redesign the leading edge so the wing would stall at higher speeds, speeds at which the pilot could still control the airplane. The new wing design would create what the government certification people called a natural controllable stall speed.

Halton told Owen he intended to proceed with the design of the airplane on the assumption that there would be an artificial stall barrier system; he had no intention of designing the airplane to have a controllable natural stall. It was completely contrary to the design objective for a high-speed civilian aircraft; the Challenger was not designed to have flawless low-speed characteristics. A stall warning system was the answer if the airplane was going to have controllable low-speed characteristics.

Owen did not agree. He did not like artificial stall barrier systems; he believed the airplane must show a safe natural stall, and he stated that the DoT would not accept the artificial stall barrier.

Halton made a pitch he knew would be shot down. He proposed to certify the airplane with the artificial stall barrier in place, and said he considered in-flight stall tests unnecessary. This was the way the FAA would certify the airplane. Owen disagreed. Halton then proposed that Canadair do the stall tests but with the artificial stall barrier system in place. He pressed ahead to get an artificial barrier developed.

For more than a year after those meetings in early 1977, Halton and Owen volleyed over the issue of an artificial stall barrier system without resolving their differences. Communication broke down along the way, and the seed of a future conflict was sown.

Nineteen months after go-ahead the first Challenger rolled out of the factory. It seemed Canadair had pulled off one of the greatest engineering and commercial coups Canada had ever seen. Unfortunately, the Challenger's originator, Bill Lear, didn't see the Challenger. Eleven days before the world got its first look, the king was dead.

The first civilian jet produced in this country came in record time and close to budget. The skeptics who said it couldn't be done were momentarily silenced by Canadair's success. It appeared that Canadair's gamble on the Challenger business jet had paid off. The day the first airplane was rolled out, May 25, 1978, TAG popped another order of 10 aircraft, bringing its total order to more than 30 Challengers. The company had a new plane coming off the production line, a bulging order book and a good-looking balance sheet. Half a dozen business schools made case studies of the program, and the first Challenger made a splash in the media.

But the Challenger, like an underage debutante, was not ready to go out into the real world. First flight after roll-out is usually a matter of weeks, but the Challenger was still no more than a shell, and it would be another five months before all systems would be installed, tested and operating. There were a lot of bugs in the engines, and there was still the matter of the excess 2,000 pounds. Harry Halton had a lot of work ahead of him. All he needed was time.

As Halton pressed ahead, completing the final stages of airplane development before first flight, Jim Taylor, the man who was selling the airplane to the world, stated in no uncertain terms that he was not happy with Halton's airplane.

"We have a serious problem," Taylor wrote Kearns two months before the first flight of the Challenger 600. "We will be delivering something less than what we sold." By the time the first Challenger was delivered, two years later, Taylor was prepared to declare the airplane an unmitigated failure. He wanted what had been promised and would settle for nothing less.

7

Prelude to disaster

As the Challenger approached a state of readiness for the first flight, the pilots and engineers who would fly and test the airplane began to take over. Ron Neal, Halton's second in command, organized the engineering side of the test program, while Doug Adkins, Canadair's chief test pilot and director of flight operations, organized the team of pilots to conduct the flight testing.

A native of Medicine Hat, Alberta, Adkins got his wings in the Royal Canadian Air Force during the Korean War, but he soon realized he was not cut out for the military. While training in Germany, the young recruit earned a reproof on his military record for blowing up in front of a superior because he, in his opinion the best fighter pilot in the squadron, had been passed over for duty in Korea in favor of a more experienced pilot. Adkins was 22. In 1954 he transferred to the RCAF Reserve Support Squadron and enrolled in Canada's only aeronautical program, at the University of Toronto. During his periodic flight training with the reserve he noticed something odd at the Avro aircraft factory. Workers were using blow-torches to cut a couple of CF-105 Avro Arrow prototypes to pieces. Over a period of two weeks Adkins watched from the air as the supersonic aircraft were dismembered limb by limb. If this was the future of Canadian aerospace, maybe he should get into another line of work. But his sickness for flying was stronger than this specter of a doomed industry, and in 1961 he got his bachelor of applied science in engineering physics.

Because there were no test-pilot openings available, Adkins started at Canadair as an engineer with the understanding that he would be made a test pilot as soon as a position opened. Once he made test pilot Adkins rarely had his feet on the ground. He tested every aircraft Canadair built during those years: CF-104s, CF-5s, CL-84 tilt wings. He worked as an engineer on the hydrodynamics of the CL-215 water bomber and was the first pilot to test fly it. By 1991 he had flown more than 13,000 hours, nearly all of them at Canadair. (Test pilots generally hang up their wings after 4,000 hours.) Adkins wasn't kidding when he said flying was an incurable sickness for him.

On the ground, Adkins was restless and impatient, particularly with aircraft regulators from the Department of Transport. During the certification of the CL-215 water bomber, Adkins's temper was frequently ignited by DoT personnel. When the Challenger program was launched and Halton made Adkins director of flight operations, he hadn't mellowed. "If DoT could figure an interpretation that would hold you up so you couldn't do something, they would do it with almost perverse pleasure," Adkins said. "They were obstructionist."

He also had problems with the other engineers. His biggest problem was Ron Neal, the American engineer Halton had hired in the first year of the program. Neal was responsible for organizing the flight test and certification program, and Adkins didn't like Neal. In fact, Adkins took exception to just about every aspect of the Challenger's flight test and certification program. If there was one thing Adkins had become convinced of in his years of flight testing, it was that the world was out to get the test pilot.

Early in the program Adkins had told Halton he would prefer to have the flight test program done in Montreal. The hassle of relocating was unattractive to the pilots, and being far away from the company's support resources would not help matters, either. Halton said that wouldn't be possible. The accelerated development program required a fast flight test and certification program, so the flight test crew would need perfect flying weather. This was hardly possible in Montreal, or anywhere in Canada, for that matter. Halton had led a flight test program in the Arizona desert, and he knew where he wanted to test the Challenger: California. Moreover, he knew of a company there that could help with the flight test and certification program. Adkins didn't like the sound of this at all.

Canadair would certainly need all the help it could get given the demanding schedule. Frank Davis, the former president of General Dynamics' Fort Worth division, told Kearns as much early in the program. He questioned whether Canadair was capable of carrying out the complex flight test program on its own and urged Kearns to look for help. It wasn't long before help came looking for Canadair.

When a new program comes along, flight test pilots usually beat a path to the manufacturer's door. In 1977 Al Blackburn, the consultant working for Canadair's marketing division, called up Bob Laidlaw, an MIT classmate and fellow test pilot who was president of Flight Systems Inc. (FSI) of Mojave Airport in California. Laidlaw, a flight test pilot with an engineering degree, had built up a business testing government military hardware for the Vietnam war effort. But the war was over, and although he was doing about $10 million a year in business, the Challenger program would be a big contract for him, one that could possibly launch his modest company into the big time. Laidlaw didn't need much convincing from Blackburn that he should get involved with the Canadair Challenger program. "The man you want to talk to is Harry Halton," Blackburn told Laidlaw.

When Laidlaw called and explained what he and his company could offer, Halton saw a potential partner. He would not contract out the flight test program, but he could use Laidlaw's resources under Halton's control. Kearns and Halton discussed the matter just after program go-ahead and decided Laidlaw and his company might be the answer. Halton called Laidlaw and asked him to come up with a proposal for flight testing, final assembly and preflight operations. From then until the start of flight testing a year and a half later, Laidlaw thought he had a chance to run the flight test program and be responsible for certification. It was a dangerous misunderstanding that Canadair would pay dearly for.

Flight testing a brand new aircraft such as the Challenger is a complex and difficult process for the simple reason that every single aspect of the aircraft must be tested. A company that progressively develops related types of aircraft may be able to benefit from commonality of systems and procedures. Canadair, however, was developing its first civilian high-speed jet aircraft.

The process of flight testing is straightforward. Engineers provide a list of items to be tested. A flight test observer plans the tasks before flight and makes the observations during flight. The test pilot carries out the tasks by flying the necessary profile. All data are recorded and analyzed by engineers, who produce certification reports. With a new aircraft there are thousands of tasks to be performed, requiring a lot of time in the air before the aircraft is approved for delivery to customers. And, with the Department of Transport's new approach, DoT test pilots would follow along each step of the way.

During the year before flight testing, FSI's Bob Laidlaw developed expectations of a significant role. Halton did nothing to discourage him, although he tried to convince Laidlaw that the new DoT approach to certification would mean the government pilots would have a large share of the flight testing responsibility.

In 1977 Laidlaw and Halton worked together to plan the Challenger flight test program. It would be located at FSI's base at the Mojave Airport, a dusty, windswept ex-Marine Air Corps base. Laidlaw and a few hobby pilots were its only occupants. As Laidlaw understood it, Canadair wanted an off-site operation in the United States, but didn't want to set up another division of the company. Halton proposed to subcontract with a company for support but not management of the flight test operation. Laidlaw was asked to make a proposal that involved the construction of a hangar, the setting up of a data system, a flight test recording system, a ground data analysis station, tooling, furniture, metal workers, secretaries, the works. Canadair would provide the engineers, the managers and foremen and the test pilots. In early 1977 the contract was awarded to Laidlaw on the basis of a preliminary proposal. Laidlaw went to work on a final proposal. He believed that Canadair was not capable of doing the flight test and certification on its own and would be so impressed with his resources and skills that it would give him a large measure of control of the Mojave program. Laidlaw contracted high-priced consultants to put together a final and very detailed proposal built around the concept of a Canadair-FSI team with FSI playing a major role. The proposal included substantial technical participation from talent Laidlaw had culled from the area. (Edwards Air Force Base was nearby.) He sent the proposal to Canadair a few weeks before the Challenger was rolled out of the hangar in May 1978, and arrived two weeks later ready to hear the response to his terrific proposal. Laidlaw was in for a big surprise.

It didn't take an aeronautical engineer to figure out that Doug Adkins would have a problem with the idea of Laidlaw and his company. During the year of discussion and preparation for testing in the Mojave, Adkins began to see Laidlaw as someone trying to

Canadair's president Fred Kearns and the CL-215 water bomber. The CL-215 was an ungainly looking but highly efficient flying fire engine that was sold successfully in Canada, Greece and France, swapped for wine in Spain and frozen out of the U.S. market.

After chaotic negotiations and false starts, Bill Lear (centre) finally agreed to sign an option agreement with Canadair to build the LearStar 600 in 1976. Also at the signing were (l to r) chief engineer Harry Halton, Moya Lear, Lear, Canadair chief counsel Bob Wohl and president Fred Kearns.

The first Challenger wing is hoisted out of its jig (above) and later mated to the fuselage (below). The designer and the sales and marketing team both wanted the plane developed in record time to beat the competition. The tight production schedule meant that design changes were being made as parts were in production, leading to occasional chaos and cost over-runs.

Courtesy of Canadair

Only 19 months after program go-ahead, the first Challenger 600 is rolled out to unanimous applause in 1978. However, the aircraft was little more than a shell and, due to further production and engine problems, would not make its first flight for another six months.

Courtesy of Canadair

Treasury Board President Jean Chrétien (above, right) was one of the cabinet ministers who supported the Challenger program. Bill Lear called him and assured him that Canadair could sell a thousand airplanes. Antoine Guerin (below, right) was assistant deputy minister at Industry, Trade and Commerce and the company's strongest supporter in government. When things began to unravel, Guerin began lobbying Canadair's board for a job with the company.

Courtesy of Canadair

Marketing president Jim Taylor (left) and chief engineer Harry Halton (right) maintained an uneasy relationship as Taylor demanded nothing but the best (as soon as possible) for his customers and Halton struggled with growing engine and certification problems.

Taylor's sales team of Dave Hurley (left) and Bill Juvonen (right) was hired after gruelling interviews and tests that one candidate said were more appropriate for a position at NASA. The job was a lucrative one for knowledgeable sales staff who were willing to work hard and the team was responsible for nearly all the Challenger sales.

Courtesy of Peter Aird

Finance vice president Peter Aird thought he had raised all the capital he needed for the Challenger project after the first bond issue. As the program progressed and costs spiralled, he found himself canvassing banks and bond markets for more and more cash, armed with letters of comfort signed by the ITC minister to guarantee the loans.

Courtesy of Canadair

Ron Neal was hired as an assistant to chief engineer Harry Halton to keep the engineers up to speed and provide an American presence on staff that would hopefully make the plane more attractive to the U.S. market.

Courtesy of Canadair

Andy Throner's manufacturing unit was charged with producing the Challenger. While his staff had experience building all kinds of aircraft, they would be almost overwhelmed by the Challenger design changes and the schedule.

Fred Smith, chairman of Federal Express (right), was the Challenger's biggest customer in the early days of the program and modifications were made to accommodate the needs of the cargo hauler. After deregulation of the U.S. aviation industry, Smith no longer needed the 25 Challengers on order. The future looked bleak until Fred Kearns (below, center) met Mansour (left) and Aziz (right) Ojjeh and their father Akram. Akram Ojjeh was a Saudi trader who signed on to sell the Challenger into the rich Arab market.

Courtesy of Harry Halton

Mojave, California was the site of the long and tortuous flight test and certification program. Before it was over, Canadair would lose Challenger One (above) and a pilot, and chief test pilot Doug Adkins (below) would take charge of the lengthy and dangerous stall testing.

Courtesy of Canadair

Courtesy of Harry Halton

The bitterly contested issue of stall testing was finally resolved when Department of Transport airworthiness director Ken Owen (right) succeeded in forcing Harry Halton (left) to reconfigure the airplane to meet DoT's tough rules on stall protection. Only then, in 1980, did the Challenger get the OK for production.

Courtesy of Dick Richmond

In the first year after certification, Canadair had hoped to deliver 70 Challengers. Instead the assembly line (opposite, top) was nearly at a standstill, in part due to continuing problems with the engine (opposite, bottom). When the problems and the cost over-runs forced the company to cut back to two aircraft a month, drastic action was needed. In 1981, Dick Richmond (above left) was brought in to take over the engineering division and Vince Ambrico (right) replaced Andy Throner in production. The GE engine replaced the Avco Lycoming and the Challenger 601 model was born.

Courtesy of Canadair

As costs soared in 1982, ITC minister Herb Gray (above, left) put a cap on Canadair's borrowing and warned of dire consequences if the $1.35 billion mark was passed. Six months later Canadair exceeded the limit and the government sent in Gil Bennett (below, left) and Joel Bell (below, right) of the Canada Development Investment Corporation to examine the books and make some changes.

Courtesy of Canadair

CBC *fifth estate* co-host Eric Malling (above) got wind of the problems and cost over-runs at Canadair and started to investigate. The result was a dynamite show that created a furor across the country. Executives were fired or demoted and CDIC trustees Bell (below left), Senator Jack Austin (center) and Bennett (right) were called before a Parliamentary committee in 1983 to explain the situation.

Once the problems with the Challenger were settled and the program began to look like the success it was meant to be, a battle broke out among the remaining executives to see who would lead Canadair into the future. After a prolonged and fruitless struggle, an outsider, Pierre Des Marais II (above), former chairman of the Montreal Urban Community was appointed. After a second salvo from *fifth estate*, marketing vice president Jim Taylor was fired and replaced by his rival Charles Vogeley (left), former vice president of Gulfstream Aerospace.

Brian Mulroney's Conservative government finally sold Canadair in 1986 to Quebec-based transportation company Bombardier Inc., headed by Laurent Beaudoin.

Courtesy of Canadair

Bombardier has continued to show confidence in Canadair and its abilities. In 1991, the Regional Jet (above), a stretched version of the Challenger based on Harry Halton's original design for the aircraft, began its certification tests.

muscle in on the glory. He thought of Laidlaw as an arrogant American trying to take something away from the Canadians. When Adkins read Laidlaw's comprehensive proposal, it confirmed his fears. Canadair had already committed to working with Laidlaw, so there was no turning back, but Adkins never trusted Laidlaw and his group.

When Laidlaw arrived in Montreal, Halton pulled him into his office for a talk.

"Bob, I've got a problem with your proposal," Halton told Laidlaw. "You give the impression of running the show, and that just won't wash here. I'm afraid you're in for a rough ride tomorrow."

The next day a program management meeting took place, and Adkins went after Laidlaw. He challenged and humiliated Laidlaw, then took great pleasure in watching an uncomfortable Ron Neal, who was responsible for the flight test program, inform Laidlaw that FSI's role would be limited to providing basic services, no more than that. Laidlaw's technical management contributions, valuable as they might have been, were not wanted. Laidlaw said he didn't believe Canadair could pull it off without his help. Neal, for one, felt embarrassed.

"For that year Laidlaw really believed he would run the program or at least have a large hand in the technical side, the challenging part of the program and the only part that really matters to a test pilot like Laidlaw," Neal recalled later. "Canadair has to be blamed for not laying it out until the last minute."

Laidlaw returned home a disappointed man. He had made many promises to his employees based on his understanding, or rather misunderstanding, with Halton. When he got back to Mojave, Laidlaw told his people, "Give Canadair what they want and no more."

It rained all week. It was a dreary Montreal November and the flight test crew was growing impatient. Everybody at Canadair was getting impatient. The Challenger had been ready for nearly a week for first flight, but each day the flight was canceled because of the weather. Near the end of the week the weather system finally broke, and on November 8, 1978, Harry Halton gave the okay for the first flight of the Challenger.

It was an unqualified success. Normally when a new airplane takes to the air for the first time, it's rolled into the hangar as soon as it has landed and work begins on fixing all the bugs uncovered during the flight. Not with the Challenger. It went so well Halton ordered the airplane into the air for a second flight, possibly an unprecedented event in the business, to conduct more tests.

A week later the honeymoon was over. It was time to find out how serious the problem was with the plane's stall characteristic. On that day Doug Adkins strapped himself into the pilot's seat and flipped the "power on" switch. He snapped a blank cassette into a tape recorder and began to talk. He noted the time, the mission and the weather conditions. He was calm and precise and gave no indication that he was about to begin the most dangerous part of any flight test program: he was going to stall the airplane in flight. The plan was to take the airplane up to about 35,000 feet, slow down until the airplane was almost stationary in the air, then wait to see what happened. Adkins was going to find out how a Challenger behaved just before it dropped, bottom first, out of the sky. No one knew what would happen, exactly, but the aerodynamic engineers had a pretty good idea it was going to be rough, perhaps dangerous, maybe even fatal.

Adkins was all business. He gave the Challenger the throttle and in several minutes he was flying at 35,000 feet. Slowly he began to pull back. The speed gradually decreased. Adkins read the airspeed and angle of attack numbers into the tape recorder.

Suddenly the left wing of the airplane dropped violently; the drop was so deep the airplane was nearly upside down. Quick reflexes helped Adkins to recover—he twisted the controls in the other direction before the drop went past 120 degrees and got the airplane onto a steady flight path.

"Well, now, that was interesting, wasn't it?" he said coolly into the tape recorder.

When the Challenger reached stall speed, it became uncontrollable. Given the position of the Department of Transport on the stall issue, certifying the airplane was not going to be easy. It was up to Halton and the Department of Transport to find a solution.

Based on his long-standing and uneasy acquaintanceship with Owen, Halton had known from the start that he was going to have a tough time getting many of his flight test ideas past him. Halton hoped he would be allowed to satisfy many of the certification requirements on the basis of design data from computers and wind tunnels. Owen knocked down nearly every attempt to do so, requesting instead that Halton satisfy the requirements with actual flight testing. Owen wanted a thorough certification program that tested the integrity of the design and construction. He would not allow any shortcuts. Halton did not complain because he knew it would be a waste of time. Owen's boss, a deputy-level transport ministry official named Walter McLeish, was ready to back him up. But when it came to the stall issue, Halton complained bitterly and refused to comply with Owen's requests until he had to admit that he had lost a major contest of wills. Eventually Halton had to agree to design the airplane to stall at a higher speed; the stall would then have more controllable characteristics.

The question of the airplane's stall speed and how to avoid dangerous flying characteristics was complicated by the problem of the deep stall, a hazard particular to aircraft with a T-tail, so-called because of the shape of the rear horizontal stabilizer that sits atop the tail fin. When the tail of a T-tail airplane sinks down, the engine exhaust blasts directly at it; at the same time the flow of air going to support the tail is cut off by the changing angle of the wing as the nose of the airplane rises. The result is a T-tail that is uncontrollable, and it is nearly impossible to recover the aircraft. The airplane drops helplessly earthward. This is the deep stall.

The first design of the Challenger didn't have a T-tail; the horizontal stabilizer was located low on the fuselage in Bill Lear's original design. This configuration didn't have the great disadvantage of the T-tail, the dangerous deep stall characteristic. But because the engines were at the rear of the fuselage, engine exhaust would interfere with the operation of the tail area. A T-tail was the only solution.

The Department of Transport's certification people were wary of the T-tail design. They remembered the British-built BAC One-Eleven prototype, the airliner that had crashed and killed its flight test crew in 1963. That crash also made the DoT suspicious of artificial stall barriers. The BAC One-Eleven crew had disconnected the experimental artificial stall barrier after a series of false stalls had caused the system to engage unnecessarily. These were the very early days of stall barrier technology, and the settings for airspeed and other flight characteristics were not precise. During flight the aircraft had gone into a deep stall; the crew did not recognize it, and the airplane crashed. Since then, the stall warning system had become a generally accepted piece of equipment on most T-tail airplanes. The technology had advanced, and there were sophisticated systems to alert the pilot by various means that the airplane was approaching critical stall speeds.

When Adkins stalled the Challenger and immediately went into a 120 degree roll, it was clear the Challenger exceeded the FAA's 20 degree wing-drop limit. At its natural stall point, the Challenger's behavior was dangerous. An artificial stall point would have to be determined and artificial stall barrier systems installed that would warn the pilot before the aircraft went out of control. Halton understood that Owen objected to such a system, but he refused to acknowledge it.

The Department of Transport made a stand in July 1978, four months before first flight. Owen said the DoT wasn't going to decide on the use of a stall barrier until Canadair had done an analysis of the Challenger's stall characteristics, and that couldn't be done until Canadair had flight tested the airplane. When Halton asked what Canadair's options would be if the flight tests confirmed the airplane didn't have safe stall characteristics, something everybody knew for a fact anyhow, he got a reply that sent shivers through program management—Owen said he could use the artificial stall barrier or he could redesign the airplane.

Every one of Canadair's staff of 70 who arrived at Mojave at the start of 1979 knew that the schedule was everything. Far away from home and under incredible pressure to deliver, the challenge to manage the flight test program without incident was immense. The staff's temporary home, the Mojave site, was nothing more than a few buildings and a lot of desert that began just north of Los Angeles and stretched hundreds of miles into Death Valley. Mojave Airport lay in an extremely windy landscape dotted with Joshua trees. The carefully planned 13-month Mojave flight test program defied everyone's best efforts and lasted 21 months.

Life at Canadair's new Mojave facility began very early in the morning. Hundreds of tasks had to be performed on the ground as well as in the air. The urgency of the schedule was immediately apparent. It flowed from the program office in Montreal, through the engineers at Mojave to the test pilots. Such pressure is not abnormal. Test programs are expensive undertakings, and they must be completed as quickly as possible. At one point the Challenger test program was costing Canadair more than $5 million a month.

Doug Adkins didn't like the decision to do flight testing in Mojave or cooperate with Bob Laidlaw's team, and he was critical of everything Laidlaw provided. This didn't help an already delicate situation. The FSI staff, all highly skilled aircraft people, outnumbered Canadair employees nearly three to one, yet very few of them were used directly in the program. At Mojave, the Canadair team kept very much to itself, and it was clear to Laidlaw that Adkins was behind this. The Challenger was Adkins's airplane, not Laidlaw's, and Adkins took every opportunity to remind him of this fact.

Laidlaw was not the only one to feel shut out by Adkins. Jim Woods, the man Ron Neal hired to be the general manager of the Mojave operation for Canadair, had been a test pilot for the U.S. Air Force. Woods was desperately keen to get involved in the flight testing of the Challenger, but he had been hired by Neal, and therefore Adkins excluded him from flight operations. In the end a bitter and frustrated Woods took his anger out on the pilots. He became a merciless taskmaster and bullied the pilots.

Adkins's appointment of Al Baker as chief test pilot for the Mojave operation was far more damaging to the program than Neal's appointment of Woods. Baker was hired because of his background as a former Department of Transport test pilot. His job was to build a working relationship between Canadair and the DoT flight test observers on site. He had been recommended by the DoT as the best person to usher through the flight testing program. It didn't work out that way. Instead Baker became a major source of antagonism between Canadair and the DoT.

The DoT eventually came to a decision on the stall issue, and the bad news came in a letter from a low-level DoT official to a Canadair engineer in July 1979. The DoT would not accept the artificial stall barrier. Halton immediately went to see Owen in Ottawa.

"You can't do this, Ken. It's crazy!" Halton told Owen. "Every other jurisdiction accepts artificial stall barriers on these types of airplanes, why not you guys?"

Owen was unmoved. He told Halton that Canadair needed to do

further tests on the configuration of the airplane. In other words, Owen was questioning the Challenger's basic design. It was a terrible blow to Halton. Owen reminded him of the Challenger's violent wing drop in a stall. "If you guys can't cure that problem, you'll just have to redesign the airplane."

Seven months into the flight test program, Owen wanted Canadair to redesign the aircraft. Halton began to research how the stall situation had been treated elsewhere. He confirmed that nearly all T-tail airplanes had been certificated with artificial stall barriers. He reread the FAA rulings on artificial stall barriers and found that the barriers met safety requirements, and that it wasn't necessary for the manufacturer to undertake dangerous stall tests to prove that the airplane didn't have acceptable natural stall characteristics. Yet Owen and his team were forcing Canadair to do just that. One FAA ruling in particular struck Halton. It was a precedent-setting decision regarding the use of artificial stall barriers in the Learjet. Twelve years later the FAA had reaffirmed the precedent, stating that the "philosophy underlying the approval of the stick pusher/shaker is applicable if it is required to create a barrier to prevent reaching the aerodynamic stall due to hazardous stall characteristics."

If Canadair had to make design changes and perform more stall testing, then the pace of activity would have to be speeded up considerably to meet the schedule. Halton and Neal realized things were already moving too slowly and that the two men they had sent down to manage the engineering aspects, Jack Greniaus and Odd Michaelson, were swamped by the details of the project. Hundreds upon hundreds of testing events remained to be organized. Halton decided to send down his chief of flight sciences, George Turek, to crack the whip.

Turek knew the work load was a problem, but he got a shock when he attended his first meeting between DoT officials and Canadair's test pilots. Chief pilot Al Baker sat at the head of the table, and as the DoT officials laid out yet another series of dangerous stall tests to be performed that day, Turek could see Baker's face becoming red with rage. Normally Baker was a soft-spoken gentleman without a trace of rancor; that day Turek was looking at a totally different person. The fissure between Baker and the DoT was profound. The DoT was continuing to demand stall tests. Baker thought the tests were dangerous and unnecessary. He was bitterly opposed to the whole process.

Turek could see Baker weakening under the strain. He began delegating important flight tests instead of doing them himself. One of those tests was the minimum unstick speed test. It is a difficult and risky maneuver that determines the minimum speed required for the airplane to become airborne. Baker gave the job to a junior pilot named Ron Haughton, who nearly crashed the plane when its wing grazed the ground on lift-off. A more serious accident, it seemed, would be just a matter of time.

The stall issue was by no means the only problem dogging Halton's flight test program. The Lycoming engine, which had been slowing the schedule since design, continued to be plagued with problems when it went into production. Avco Lycoming asked for a special inspection of the engine weeks before the first flight was scheduled. They found defects, and the completed engines had to be returned to the factory. This delayed the first flight. It was also the beginning of a long series of reliability problems with the engines. When flight testing was underway Canadair discovered engine instability at high altitudes. Then the engine ground tests showed fan gear failures. Halton knew that Avco Lycoming had had gear problems on two military models but understood that the problems had been fixed after a redesign effort. If Avco Lycoming was going through the same problem again, there could be significant delays. Avco Lycoming placed speed restrictions on the engines it had belatedly delivered.

Another problem was the specific fuel consumption (SFC). The SFC separates the gas guzzlers from the fuel-efficient airplanes. Avco Lycoming had delivered engines that it admitted barely met the sea-level SFC guarantees of the contract. Then Avco Lycoming said there was a two percent degradation of the SFC at sea level on production engines; a fix was in the works, it added. When Avco Lycoming and Canadair did high-altitude SFC tests in March 1979, five months after first flight, they got a big shock. The tests showed how far the airplane could fly on a full tank of gas, and they showed that the SFC shortfall at altitude was a lot worse than Avco Lycoming had projected. A two-percent SFC degradation would have been a serious problem. Canadair discovered that the SFC shortfall at altitude was between four and six percent, and some unsubstantiated data pointed to a ten percent degradation. That would make the Challenger less fuel-efficient than promised, with a shorter range, around

2,700 nautical miles instead of the promised 3,600. The Challenger could not be an intercontinental jet at that range. And there was no way the aircraft could fly from Jeddeh to London against head winds, something that was pointed out to TAG by Jim Taylor. For Taylor, who had boasted to customers that the Challenger would hop continents with ease, the Challenger's range deficiency was truly bad news. He risked losing his credibility. Avco Lycoming disputed the results but didn't supply their own confirmed SFC results for almost another year and a half. This left Canadair with a bad SFC figure it couldn't substantiate. Customers wanting to know the SFC were left in the dark, as well. Taylor, already frustrated because the Challenger had engines he had opposed from the start, increased his campaign to get Avco Lycoming out of the program.

Halton had to admit that Avco Lycoming was at least diligent in acknowledging most of the problems, but they were less diligent about solving them quickly. Each problem wasted time, and every solution took longer and longer to arrive. From the start of the test program, the engine difficulties compounded the pressures already building in Mojave.

Six months into the flight test program rumors began circulating among customers that Avco Lycoming and Canadair were having reliability problems with the engine. Test pilots complained of in-flight failures and delays in receiving parts, and word spread. Dick Van Gemert of Xerox, who kept close to the program, picked up on these rumors and asked Avco Lycoming's program manager, Bob Schaefer, who succeeded Ned Dobak, if there were any problems. "You better ask Canadair about that," Schaefer told Van Gemert.

Fred Kearns still believed there was no problem that could not be solved. Kearns was not interested in changing his decision to select the Lycoming engine. He had faith in Avco Lycoming, and he held that faith right to the bitter end. He steadfastly refused to entertain a proposal from General Electric, despite the repeated requests from Jim Taylor, until the summer of 1979, when Halton told him the problems with the Lycoming were so bad that perhaps Canadair had better prepare an alternative.

Halton had been seeing people from GE since the start of the flight test program in early 1979. GE's Art Adinolphi had come to Halton and said GE had done more development work on the TF-34, the engine it had half-heartedly proposed in 1976. GE had since made a corporate commitment to certify a civilian version of the engine and was looking for business. To back up his point Adinolphi offered to run the engine on a Challenger model in the wind tunnel at GE's expense. It was a good deal: GE would do the tests and modifications and Canadair would own the results. Halton, sensing major problems with Avco Lycoming, gave his blessing to GE. Canadair lawyer Bob Wohl reviewed the Avco Lycoming contract for any clauses that might prevent Canadair from allowing such tests and agreed, on the condition that the deal was kept strictly under wraps. Kearns didn't like the idea because he still believed in Avco Lycoming, but he agreed to the tests.

Taylor's campaign to denigrate the Lycoming-powered Challenger 600 in favor a GE-powered model picked up momentum. At first Halton refused to consider another engine because of a lack of resources and because he hadn't finished development on the first Challenger model. That changed when Kearns said maybe it wouldn't be such a bad idea to start thinking of a follow-on model, but not another business jet. Even with all the weight problems on the 600, what Kearns favored was a 20-foot stretch, powered by the General Electric engines, that could serve as a short- to medium-range cargo-passenger airliner. Of course, Jim Taylor didn't like this version since it wasn't a business jet, but Kearns wasn't interested in developing a model that would compete with the Challenger 600. He wanted to take another shot at the cargo market.

Still, Jim Taylor was delighted to have Kearns seriously considering any GE-powered Challenger. The initial sales campaign for the Lycoming-powered Challengers had peaked at 120 orders; almost no new orders came in after that. Taylor's marketing effort had begun to stall. Rumors of delivery delays due to problems with the flight test and certification program swirled through the bizjet market and made selling airplanes extremely difficult. Then the orders Taylor did have began going soft. A frantic process of buy backs and resales started. (This would cause panic in Mahogany Row later on.) Taylor feared the worst, that the plane's market potential would collapse before the first airplane had been delivered. He knew the airplane was overweight by 2,000 pounds and the engines were substandard, and there were likely other problems he didn't even know about yet. To make matters worse, Grumman had finally launched the G-III program after numerous delays and planned to deliver them the same year Challenger deliveries were to start. Taylor felt that Kearns had only one choice: drop the Lycoming-powered Challenger and convert orders to a GE-powered model as soon as possible.

But Fred Kearns had come to the conclusion that the Canadair business jet wouldn't be enough to keep the program running. Before the first airplane had been delivered, the company was making parts for airplanes that didn't have firm orders. While building parts for unsold aircraft is not uncommon in the industry, for Kearns it spelled trouble. The whole program was based on the assumption that a large number of aircraft would be delivered every year, allowing the recovery of development costs in a reasonable period of time. But with sales stalled, delivery schedules being pushed into the future and a performance level that fell below that announced at the start of the program, an early recovery no longer seemed possible. To deal with the order book problem, Kearns had a choice: cut back production, lay off people and admit that a major assumption of the program was no longer valid; or launch another Challenger model. The consensus among Kearns's top management people was for the new model, although it was obviously the greatest risk.

Taylor continued to hope that eventually he would have a GE-powered Challenger to sell. He was supposed to be out there marketing the Lycoming-powered Challenger, but he gave Avco Lycoming little more than lip service. Sometimes even that was hard to come by. At an Avco Lycoming-sponsored customer seminar, Taylor and his people gave little Canadair support to Avco Lycoming's statement that the engine was proceeding well. It didn't go unnoticed by the supplier. "You know," Kearns told Halton afterward, "Lycoming felt that we really let them down at that seminar and I can't say I blame them." Avco Lycoming evened the score when they failed to put in much of an appearance at Taylor's Challenger exhibit at the NBAA show in St. Louis a few months later.

As the flight test program progressed, it was evident that the Challenger would have at least a ten percent shortfall in performance. Taylor knew the shortfall could be fixed with the more powerful GE engine. Taylor wanted Canadair to make an extraordinary confession: to tell the customers the Lycoming engine was a mistake. If Canadair announced the introduction of the GE engine, maybe no orders would be lost. Kearns would not go that far, but he was very concerned by the poor performance of the engine.

Several months into the flight test program Taylor told Kearns he had a good idea why things were going so badly at Avco Lycoming. Ned Dobak, the Lycoming engine program manager, had resigned after being passed over for a vice president's position. Over lunch Dobak had given Taylor a withering criticism of his former employer. A delighted Taylor passed Dobak's comments to Kearns in a memo: "Dobak confided to us that Lycoming is having a lot of problems they hadn't anticipated. The company has simply no depth of past experience, no corporate memory, no other ongoing turbofan engine programs from which to draw for broad technical support. Our credibility is at stake. We've got to come clean or we'll lose it." His advice: switch to GE before it was too late.

Mahogany Row couldn't ignore Taylor's comments completely. Named at the start of the program as president of Canadair Challenger Inc., the newly created U.S. subsidiary of Canadair, Jim Taylor had been given considerable resources and was a highly visible figure. He was responsible for more than just advertising and sales in the United States. He established a new service center at Bradley International Airport, created product support groups all over the country and formed alliances with service centers worldwide. (This last was a source of antagonism between Taylor and Canadair's product support people, who felt the function should have stayed in St. Laurent.) Taylor didn't have de facto control of worldwide sales but he acted as if he did, and often criticized marketing efforts originating in Montreal. In fact, there wasn't a Challenger sales office, apart from government sales, in Canada. From his office in Westport, Connecticut, Taylor managed a formidable fiefdom that rivaled Montreal for control of the program's myriad aspects. To many people, there were two Canadairs, not one, and on issues such as engine selection the two were constantly at odds with each other. As far as Taylor was concerned, if the Challenger program was supposed to be market-driven, then the program was in trouble because the market didn't like the Challenger 600. It was fat, its range was poor and it was unreliable.

Although Mahogany Row paid serious attention to its marketing president, it wasn't about to drop Avco Lycoming from the program. Instead, Kearns decided to do whatever it took to bring the Lycoming-powered airplane up to the level of performance Taylor wanted. Taylor wasn't satisfied with that; he wanted nothing less than a new

GE-powered business jet. To convince the company of the necessity of a GE-powered model, he needed details about the existing Challenger.

Getting the inside information wasn't easy because Taylor was out of the information loop as far as engineering matters were concerned. Halton didn't volunteer details, and Taylor did not confront him about all the rumors the customers had been hearing. Late in the summer of 1979 Taylor decided the best way to get the full story was to gain Halton's confidence and get him to speak candidly. He called Halton and told him he was coming to Montreal. Over lunch in Canadair's executive dining room, Taylor said he and his people were becoming very worried about the rumors surrounding the Challenger. He needed Harry to level with him, to let him know what the problems were so Taylor could fashion intelligent responses instead of saying he didn't know.

Halton suspected that marketing was the source of many of the rumors, or at least it wasn't doing very much to discount them, and he was reluctant to let down his guard. In particular, Halton felt that marketing's continued criticism of Avco Lycoming was weakening Canadair's negotiating position on matters such as the schedule of engine deliveries. But Taylor was a division president and was entitled to know what was going on. Halton didn't know if he could trust Taylor, but he knew of Kearns's belief that Canadair had to break with the past and make marketing a close player in the overall management of the program. Halton weighed these thoughts and decided to give Taylor the facts. It was a big mistake.

A few days after that lunch, Kearns stormed into Halton's office and threw a memorandum on Halton's desk.

Halton read the memo and flushed. It was from Taylor to Kearns, and in it were all the details of the lunch conversation. Only the problems, no potential solutions or actions undertaken to solve them, everything negative, not one thing positive. Taylor had taken Halton's litany of problems and thrown them in Kearns's face. Halton felt betrayed. He had told Taylor of his problems with the certification and flight test program in confidence, and there they were in a memo to Kearns. Further, the memo suggested that marketing had been shut out of the engineering decision process long enough and recommended that engineering get approval from marketing before proceeding with any further changes or improvements to the aircraft. There was an implication that past changes had been on Halton's whim and that they were the cause of many of the problems with the program.

"I'm not looking for sympathy," Halton wrote to Kearns in response to Taylor's memorandum, "all I'm looking for is some measure of understanding and Jim [Taylor] does not appear to be either able or willing to give it." It was clear to Halton that Taylor did not appreciate how much Halton and the others were doing to deliver the airplane Taylor had promised to the market.

However, there were some things Halton was powerless to fix. Reports from Avco Lycoming via his consultant, Thor Stephenson, said the company still wasn't putting enough development time on the engines. Avco Lycoming wasn't delivering the resources originally promised to do the development work. Halton told Kearns that unless Canadair got better action out of Avco Lycoming, it would have a crisis on its hands within the year.

This wasn't the first time Halton had requested action. When things began to go wrong at the start of the flight test program, Halton had demanded action from Avco Lycoming and had flown down to Stratford with Kearns to meet Avco Lycoming chairman, Jim Kerr, and general manager, Joe Bartos. For everyone to hear, Kerr had said, "Joe, no money spared. I want you to get behind this program." That was it, the word from the top. Yet months later it was clear from Thor Stephenson's reports that Kerr's words had not been enough. As Halton got ready to see Kearns for a second time on this question, he wondered what Kearns could possibly do to convince Avco Lycoming to spend more effort on Canadair.

"I think you've got to write a very strong letter, Fred," Halton told Kearns. "Our flight test and certification schedule is going all to hell because of Avco Lycoming. You've got to tell Jim Kerr that Avco Lycoming is screwing up our program."

In the summer of 1979, Fred Kearns felt pinned to the wall by Avco Lycoming. Things were getting out of control. The flight test and certification program was in trouble. The industry was rife with rumors about Lycoming engine reliability problems. The FAA had issued a warning to the Department of Transport about engine fan gear failures. And Taylor's continuing campaign for the GE engine was undermining Canadair's position with both Avco Lycoming and GE. Avco Lycoming felt it had a customer that didn't deserve more

than it was getting; GE felt that sooner or later the program would
fall into its lap. Taylor's campaign might have spurred Avco Lycoming into action were it not for an exclusivity clause in the engine
contract that prevented Canadair from using other engines on the
program. Kearns felt that Taylor was doing serious damage to the
program, and told Halton this. He wanted to fire Taylor but he knew
that might create more problems than it would solve.

Kearns and Halton didn't want to make any problems public
because they believed that all would be fixed. Mahogany Row had its
own concerns about credibility and didn't want to admit it was losing
control over the program. But despite its best efforts, Canadair
couldn't keep certain things secret forever. When the first Challenger
was flown to the Paris Air Show in the late spring of 1979, the
airplane's stop for refueling was kept secret because it would have
publicized the range deficiency. Even Canadair employees were told
by Kearns that the Challenger had made the journey nonstop.
However, one wily customer called Canadair's flight operations after
the Paris flight, and asked for and was given the flight log information. From this he was able to figure out that the airplane's promised
range of 3,600 nautical miles was more like 2,800. The Challenger
had already done some 300 hours of flight testing, and customers
were beginning to ask what the specific fuel consumption was.
Canadair was loath to admit just how bad the SFC problem was and
decided to keep that a secret, as well.

Kearns knew that Avco Lycoming's chairman, Jim Kerr, was having problems of his own. The company's biggest contract, to produce
a state-of-the-art gas turbine engine for the Abrams XM-1 main
battle tank, was in trouble. The weapon system was late, over budget
and technically flummoxed, and it was facing growing Congressional
opposition. The Chrysler Corporation, the prime contractor for the
XM-1, had lost its enthusiasm and was anxious to get out of the tank
business altogether. Kerr also had to deal with a three-week strike
and a major management reshuffle. They were not easy days for Kerr.
But somehow Kearns had to get through all the interference to
communicate the seriousness of his own situation. Canadair was in
trouble, too, and it wasn't getting any relief.

By this point Canadair's reliability problem with Avco Lycoming
was the aircraft company's worst kept secret. Gossip was rampant,
and Canadair knew it wouldn't be long before it hit the trade press. A

month after Kearns's letter to Kerr, the press began reporting sub-
stantiated stories of problems with the Lycoming engine. Avco
Lycoming's reliability, the basis of any engine manufacturer's credibility, was called into question. Stung by Taylor's cocky advertising
in the past, the competition stung right back. Grumman, Canadair's
principal competitor, ran this ad: "When you're spending 8 hours or
more up here [in the sky] engine reliability is something you want to
take for granted." This particular advertisement was a blow to
Kearns. His letter to Kerr was a desperate plea for help.

"Up to now, I have believed that we at Canadair were in fact
masters of our own destiny," Kearns wrote. "Events in recent weeks,
however, have shown that this is no longer the case . . . [we] are now
entirely dependent on actions undertaken by Avco Lycoming." He
listed the problems: the compressor stalls, the gearing failures, the
delayed certification of the engine—the engine certification was
already nearly a year behind schedule—the speed restrictions, and
most serious, the fuel consumption problem. Kearns concluded,
"You and we, at this point in time, really don't have an overview of
the engine program." Not having an overview of the engine program
was like admitting that Canadair didn't know what was going on with
half of the aircraft program.

Kearns never received a response to his plea. Finally he gave Halton
the green light to send a letter out to customers explaining that
delivery delays were being caused by three major engine problems. In
the letter Halton made the first reference to the SFC problem.
However, he presented it very optimistically. He wrote that there
"would be about 300 nautical miles less than the 3,600 nautical miles
that we had promised." It was more like 700 nautical miles less, but
Halton was still betting heavily that his Performance Recovery Program, which included a combination of weight reductions and aerodynamic improvements, would perform a miracle.

Meanwhile, with the slipping fortunes of the Lycoming-powered
Challenger, Kearns decided the time had come to launch a GE-
powered Challenger.

Kearns continued to count on FedEx as an important long-term
customer, and that meant he had to honor his promise to launch the
stretched version of the Challenger, which would be called the

CL-610. Jim Taylor warned Kearns there wasn't a market for the 610 and once again challenged FedEx chairman Fred Smith's sincerity. He said as much to *Aviation Week and Space Technology*, the influential aerospace weekly, in its story on the FedEx order. Taylor warned Kearns that Smith was still "whimsical" and "fluid in his thinking" and that Kearns shouldn't rely on Smith as a long-term customer. Taylor also discounted Kearns's overtures to representatives from the People's Republic of China about a purchase of the stretched version; again he thought Kearns was wasting his time. But Kearns had made up his mind that the stretched airplane was going to put steam back into the program. He didn't want to hear any more from the business jet market, at least not for now.

There was a second reason Kearns did not want to consider another business jet: Canadair's contract with Avco Lycoming included exclusivity terms, and he didn't want to make trouble with Avco Lycoming by launching a GE-powered business jet that could be interpreted as a violation of that agreement.

Kearns eventually asked Bob Wohl, Canadair's legal counsel, to contact an outside counsel, Roger Harris of the New York law firm Windels, Marx, Davies and Ives, and find out if Canadair could be sued for promoting a GE-powered Challenger. Harris said there was a strong possibility of a suit if Canadair moved too boldly. He said it would be difficult to argue that the Lycoming engines had hurt sales if 120 Lycoming-powered airplanes had already been sold. If, on the other hand, the market started asking for GE engines, then that would be a different story. The recommendation: introduce the GE engine into the program cautiously. Kearns interpreted this to mean he could introduce the engine on a bigger non-business jet, a jet the Lycoming engine clearly wouldn't be enough to power.

The marketing effort got underway, but right from the start it served to further alienate Jim Taylor. The 20-foot stretched Challenger, the CL-610, was for airlines and cargo carriers. There was nothing in the model for his marketing group, since their contacts were strictly in the business jet market. Canadair's elaborate and sophisticated marketing division in Connecticut remained largely removed from the new program. Selling the 610 was done mostly by Kearns and finance VP Peter Aird, who had also come to the conclusion that the order book needed a boost. They both saw the virtue of dealing with the airliner market—the large operators bought airplanes by the dozen. This had been the attraction of Federal Express before it dropped out of the 600 program, and the prospect stayed alive when Canadair got FedEx to sign on for the 610. Taylor thought this too incredible to be true, given what Canadair had already gone through with FedEx.

Meanwhile Taylor was pulling out the stops to get a GE-powered business jet into the program. He continued to talk to GE, telling them it would be just a matter of time before the engines would be on a Challenger business jet. He told customers the same thing, and occasionally Halton received calls from customers asking when the GE-powered version would be ready for delivery. When Taylor brought potential Challenger 600 customers to Montreal, if discussion veered away from the engine or range problems, he promptly steered it back. On one occasion, when Taylor brought the chief pilot of a potential customer to Montreal to meet Fred Kearns, it became so apparent to Kearns that the pilot had been coached by Taylor that he stopped the meeting and asked if the weight and range problems had been emphasized by Taylor. The pilot admitted they had. That incident made it clear to Kearns that Taylor, the man he had hired to sell the airplane, was mounting a campaign against the Challenger 600.

This was a blatant violation of an earlier edict issued by Kearns to Taylor the previous June. In a terse two-paragraph letter to Taylor, Kearns had warned Taylor that anyone in marketing found promoting the idea of a GE-powered Challenger business jet would be "guilty of insubordination and . . . subject to instant dismissal." Much to Kearns's chagrin, Taylor ignored the warning and continued his campaign. It was a direct challenge to Kearns's authority and leadership within the company, and Taylor kept up the pressure. If Canadair wanted to sell any more aircraft, then it should listen to the message from marketing: "Customer A is nervous about the Lycomings. Excellent prospect for a GE-powered Challenger." Over lunch one day Taylor told Halton he could practically guarantee that every existing customer would convert his order for a Lycoming-powered 600 to one for a GE-powered aircraft, even at $2 million more in price. Taylor didn't care what happened to the canceled orders for the 600 because he wanted the Lycoming-powered 600 to disappear.

As Avco Lycoming's problems worsened, Kearns began to realize that the engine problems could affect the program for years to come and that it would be wise to consider another engine for the standard Challenger. The plane with the new engine would be called the CL-601. It wouldn't be actively marketed, but a small number would be there if the market asked for them. Indeed, the 601 had strategic significance: it served as a warning shot across Avco Lycoming's bow without sinking the relationship all together.

Pressure on Kearns to launch a new model grew in early 1980. Gulfstream, formerly a division of Grumman but now an independent company, had plans to bring the Gulfstream G-III to market in mid-1980, the same time as the Challenger. With a longer fuselage and a much improved wing, the G-III laid claim to the long-range "big iron" market with no competition. The 600 couldn't match it for range.

"Time is running out," Taylor warned Kearns in early 1980. "You must make your decision soon."

Under great pressure to do something to recapture momentum, Fred Kearns went to Canadair's board of directors in March 1980, six months before the first Challenger 600 was delivered, seeking approval to launch a two-pronged program. He proposed launching a 105-inch stretch GE-powered Challenger 610 (he dropped the 240-inch stretch as too complicated to develop quickly), and later the gradual and inauspicious introduction of a GE-powered version of the standard-body Challenger, to be called the 601. He had 20 orders for the 610. There was one order for the 601.

The idea, flawed as it was, had a certain elegance. It would open a new source of revenue, something the company desperately needed; it would bring Federal Express back into the program; it would give Avco Lycoming a nice kick in the pants; and it would get the order book breathing again. The board accepted the idea, and the program was officially launched. News of the launch stunned the competition. Allen Paulsen at Gulfstream could not believe Kearns planned to certify two more aircraft before finishing the first model, particularly in light of all the trouble both Canadair and Gulfstream were having with certification under the new guidelines of FAR Part 25. (Gulfstream's problems were not nearly so severe as those of Canadair.) Paulsen knew through his contacts that Kearns's total program cost was way over earlier estimates and that he was short on cash. As a business jet maker, Paulsen could appreciate better than anyone else what Kearns was trying, and he could only shake his head in disbelief.

While engine problems continued to pace the program, the dispute with the DoT over the stall issue continued to drag on. Harry Halton ignored the DoT's letter of July 1979 instructing Canadair to comply with its stall certification requirement, specifically, to come up with a natural controllable stall instead of using an artificial stall warning system. The DoT had become increasingly frustrated with Canadair's refusal to comply with the directive, and a showdown between Halton and Owen came on February 13, 1980, in Halton's office. Halton was managing the certification issue single-handedly. Even though Ron Neal, Harry's chief program engineer, was responsible for the flight test and certification program, Halton took care of all the crucial negotiations. It was just as well, since Owen discounted Neal's knowledge of certification matters. Owen was not impressed with Halton's skill in this area, either, and felt he needed professional airworthiness managers—high-priced consultants who did nothing but run certification programs for airplane manufacturers, something Bob Laidlaw of FSI had tried to offer Canadair without much success.

It was Halton's last attempt to defeat what he considered an absurd and unreasonable request. He hauled out his large folio and related his research into stall barriers in other jurisdictions, including the FAA. He listed all the T-tail types of airplanes that were certified with an artificial stall barrier. He stated that the Challenger needed the artificial stall barrier.

Owen wouldn't budge. The DoT was not prepared to buy into a stall barrier system. "We haven't been able to establish a reasonable set of requirements at DoT on the use of the system," Owen said. "For instance, the pilots want to be able to disconnect the system, but our engineers won't permit such a disconnect of the system if it is to be verified. We can't agree in-house on how to design it." Owen paused. "Anyhow, Harry, I think it's clear you guys haven't really tried to redesign the airplane to show an inherent and safe stall characteristic. It would be a lot simpler for everyone if you just came up with an inherent stall characteristic which doesn't require an artificial stall. Besides, I don't think we could get an artificial stall system past the FAA."

"But, Ken, I've just shown you the FAA has bought into the artificial stall barrier system!" Halton yelled. "What you're suggesting is just not true!"

Owen explained to Halton that the FAA had recently been decentralized. As he put it, "The FAA doesn't really exist. It's just a bunch of regional offices now, and very often they don't talk to each other. One region may buy into the system while another does not. Anyhow, it doesn't matter what the FAA says because you guys have to satisfy us!"

The dispute between the FAA and the DoT had finally been acknowledged, and Halton felt defeated. He thought Owen's arguments had no substance, but there was nothing he could do about it. Halton should have been delivering airplanes already and instead he had to go back to the drawing board to redesign a vital part of the airplane, the leading edge of the wing, to meet the DoT requirements.

Halton had no choice. He would have to launch a major change to the flight test program and implement another series of dangerous stall tests. This change disrupted the whole flight test program.

The day Halton informed his staff he had been defeated by the DoT on the stall issue and that the Challenger would have to demonstrate a natural controllable stall will be long remembered by those who were involved in Mojave. The employees felt betrayed when the company appeared to roll over on this critical issue. Al Baker, the test program's chief pilot, went into a rage. The request came at a crucial moment, the point in the schedule when Canadair should have been delivering airplanes. The Mojave team had been working flat out and making every effort to protect a schedule that was slipping because of engine problems and design changes from Montreal. Frustration was high, and the timing of the DoT decision couldn't have been worse.

The task of coming up with a controllable stall was left to Canadair's aerodynamicists. They had worked very hard to design a high-speed wing with extremely efficient lines for stable air flow. Now the DoT wanted them to mess it all up for the sake of a low-speed stall characteristic, something that could have been solved with an artificial stall barrier system. They knew the solution—they would have to place a metal strip on the leading edge of the wing to mess up the air at low speeds. The strip would go on the supercritical portion of the wing, the part of the wing they had worked hardest to refine.

Searching for an acceptable stall using the stall strip was a time-consuming process. One metal strip configuration could be tried each day. Metalworkers put on a strip, pilots took the aircraft up and tried to put the aircraft into a stall, found out the strip didn't work, and the metalworkers went back to the shop and readied the aircraft for the next day with a new strip. Once an acceptable configuration was found, it had to be tested at all the different flap positions. For four months, seven days a week, the flight test group searched for an acceptable stall point.

Doug Adkins estimated that the Challenger was put into about 5,000 stalls. The Douglas DC-9 was another T-tail airplane that had been certified with a natural controllable stall—because sophisticated artificial stall barriers had not yet been developed. Douglas used stall strips as well, and managed to achieve certification after about 2,000 stall tests. During the tests, pilots, engineers and technicians at Canadair were all pushed to the limit. Exhaustion and fatigue began to set in. The engineers were unhappy because Baker wanted to rotate pilots for the stall testing. (The tests were highly stressful.) Every new pilot had to be updated. This took time. The engineers were also frustrated by the fact that they were being asked to design a stall characteristic into an airplane originally designed not to have such a characteristic.

The staff had a problem, and they felt management in Montreal was not sensitive to it. They felt separated, insecure, abandoned by senior management. As Halton noted, "When you take people out of the company and set them up in a separate environment, you can expect that they change in ways you can't predict or see immediately."

Just how they were changing was explained by Bill Greening, a flight test engineering observer and a Canadair engineer. Greening was responsible for planning the tasks for the pilots, and the last task, the stall testing, was creating a lot of trouble for the people at Mojave. "It was a lot of people, strangers to each other for the most part, thrown together for a common cause. We became a tightly knit community and we all shared in the pressure that was being placed on us. There were many layers of pressure, of course, and most of the people at Mojave at the time were feeling all of them," Greening said.

It was impossible for the people at Mojave to believe that one man at the Department of Transport, Ken Owen, could have exerted so much influence over the program. Instead, they began to blame their management, pointing the finger at those guys in Montreal. "We felt it was wrong that the pilots were not included in the meetings with Owen," Adkins said. "There should have been someone to argue the technical points . . . . In fact, we were mad at our own management for capitulating to DoT because every time they capitulated we ended up getting the squeeze from management to meet DoT's whims. It was, after all, easier to squeeze someone you control than someone in DoT you don't."

To a knowledgeable outsider, Canadair's flight test program might have seemed out of control by the spring of 1980. Normally the stall program is completed very early in the flight test program, since the results provide the reference points for much of the subsequent testing. Canadair was doing stall tests sixteen months into the program. The flow of flight test requests was chaotic and unending. There was now so much going on it was only a matter of time before something went wrong. It happened on the day before Good Friday, April 3, 1980, sixteen months into the flight test program.

8

The crash of Challenger One

Norm Ronaasen arrived at Canadair's flight test facility early Thursday morning, April 3, 1980, rested and ready for yet another day of stall tests. There was still a problem with his aircraft, Challenger One, but Ronaasen knew it wasn't enough to hold up the tests. He had to fly, like it or not. And he didn't like it.

Much of the difficult flight test work had gone to Ronaasen, a former test pilot for the RCAF. He was the hands-down favorite as the most popular and respected pilot in the group. At 52, he was the most senior member, and he had a spotless flight test record. He was also an Officer of the Order of Military Merit for his flight test work on the CF-104 Starfighter. As the Department of Transport continued to make extraordinary demands, Jim Woods was cracking the whip to keep the flight tests moving and finish the stall tests. The pressure on the pilots was tremendous, and it was Ronaasen who held the group together. The FSI group had stayed on the sidelines and become withdrawn under the stress of dealing with the DoT. Ronaasen became the leading spirit in the pilot group.

There had been a row the day before because of a problem on Challenger One. On Tuesday Ronaasen had heard banging noises during the flight test, and he asked the ground crew to check them out. These were no ordinary noises; they sounded like a grand piano was being dropped repeatedly onto the fuselage. The crew was unable to find anything to explain them. On Wednesday the noises, which usually occurred during an attempted stall, returned just as Ronaasen was starting out for another day of flight tests. Half an hour into flight he decided to abort the test card.

When Ronaasen got back to base an angry Jim Woods was there to greet him. "What the hell do you think you're doing aborting a flight test?" Woods demanded.

"Look, Jim, there's a problem with this plane and I think we've got to find out what it is before someone gets hurt," Ronaasen replied calmly.

"Oh, yeah? Well, I think you aborted because you're chicken! You're not to pull that stunt again, you hear me?"

Ronaasen went and told the ground crew he bloody well wanted the source of the banging found. All that night technicians examined Challenger One inch by inch. Extra ground crew members and overtime authorization were okayed. Nothing was found. The technicians installed nylon spacers at the wing spar and fuselage joints to try to eliminate the noise.

No pilot likes an unexplained problem during flight testing. But Ronaasen, copilot Dave Gallings and flight engineer Bill Scott took the airplane up for another series of high-altitude stall tests early Thursday morning. During the tests the banging noises were heard again, but they were not as loud. At the end of the test card Ronaasen radioed to base that they were finished and were on their way home.

Then Bill Scott, the flight engineer, had an idea—to move the water tank, a huge container of water mounted on tracks that was used to change the airplane's center of gravity. He wanted to move it aft and do a stall. That way, he said, they could eliminate the aft tank position as a source of the noise.

They moved the tank and did the stall, and no noises occurred. Ronaasen decided to do one more stall. He took the plane to 17,000 feet. He proposed to go into a left turn and hold it in the stall, so Scott could look around.

Slowly the nose began to go up as the airplane's airspeed decreased. The crew could feel the heavy buffet of the stall, and Scott scrambled around checking for the source of the noise. He was about to say everything was okay when Gallings noticed the angle of attack indicator and started shouting.

"We're into a deep stall!"

"We've lost the right engine!"

Ronaasen and Gallings threw their bodies against their sticks, and slowly they got the nose of the airplane level. But they couldn't get the nose to drop any farther, and they were still stalled in the air.

Ronaasen ordered Gallings to deploy the anti-spin parachute attached to the rear of the airplane. It was designed specifically to recover the airplane from such a situation. The chute did its job, and the nose of the plane began to drop, but Ronaasen's problems had just begun. When Gallings tried to eject the drag chute, both the primary and backup ejection systems failed. The airplane continued to drop like a rock. The rate-of-descent indicator was pinned to 6,000 feet per minute. The crew should have bailed out at 12,000 feet; they were already closing in on 6,000 feet. It was impossible to tell how high up the airplane was by looking out the window, because the bushes on the ground were deceiving and because there was no time.

Ronaasen was out of the deep stall, but the engines had quit. With no power and a drag chute stuck to the rear of the airplane, Ronaasen had no choice. He ordered Gallings and Scott to bail out. He kept the airplane stable while they exited, then he tried to restart the engines. If he could start the engines he might get the airplane back in flight even with the drag chute attached. Suddenly he realized he was very close to the ground. He bailed out, but the plane was only 150 feet above the ground. His parachute didn't have time to open. He landed head first and was decapitated.

Romauld Foran was on duty as day shift foreman when the distress call came from Challenger One. It had been a routinely busy morning for Foran and his ground crews. Challenger One and Challenger Four had been prepared for a flight test and taken off. About an hour later, around eight o'clock, Norm Ronaasen came over the hangar loudspeaker to say Challenger One's test card was completed and they were returning to base in seven minutes. Foran ordered three mechanics to meet the aircraft, and they were on their way out to the ramp, wheel chocks dangling from their shoulders, when the loudspeaker crackled to life again. Foran recognized the tone in Ronaasen's voice: he was in trouble. Even before Ronaasen completed his distress call, Foran had jumped down from the engine stand where he was working and was running with everyone else toward the ramp. They strained their eyes toward the approach to Runway 30, where Challenger One was due to land. They heard a muffled explosion, then they saw a rising column of black smoke.

A reserve helicopter on a training mission out of nearby Edwards Air Force Base was in the crash area, and the pilot was diverted to the scene as soon as the distress signal went out. Foran and his crew listened as the helicopter pilot radioed that he was observing two parachutes descending. Foran realized that someone didn't make it. The group continued to monitor the helicopter pilot's transmission: two survivors on the ground, one standing, one down. (Co-pilot Dave Gallings broke his right leg in landing.) No sign of the third crew member. The helicopter pilot brought his vehicle down near the survivors and flew them to Antelope Valley Hospital, 30 miles away.

The test site's safety committee chairman, Ronaasen, had been on board Challenger One; it was up to Foran to marshal a crash crew and secure the area. He and his crew got into his truck, the same truck he had used to move his family from Montreal to the California testing ground more than a year earlier, and headed out. The rescue helicopter had radioed him a crash location about seven miles north of California City, a small desert community about 20 miles north of the airport. Foran didn't have any difficulty locating the crash once he was on the road: he could see a dense tower of black smoke rising heavenward.

Foran slowed to turn off the highway and drove across the desert in the direction of the crash site. What he saw was a scene of total destruction. Foran couldn't believe that so little remained of the airplane he had worked so hard to complete. A small tanker from the California City fire department applied a stream of water to the last pockets of flames. The only recognizable parts were the baggage door, which had been blown a hundred or so yards beyond the wreckage, and the number one engine, a short distance farther away. The fire hadn't consumed the T-tail and the anti-spin chute, which had trailed behind and was caught in the sage brush. The rest of the airplane was totally unrecognizable. Off to the left of the wreckage were the remains of pilot Norm Ronaasen.

Foran and his crew took out some white nylon rope and cordoned off the area to keep out souvenir hunters. A short distance away a couple of rabbit hunters sat staring at the scene from their dune buggy. Foran assumed they were in shock, because they sat completely motionless. They had watched the airplane glide over their heads and crash right in front of them.

The county coroner arrived and made a quick survey of

Ronaasen's remains and the crash scene. As he was leaving he picked up a stick and began poking at a deadly but severely injured side-winder snake. A sheriff's deputy came over and put the snake out of its misery with a .38 bullet in the head. It was a scene Foran would never forget.

That night Ron Neal and Doug Adkins flew down to Mojave. Jim Woods met them at the airport. Woods was emotionally shattered, and it didn't take long for his distress to affect Neal.

At the test site the pilots discussed what they were going to do. They felt they had been ignored long enough. They went over all the problems and rehearsed what they would tell Neal, Woods and Adkins the next day. One of their concerns was that the company would try to hide the incident, and they were determined not to let that happen. They knew they had the power to irreparably damage the program by going public, but no one wanted that. But they were not going to let management ignore their pleas to correct a situation gone wrong.

The meeting lasted less than an hour, and the pilots' comments didn't come as a surprise to Neal, Woods or Adkins. Some were direct attacks aimed at them as Canadair management, others were directed at more senior levels of responsibility. The pilots were fed up because decisions had been made without their input. Management didn't seem concerned about the dubious state of flight safety in the stall program. The engines, they said, were degraded to a dangerous level. Strange noises were showing up. They did not know if the crash was caused by an unsafe aircraft, but they were intimating the worst — that their safety was being put at risk by managers who were asking them to fly an unsafe aircraft.

The pilots wanted to know why Canadair had given in to the Department of Transport. Bill Scott, the flight engineer who bailed out of Challenger One, said, "To think that Fred Kearns is having lunch with Ken Owen and doing mental battle with that man is crazy. He doesn't have the technical expertise to be doing it. And turning round and telling [Neal] what to do, who tells Jim what to do, and Jim has to put pressure on us, we should have been able to say no."

The right to say no. There was certainly no opportunity for that during the flight test operations. The flight test committee, made up of management and pilots to discuss important flight testing issues in Montreal, had been disbanded after the move to Mojave.

Later Harry Halton would say Scott had a point. "It's true. Kearns half the time didn't know what Owen was talking about. But Kearns was having lunch for what he thought were political reasons. Kearns was told . . . that Canadair's technical people were not listening to Owen. Kearns said he would listen to Owen because he believed that . . . Owen had Canadair's interests at heart and that in the end Kearns and Canadair would get what they wanted despite their difficult dealings with Owen."

Canadair wasn't going to get what it wanted. Once again Kearns's faith had been misplaced. Walter McLeish, Owen's boss at the DoT, backed Owen on the stall issue right to the end.

The second most important comment made at the meeting also came from Scott: "We didn't know where we were going, we didn't know the ground rules. We violated every principle that was ever taught to us at test pilot's school." That was true. The pilots were asked to find something that was impossible to find, a natural stall that would please everyone. It wasn't a matter of going up, testing something and coming back again according to the book. They weren't testing something that was clearly defined. They were looking for something that wasn't defined at all. But Scott was closer to the truth than he realized. The crew had violated a principle during the crash flight, but not the one he thought.

Challenger One had gone down while the crew was conducting a test that was not on the test card. This violated some of the test pilot's basic principles for survival. For one, never conduct a flight test independent of the flight test process. For another, many test pilots would not have flown again until the apparent problem—the source of the noise—had been resolved. Ronaasen, harangued by an irate Woods, didn't want to hold up the test program. When the technicians failed to find the problem the crew decided to experiment.

When the pilots finished speaking, Adkins didn't say a word. He had made his feelings known in the past—the world was out to get the test pilot. The accident was proof that he was right. Woods and Neal declined to make any comments; there was nothing left for them to say.

On the Saturday morning following the meeting Neal called

Halton at home. It was the first time they had spoken since the crash. In a faltering voice, Neal said the situation was out of control and that Halton should come down as soon as possible.

That afternoon Halton flew down in Canadair's Learjet and was met at Mojave by a weeping Woods and a distressed and silent Neal. At the test site Halton listened to the tape recording of the pilots' meeting, then he left to visit Gallings in the hospital. By the end of the day Halton agreed with Neal that things were indeed out of control. People were blaming each other, yelling at each other, and the anger frightened Halton. He began mulling over a difficult proposition, to close Mojave down and bring everyone back to Montreal. That evening he called Kearns and said he was considering closing down the Mojave operation.

"That's your decision to make, Harry," Kearns said. "Call me back tomorrow when you've made up your mind."

For 24 hours Halton wrestled with the question. A return to Montreal would be a terrible admission of failure and might deliver a fatal blow to the program. Despite all the problems with the engines and the design changes, the team was on the verge of completing a flight test program in record time. Halton thought the flight test people at Mojave should have felt a tremendous sense of accomplishment, and instead they felt victimized and abused. People were losing sight of the fact that, until the crash, the flight test program would have been considered a great success by anybody in the industry.

The future of the program hung on Halton's decision. In the end he decided to let time, something in very short supply, heal the wounds. He elected to continue flight testing in Mojave for the moment. If things did not improve, he would close Mojave down and move the testing to Montreal.

A few hundred people from Canada and the United States attended Norm Ronaasen's funeral, and Halton, with Ronaasen's friend and mentor Jack Woodman, gave the eulogy. There was a wake at a Mojave desert flying club, then Greg Ronaasen flew up in his father's privately built aircraft and scattered Norm's ashes over the countryside of the Tahachapee Valley. A few years later Halton wrote: "I cannot remember a period in my life when I felt sadder and more frustrated by what appeared to be rules and regulations and interpretations which were wasteful, unnecessary and unjustified. And the pity is that all subsequent events have proven me right."

Few people who were involved with the flight test program are willing to talk about those days. Al Baker, who resigned shortly after the crash of Challenger One, said recently, "Those days will forever be too painful for me to talk about." The crash created deep emotions. Halton recalled, "People, grown men, were crying, yelling at each other, passing blame freely about, and I tried to figure out whether . . . these feelings were coming from some sort of guilt, of having done something wrong to cause the crash. Only later did I realize they weren't feeling guilt. They were feeling a profound frustration with management, with the flight test subcontractor, with the aircraft, with the certification officials, you name it, they were frustrated every step of the way. With the crash of Challenger One, all this frustration spilled out. Unless you were there from the beginning you couldn't understand or appreciate that. I didn't understand it at first and so those days after the crash were for me the darkest days of the program. For a few days it looked even to me that the Mojave flight test program had been a colossal failure. Of course, it was quite the opposite. Given what we were up against, it was a tremendous success."

The Challenger One was an experimental airplane, so the U.S. National Transportation Safety Board did not give the crash priority. There was no field team, only a surly local investigator who told Halton's people to stay out of his way and not to expect a report for at least six weeks. Halton needed to know a lot sooner if there was a problem with the aircraft. He initiated a Canadair in-house accident investigation.

Halton called on Maurice Holloway, a Canadair technical representative who had conducted crash investigations for Canadair before. Holloway was an unassuming gentleman with a reputation for being a quiet hero. During World War Two he escaped from a German prisoner-of-war camp and led six hundred prisoners and war refugees across the savagely inhospitable Russian frontier in the dead of winter. If there was a problem, Holloway could be counted on to get to the bottom of it. If Canadair was responsible, Holloway was one man Halton could count on to tell him the truth.

There wasn't much left to work with at the crash site. Tangled among the desert grease bushes were pieces of cassette recording tape from Challenger One. Holloway took them to an FBI laboratory for analysis. The fragments gave a sketchy picture, but he did get the words of Dave Gallings as the angle of attack shot up. Why had this happened?

The angle of attack—the angle of the aircraft in relation to the flow of air—was sensed by a vane attached to a boom on the nose of the airplane. The vane was the most important reference instrument during stall testing. Since no stall protection systems could be engaged during stall tests, this indicator was the only thing between the pilot and a deep stall. When Holloway examined the remains of the vane, he discovered that it had been clogged with sand because the dust cover was missing. That explained why the angle of attack shot up so quickly: the device must have become jammed as Ronaasen put the airplane into the stall. Had the boom device been properly maintained, Ronaasen would have been aware of the stall sooner and could have averted the crash.

Holloway then examined the chain of equipment failures that had followed. The remains of the anti-spin chute device revealed that the system had been filled with incorrect fluid. Holloway looked at the service reports and found that ground personnel knew the fluid was incorrect but did nothing to change it. The ground personnel hadn't realized the incorrect fluid would cause the chute release system to fail. In the backup system, Holloway found solder flux in the switching device.

Holloway had uncovered some mechanical failures, but didn't feel they explained how the crew had gotten itself into a life-threatening situation. Why was Ronaasen not aware of his altitude? Holloway began to interview people involved with the flight test program. He decided the errors in pilot judgment and awareness displayed by Ronaasen were caused by fatigue because of the extended and dangerous stall testing. Holloway stressed this point in his report to Halton. When Halton reviewed Holloway's report, he deleted all reference to the stall program, even though he agreed with Holloway's conclusion. Holloway's opinions were based on hearsay rather than fact. Furthermore, the stall program wasn't over and Halton didn't want to create more trouble with the Department of Transport. Unknown to Halton, the crash had made the DoT more adamant about the natural stall.

Two months after the crash, and true to its stiffened resolve, the DoT announced that Canadair would have to do test stalls on selected production aircraft, rather than test aircraft outfitted with

an artificial stall barrier system and a spin chute safety device. The
request nearly caused a riot in Canadair's flight operations. Even the
DoT's test pilots said the request was absurdly dangerous. This time
Canadair didn't roll over.

"Hell will freeze over before I let you use production aircraft
without a stall barrier in place and activated," Halton told Owen.
The request was withdrawn.

Doug Adkins moved to Mojave to take over the stall testing.
Ronaasen was dead and Baker had gone. Ron Neal, the man responsible for the flight test program, was about to quit. It was up to
Adkins to lead Canadair out of the mess. After a three-month hiatus,
Challenger Two was set up for the stall testing, and improvements
were made to the chute release system. New rules were established to
address the problems raised by the pilots. But the measure of safety
was vague, and the stall testing objectives remained ambiguous. In
those first mornings at Mojave, Adkins watched the sun come up and
wondered if these were going to be his last days on earth.

In August 1980 Harry Halton got his Canadian certification. Despite the problems during the flight test program, Halton had every
reason to feel pleased. Canadair had achieved certification of a new
airplane under new rules and harrowing government interpretations,
and had done it in 21 months. It was a considerable achievement.
Unfortunately, Halton had been forced to make changes to the
airplane that rendered it less than what had been promised in 1978.
Because of the stall strips, the Challenger had significantly diminished low-speed characteristics; it needed more runway to land and
take off because of increased minimum landing and takeoff speeds.
The Challenger would have extremely limited landing and take-off
performance from high altitude airports, particularly on hot days.

Halton dearly wanted to get rid of the stall strips, and there was a
way. Canadian certification was needed principally so that Canadair
could export the Challenger to the United States. It was certification
in the United States, the Challenger's largest market, that was important to the marketing of the airplane. An FAA certified Challenger
need not be the same as a DoT certified Challenger. Halton began
thinking he might certify the Challenger in the United States without
the stall strips.

The Department of Transport scuttled that maneuver. In a letter
to the FAA during U.S. certification, Owen said the Challenger was

an unsafe aircraft without the stall strips. The FAA, weary of the DoT by this point, asked Canadair to keep the stall strips on for the sake of a speedy certification, which was completed in November 1980.

A year later Owen was replaced as the DoT's director of airworthiness. His successor reversed the DoT's position on the use of artificial stall barriers, and by 1982 the Challenger was certified without the stall strips. The natural stall test exercise had all been a complete waste of time.

By late 1980 the incredible stress and pressure of the four-year development phase was beginning to pull at the seams of the program. As the first Challenger 600s were delivered to their customers in the fall of 1980, Harry Halton had become convinced there was something terribly wrong with the attitudes of some people in the program. Here he was, just four years after program go-ahead, with the world's most advanced small jet. The Challenger had been designed, developed and certified in record time. The achievement was remarkable, and yet people were whining about the problems rather than feeling pleased with the achievements. The problems would have been considered normal in any new aircraft development program and could be solved with time and effort. The airplane was 2,500 pounds overweight, the engines had reliability problems, and the airplane was, in its present state, not the intercontinental airplane Taylor had promised his customers. But the Challenger could hardly be considered a failure. Nonetheless, the problems fed the fears of some in Canadair's management that the Challenger 600 was not going to bring the company the success it needed to recover its huge development costs. Fred Kearns had not given up on the Challenger 600. Instead, he was plunging the company into greater difficulties by demanding that the airplane be brought up to the promised (though unattainable) standards by whatever means possible.

The Challenger 600's moment of truth had come in the summer just before certification. At the August 1980 customer seminar Harry Halton had to admit that the first airplanes fell short of earlier promises. Increased weight, stall strips and engine problems had conspired to make the Challenger a jet with a list of diminished capabilities. That didn't bother the first group of pilots and owners who had an opportunity to fly the Challengers. They recognized immediately that Halton had come up with a winner and raved about the airplane's handling characteristics. Many customers asked Halton not to trade away any of the good features just to improve the range. But the performance and range were clearly less than promised, and Taylor was putting the screws on Kearns to keep to his plan to deliver the airplane he had promised. Halton announced a series of performance improvements to be done at company expense. The cost of these post-development improvements contributed to the program's escalating costs, and the added work load of the improvements heightened the stress in the program. Program costs are based on the assurance that changes go down with time. With the Challenger, the number of changes went up and up as Halton tried to bring the aircraft to the level of the initial promises of weight, range and performance. Furthermore, the delays in delivery caused by the improvements probably did more to damage customer confidence than if Halton had simply delivered the airplanes as is. The attempts to bring the Challenger 600 up to the level demanded by marketing cost the company hundreds of millions of dollars, and likely scared away customers who didn't want to go through all the hassle of having their new airplane stuck in completion centers for months, in a few cases years, waiting for improvements.

By the fall of 1980, Canadair had become a pressure cooker. The company had one airplane program going into high volume production with a host of post-development problems and fixes, and development had begun on the GE-powered 601 and the stretch 610. Halton was in way over his head.

"If only I had more time to begin with," Halton would say later.

In November 1980, with the aircraft certified and deliveries ready to begin, production took over as the focus of the 600 program. From the start, Andy Throner, Canadair's vice president of manufacturing, felt as if he was sinking in a sea of paperwork. Production was underway but the continuing effort to upgrade the Challenger meant changes in design, modifications to systems, and delays in parts deliveries, including the engine. The problems were playing havoc with his factory. There wasn't one schedule, there were dozens, and he was behind on all of them.

Since program launch, manufacturing had done a pretty good job of building the airplane according to Halton's design. He had designed an airplane with innovative features and state-of-the-art systems, and Throner's manufacturing group had risen to the challenge. The wing had been particularly difficult to build. It was made from a large machined component with a profile that was designed to very precise, or close, tolerances. The innovative engineering-production design for joining the wing and fuselage was also difficult. When the wing and the fuselage were mated they were attached at four principal points, a technique used in fighter aircraft assembly. Fred Kearns for one remained skeptical that manufacturing was capable of producing such a design, and he must have asked Throner fifty times, "Are you sure you have your tools mastered enough to do the job, Andy?" Kearns wanted an airplane that would be comparatively simple to assemble to keep costs down, but not too simple. The job required flawless tooling and assembly, and it was the only aspect of the design of the Challenger that really concerned Kearns; he feared a wing separation, even though it was an impossibility.

Throner was proud of his manufacturing people, but they were hampered by engineering's inability to deliver the drawings required to keep up with the changes. The continuing modifications resulted in the same problems that had plagued development—incompatible parts and mistakes. The shop floor was chaotic, and Throner was tremendously frustrated, particularly when Halton downplayed the gravity of the problem. Kearns's dictum was the rule Halton followed: "Stop crying and start trying."

If certified at 40,100 pounds, the aircraft could carry the Branson fuel tanks. The tanks were a key component of Canadair's plan to improve the airplane's range. The new tanks were by far the costliest modification of the program. Branson, the supplier, was a small outfit that had been contracted to build both the prototype and the tooling. The tanks were extremely complicated. They were to be placed in the pressurized part of the cabin under the floor and had to be designed with safety features such as a double lining for the fuel containers and the piping. Since the full tanks were very heavy, they had to be anchored securely. Canadair got a shock with the first prototype. It was obviously made by hand, the drawings didn't match it or the airplane structure where it was to be installed, and it leaked. Throner and his people found it useless for production purposes. The whole thing had to be redesigned by Canadair.

These and other problems made the cost of manufacturing the first airplanes horrendously high. Each time a design was changed to reduce weight, manufacturing had to build a new part. If a change came in while a worker was making a batch of parts, the batch would have to be retooled or, more likely, thrown out. It was not the way to build an airplane; the way to build the airplane was to perfect the prototype before starting production tooling. Everyone on the shop floor could see that engineering was redesigning the airplane as it went along. The question was, why? It was generally believed the company was going to such extremes over the weight issue because sales contracts would otherwise fall apart. But Throner suspected that the weight and performance issues were an obsession created by marketing. In Throner's opinion, Halton was trying to deliver the impossible and was not paying attention to the problems he was creating. To make matters worse, as costs went up and the machine shop and assembly areas were hit by layoffs and attrition, fewer and fewer people were expected to handle the ever-increasing work load.

The problems caused by the design changes got Fred Kearns's attention shortly after Canadair started delivering Challengers to the completion centers. At the centers, hundreds of modifications and changes to systems and components were incorporated on the delivered aircraft, and the costs started appearing on the books. Kearns, Halton and Throner descended on one completion center to discuss the escalating costs. The center's director told Kearns about the volume of changes, and Kearns asked Halton if this was true. No, no, Halton protested. Not so many. The change traffic was normal, and the completion centers had no reason to complain.

It began to dawn on Kearns that Halton was underestimating the seriousness of the problem. Canadair was paying a premium for changes at the completion centers, more than double and sometimes triple what the work would have cost in Montreal. But Canadair had to continue this way to meet contracted delivery dates. Kearns asked Throner to keep his own figure on the number of changes and let Kearns know directly how many there were. He wanted to make sure engineering's numbers were good. Out of curiosity Throner took out a calculator and tried to figure out what the changes were costing the program. He was astounded, and for the first time he worried about how Canadair would ever get out of this mess.

Meanwhile, he pushed and cajoled engineering to honor the detailed planning sheets that contained the schedule of changes. He didn't like doing this; as head of manufacturing he felt that it wasn't his job.

"Harry, you've got to get somebody riding herd on those engineers," Throner pleaded to Halton at the height of the design changes. "Your section chiefs are busy enough already and you need somebody cracking the whip up there. The detailed design work lacks supervision."

"You cannot manage engineers like you manage tradesmen," was all Halton would say on the subject.

With all the production problems, the idea of proceeding with the development of the 610 and 601 seemed preposterous. Just why the owners and the bureaucrats could not see what others in the industry could see—that the venture was an ill-timed big gamble on two more airplane models—had to do with Kearns's ability to convince people there was no problem that could not be fixed. With time and effort, success was a certainty at Canadair. The Challenger would overcome its technical difficulties, and Kearns was optimistic that it would be sooner rather than later. But his optimism was a matter of faith. He was not an engineer, and his faith was based on the belief that Harry Halton would surmount all obstacles and bring the Challenger 600 to the level of success it deserved. As a close friend said of Kearns, "The man simply had no problems."

By the end of 1980 Canadair's board of directors began to question his optimism. The board had become concerned by Taylor's acknowledgment that, largely because of the technical difficulties that delayed airplane deliveries, there were now more cancellations than orders. The board wanted to know just how bad the failure to meet specifications was. Halton was called in to explain. Before the start of the board meeting, Kearns brought Halton into his office and closed the door.

"Go easy on this, Harry," Kearns said. "They're not engineers in there, and I don't want to panic them with a litany of problems they don't understand. Don't bother telling them that we have a problem if we're fixing it. There's nothing they can do about it anyhow. Just tell them about the problems we haven't got a fix on yet."

Halton didn't like this. He felt the world should understand why

there were so many problems in the first place, problems caused by
Canadair, by Avco Lycoming and by the Department of Transport.
But he agreed.

At the meeting, Halton told the directors that there was a fuel-
consumption problem and therefore the range of the aircraft was
going to be just over 2,900 nautical miles. This alone should have
been a clear sign to the board that the program was way off its goals.
Kearns was right, though; most of the directors didn't understand the
significance of what Halton was telling them. The few directors who
did kept poker faces. Directors like Walter Ward, retired chairman of
Canadian General Electric, who received a separate and confidential
briefing by Halton before each meeting, and Don Watson, president
of Pacific Western Airlines, were sympathetic to Kearns's problems
and didn't want to encourage panic on the board. Things were tough
enough already. But they understood that the aircraft was in trouble.
A range of 2,900 nautical miles was a long way from the intercontinental range promised to customers in the beginning. Halton told the
board that he would meet the guaranteed range by aircraft number
81, which would come off the line in a year or so. Airplanes 1 through
80 would be modified and contracts would be renegotiated. The
board didn't challenge Halton's assumptions. Ward and Watson
hoped to heaven that Halton could pull it off.

Halton came out of the board meeting expecting Kearns to be
pleased. He was in for a surprise. "Geeze, Harry, you really laid it on
thick in there," Kearns said, disappointed. Halton was taken aback.
He hadn't seen Kearns like this before—he was an unhappy and
visibly worried man. He seemed frustrated by his loss of control of
the situation. Technical problems were overtaking the program, and
costs were rising quickly. Time was running out. Kearns wanted to
regain control of the program before the board and the government
found out.

For more than a year Kearns had been concerned about the possibility of government interference in the program. In 1979, he had
had his first taste of what would happen if the government took an
active interest in his program. That year the short-lived Conservative
government of Joe Clark came to power, and it was shocked at the
letters of comfort the Liberal administration had relied on.

Privatization was a top item on the Clark government agenda. One of the first things the government did was conduct a study of Canadair as a candidate. Finance Minister John Crosbie's Gaelic sensibilities were piqued when he learned that Canadair had a negative tangible book value of $28 million, nearly $300 million in development money hanging on the Challenger program, and still a year to go before the first delivery. The report wisely said it wasn't the time to sell Canadair because of the debt load and the fact that the Challenger, the main source of revenue to repay the debt, hadn't begun deliveries. It would have been pointless to risk the program through a sale of the company.

During the days of the Clark government, costs continued to rise above predicted maximum expenditures. With no revenue coming into the program Canadair was out of cash at the time and risked missing a payroll. Aird had arranged a potential loan with the Fuji Bank, which wanted the usual letter of comfort. When Canadair went to Crosbie, the minister balked. He didn't like the letters of comfort, and preferred to seek a guarantee from Parliament. Canadair couldn't wait that long. Aird went to Ottawa and pleaded with Crosbie to issue the letter. If Crosbie refused, the program would grind to a halt and layoffs would begin immediately. He relented but passed the word down to his assistant deputy ministers that this had better be the end of the requests for letters of comfort. Later that year the government's review committee met with Canadair in Montreal and was assured that no more money would be required.

At the same time, the Challenger's development problems were still plaguing the program, and Kearns was concerned that the Clark government might release details to the public. He sent a three-page letter to all Canadair employees. "I feel that it is very important that you hear first hand from me and senior members of my staff about the progress of the company," Kearns wrote; he alluded only vaguely to program problems. Two months later the Liberals were back in power, the flow of letters of comfort resumed, and the government's review process continued to monitor an increasingly distressed aircraft program. Three months after that, Canadair was asking for more, this time $300 million.

The review process failed to expose the full extent of the Challenger's problems to the politicians because, as problems worsened, there was a sense of self-preservation and a closing of many eyes. The review committee was composed of representatives from four ministries: Treasury, Finance, Transport and Industry Trade and Commerce. The committee had access to all the information, but the true dimensions of the problems were buried in reams of data. It did not have the authority to withhold funds that it would have had under the grant system. The process had no teeth, and ignorance was embedded in the system.

The link between the government and Canadair was ITC assistant deputy minister Antoine Guerin. Guerin was a long-time bureaucrat who had come from the textile industry. He sat as the deputy chairman on the Canadair board of directors and had been there since 1976 when the government reacquired the company. He oversaw the preparation of reports for the minister on the company's status and acted as Canadair's protector within the government. Over the years Guerin had become a supporter of Fred Kearns, and he would not tolerate anyone in government who wanted to rock the program with criticisms and dire warnings. It would have been difficult to prove any criticisms since details were confidential and the reports Ottawa received concerning the Challenger were upbeat and positive.

Frank communication between Ottawa and Canadair was not encouraged. One day Peter Aird and his comptroller, John Mackenzie, went to Ottawa for a routine meeting with ITC officials, and they dropped in to say hello to Guerin. When Guerin asked the two how things were going, Aird and Mackenzie proceeded to give him an extensive account of Canadair's problems. The more Guerin asked, the more voluable they became about the program's problems. Aird and Mackenzie didn't realize it, but they were scaring the daylights out of Guerin. As soon as the two had left, Guerin was on the telephone to Kearns demanding to know if what Aird and Mackenzie had told him was all true. No, no, Kearns assured Guerin. Everything was under control. Kearns explained that the two executives had been simply under a lot of pressure lately and it was obvious their emotions were getting in the way. When Aird and Mackenzie returned to Montreal, Kearns came down on them like a ton of bricks for being so negative about the program before a government representative.

If there were red flags flying, Guerin claimed he didn't know about them. At the same time, junior bureaucrats were getting all sorts of informal indications that things were going badly for the program, but these hints of trouble never found their way into the reports to the minister. Guerin rarely saw his minister, Herb Gray, who continued to sign multimillion-dollar letters of comfort. Rumours of problems with the 600 model were widespread within the ministry, and when the 610 and the 601 models were launched, bureaucrats responsible for Canadair believed it would be only a matter of time before the minister finally realized he had a disaster in the making. Guerin himself sensed as much. With his career in government about to enter a rocky period, Guerin started asking Canadair board members about a job at Canadair.

The problems with the 600 persisted. The last thing Halton needed was another airplane to worry about. But to outsiders it appeared that with certification of the Challenger 600 nearly complete and the development phase of the program nearing its end, Canadair could turn its attention to another project. The demands of the 600's post-development program meant that Halton had little time to spare. His mistake was to give the impression that everything was okay and that Canadair could develop more models with a minimum of expense and difficulty.

By the summer of 1980 a chronic shortage of working engines was pacing the 600 program. The twelfth aircraft was on the line for final assembly, yet Avco Lycoming had delivered only six engines. Avco Lycoming was never able to catch up with their delivery schedule. The engines that came in were sloppily put together: badly installed oil clamps, lost wire locks, fouled fuel and oil lines. One engine had a major component assembled backward. Halton began to wonder who was in charge of quality down there.

As the engine delivery delays and the modifications increased, concessions had to be made to customers in order to protect the order book. By mid-1980, the biggest customer was Akram Ojjeh's TAG, with more than 70 orders for Challenger 600s and 610s. Fred Kearns went to great lengths to keep them happy.

Kearns's commitment to serve TAG sometimes bordered on the absurd. He pulled a group of shop people from the line and put them to work on completing an aircraft for TAG in time for the birthday of one of the Ojjehs. The effort was an unmitigated failure. The team missed the birthday, and after the airplane was delivered it had to be returned and completed all over again. When Aziz Ojjeh came to visit

Kearns at Canadair, an aide told Kearns it was Aziz's birthday. Kearns knew Aziz coveted a painting of a Spitfire that hung in his office. The painting was Canadair property, but the company was Fred's fiefdom, and he gave the painting to Aziz for his birthday. Canadair was certainly market-driven.

Kearns found himself giving away more than just paintings to the Ojjehs. TAG ended up with a much better contract in terms of risk than did Federal Express. TAG managed to get Canadair to delete a series of "excusable delays" in aircraft delivery, meaning TAG could more easily walk away from an aircraft delivered late, which it sometimes did. When the Challenger One prototype crashed TAG got nervous. Because of the delivery delays and performance short-falls, TAG argued that Canadair was in default of its agreement and let it be known that it could walk away from its orders because the delays were not "excusable." Management took the threat seriously. The possibility of a mass cancellation would have been fatal.

TAG started calling some shots at Canadair. In 1980 TAG said the only way it would continue in the program would be if it was a partner in Canadair. Kearns had resisted the idea from the very beginning, but this time he had no choice. He had to keep TAG happy. In the summer of 1980 TAG got new concessions in a revised distributorship agreement. If TAG hadn't had the right to walk away before, they certainly had it now. Moreover, TAG would receive compensation for late deliveries. But most significantly, the new agreement made TAG a partner of sorts in the program. In the contract it was stated that TAG would have a greater role in the future of Canadair. TAG even got an office in Mahogany Row.

As Canadair's financial situation was deteriorating and its delivery and performance problems with the Challenger were rising, TAG began demanding concessions. In March 1981 Canadair renegotiated its contract with TAG, and then again in 1982. Under these renegotiations, more and more concessions were made to TAG. The concessions soon began to cause a lot of anger within the company. For example, Canadair had agreed to make TAG a preferred customer. This meant that if two airplanes were waiting for one available part, the TAG aircraft would get the part. Peter Ginocchio was head of Challenger product support, which reported to Challenger market-ing. When he discovered these special-treatment clauses, he fired a sharp letter to Jim Taylor. He wrote, "This kind of unthinking agreement makes any professional customer service organization want to vomit . . . I have instructed my guys to disregard this."

Despite all this, the personal relationship between Kearns and Akram remained extremely cordial. Akram had little to worry about. He was protected in nearly every regard save for a guarantee on the deposit money already held in the program. Akram also had an exclusive hold on distribution in what was still considered a lucrative market, the Arab nations, and had certain rights to the European and African markets. Kearns, meanwhile, continued to have faith in Akram's ability to sell the dozens of aircraft he had on order.

Through 1980 the new 610 and 601 programs proceeded at a snail's pace. Halton saw one virtue of the new projects. He could keep his budgets and worker levels high enough to deal with the problems that continued to plague the 600. But he didn't have much time for the new programs, and his progress with GE was slow. About four months after program go-ahead for the 610 and the 601, Taylor complained to Halton that GE was still waiting for the Canadair specifications and data on the 610 and the 601. Canadair's legal and contracts department was also taking more time than expected to get a deal with GE down on paper. The legal department's slowness was due partly to the fact that they were swamped with demands from customers to renegotiate purchase agreements on the 600 program. Meanwhile GE was beginning to take advantage of Canadair's vulnerability by demanding it take a greater share of the development risks. Canadair balked at this. GE had a pretty good idea of the trouble Canadair was in, and even though it knew Canadair would sooner or later overcome the teething problems with the Lycoming engine, it also knew it could prey on Canadair while the aircraft company was in such a weak position.

If the Challenger 600 was to have been a program done on the cheap, the 610 was supposed to be even more so; escalating costs for the 600 made Canadair unwilling to spend more time or money than absolutely necessary to get the new program rolling. This much was apparent to the engineers, who recognized early on that the 610 project was going nowhere fast and that delays in announced certification and delivery schedules would be inevitable.

The launch of the new projects achieved at least one of its desired results. After Canadair's March 1980 announcement of the deal with GE for 100 engines to power the 610 and 601, Avco Lycoming sat up and took notice. A top-level meeting was called between Canadair and Avco Lycoming. When Taylor heard that Kearns was to meet with Avco Lycoming, he suspected some sort of deal to get Canadair to back down on the commitment to GE in exchange for some concessions. "Don't do it, Fred," Taylor urged Kearns.

Fred was willing to deal because he still had a bad situation on his hands with the 600. Of the program's 128 orders, more than 70 orders were under negotiation, and 31 positions on the production line were looking for customers. Delivery delays, performance problems, declining credibility, inadequate responsiveness to problems and the resales and buy backs were turning the Challenger program upside down. Kearns had to focus all Canadair's efforts on getting the Challenger 600 out the door.

All Kearns had to bargain with was a promise to cut back on production of the 601 business jet if Avco Lycoming promised to clean up their act on the 600 model. Cutting back on the 601 was not a big deal. Orders for the 610 outnumbered those for the 601 by ten to one, and Kearns felt this proved the company had tapped out the business jet market. After meeting with Avco Lycoming and getting a renewed commitment from them to meet delivery and quality targets, Kearns ordered the production cutback on the 601 and raised the production figures for the 610. Everything was riding on the stalled 610 program.

More and more, people in Canadair management began to zero in on Harry Halton. Peter Aird, Canadair's VP finance, was hoping perhaps more than anyone else at Canadair that the 610 would be a success. The company desperately needed a source of revenue and it couldn't afford to have another project snarled in engineering problems. Given all the problems with the 600 model, Aird joined the chorus of senior officers insisting that Kearns do something about the overall management of the program. They were concerned that the program had become more than Halton could handle on his own. Not long after the start of production, Aird had become very concerned about the high number of production man-hours. He went to Kearns and told him that he should, for the sake of the 610's success, seriously consider getting in a top-level engineer to assume control of the program. Kearns already had someone in mind for the job, a former Canadair engineer named Robert ("Dick") Richmond.

Harry Halton and his airplane were in trouble. Halton had recommended the Lycoming engines. He had set the weight limits which he was unable to meet. He was responsible for the flight test program, which, despite the success of achieving certification in 21 months, had gone terribly wrong. He was responsible for all the engineering changes that were plaguing manufacturing. And he was the one who had said the 610 could be done relatively quickly and cheaply.

Harry Halton was ready for a fall.

9

The fall of Harry Halton

Nobody would give Harry Halton's airplane a fair chance. Marketing was complaining and, because of this, so were the customers; manufacturing was whining because of their work load; senior management was unhappy; and, in the spring of 1981, control of the program was passing from Harry Halton to an engineer who was going to try to save the Challenger 600 program before it was too late.

The aviation business is full of rivalries and professional jealousies, and Dick Richmond, Canadair's newly appointed executive vice president of operations, was perceived by many as Harry Halton's rival. Richmond was the opposite of Halton. He was a grim-looking no-nonsense Scottish Canadian. He was conservative, the opposite of entrepreneurial, and a penny-pincher. Richmond had the reputation of being a tough manager. He ruled with an iron fist, and some of the engineers in his employ were afraid of him. He would puff on his pipe and make them feel incompetent and lazy. In engineering meetings this was often the case, particularly if some hapless engineer didn't have the facts straight. To many, Richmond was a demanding son of a bitch who often dealt with a problem with the full force of his tough personality.

He was also very frustrating to work for. He was highly critical of Halton's style of management, but his philosophy—get it right the first time—often resulted in agonizingly long processes of decision-making. Indeed, Canadair could not afford to make any more hasty decisions. Where Halton would make fast and sometimes intuitive engineering decisions, Richmond would delay until he was fully satisfied that a decision was the correct one. Engineers were frequently sent back to do more study or work on a problem, and they also came to know that if Richmond didn't agree with a decision early in the discussion, the suggestion was all but dead. As Halton would say again and again, "A Dick Richmond simply wouldn't have been able to get the Challenger program going. He takes too long to make a decision." This was perhaps true. Halton, charming and persuasive, could drive a new aircraft program. But then Richmond wasn't hired to launch a program, but to clean up the mess created by one.

Richmond was an odd choice to help get the Challenger program back on track, since he had doubted the wisdom of launching the Challenger program as conceived. When news of its problems began to slip into circulation on the industry's cocktail party circuit, he was able to say, "I told you so." One person he said this to was Gary Rutledge, a well-known Canadian aerospace engineer. Rutledge had come to Richmond in 1976 with a pamphlet describing the proposed Challenger. Richmond had already done his assessment and figured the Challenger would be an over-weight airplane. "Don't you believe it," he had warned Rutledge. "They can't possibly build that airplane."

Richmond had often dealt with the messes left behind by others. A trained aeronautical engineer, he began his industrial career at Fairchild Aircraft Company in Montreal. All ill-timed diversification program bankrupted Fairchild, and in 1947 Richmond joined Canadair. He became vice president of the missiles and systems division when the two programs he directed, the Velvet Glove and the Sparrow II, were canceled shortly before the demise of the Avro Arrow CF-105, the airplane the weapons were intended to arm. By 1958 he had many engineers on staff with nothing to do, and he spent his time organizing their lease to other companies. In 1960 he joined Pratt & Whitney Canada (then known as United Aircraft of Canada Limited) as vice president of operations, something quite unrelated to his previous experience. It was an interesting job, and Pratt & Whitney had just launched its PT-6 gas turbine engine. The company needed a tough manager to bring the factory into line. After several years as second-in-command, Richmond was again restless. When Don Douglas Jr., son of the founder of the Douglas Company, asked Richmond if he was interested in joining Douglas Canada as its general manager, Richmond accepted.

Douglas was in desperate straits financially because of costly materiel shortages during the Vietnam War effort. Shortly before Richmond became vice president and general manager, the Douglas Company was taken over by the McDonnell family of St. Louis. After getting the DC-10 wing production underway at its Canadian facility, Richmond was made president of McDonnell Douglas Canada. While he was able to congratulate himself for being the first Canadian to make it to the president's office, to his disappointment McDonnell Douglas Canada had become a tightly controlled branch plant with little business latitude. Richmond recognized that the glory of the president's office was diminished due to a major disappointment caused by Air Canada. McDonnell Douglas had committed to producing the DC-10 wing at the Canadian facility, in part on the assumption that Air Canada, a past Douglas customer through the purchase of the DC-8 and DC-9, would again be a customer. McDonnell Douglas was miffed when it found out that Air Canada preferred the Lockheed 1011 Tristar, however it was too late to reverse the decision regarding the DC-10 wing production. Gord McGregor might have gone for the DC-10, since he had been pleased with the DC-8s and DC-9s. But Air Canada had a new president, Claude Taylor, and he felt the Lockheed was a better airplane. All Richmond could do was watch and wait.

The Air Canada defection was bad news for McDonnell Douglas Canada. Head office in St. Louis began to take a dim view of its Canadian operations. Attempts were made to launch new commercial ventures for the Canadian facility, but none went anywhere. Richmond had cut costs and improved efficiency in the operation, but he found himself in a position with a limited future. Without a new development program or a new product, Richmond became restless, and in 1974 he moved to the president's office at Spar Aerospace.

When Richmond joined Spar many in the industry were surprised. Spar was run by its founding chairman, Larry Clarke, a freewheeling entrepreneurial risk taker, the antithesis of the conservative Dick Richmond. Spar Aerospace was a de Havilland spin-off—Special Products and Applied Research—and Clarke had made it work by taking risks and acting quickly and intuitively. Nobody who knew Richmond was betting on a long stay with Spar. But for the moment, the company needed him. Spar's board of directors had put pressure on Clarke to bring in an operations man and get the house in order before Clarke embarked on any more of his risky endeavors.

When Richmond arrived at Spar it was losing money on all its products except one—a satellite contract with the federal government. York Gears Inc., a gear maker Spar had acquired, was bleeding the company. Spar's engineering talent was still pretty thin, and it was getting itself organized to take a shot at a NASA program. Spar was proposing to develop a remote manipulator, called the Canadarm, for the space shuttle program. It had managed to get some seed money from Industry Trade and Commerce, but Richmond saw that the space arm involved technology development on a very grand scale and he was worried that Spar might become another victim of the too-much-too-soon syndrome.

Richmond might well have been associated with the success of the space arm were it not for his fundamental disagreements with Larry Clarke. Richmond disagreed with Clarke's desire to extensively divisionalize and questioned plans to spend more on marketing and on research and development. He was also opposed to Spar's costly acquisition of RCA's Canadian satellite operation in Montreal. It was no surprise when, at age 62, in 1980, Richmond was forced out of Spar by Clarke.

While he was working as a consulting engineer for the Urban Transit Development Corporation, Richmond ran into Fred Kearns. UTDC was developing a new-technology urban transit concept, and Canadair had a contract for the program. Kearns was seeing a customer and asked Richmond to meet him for a drink.

It was obvious to the two men that they needed each other. The stress of overcoming the Challenger 600's development problems was tremendous, and Kearns was under pressure from his senior management to bring in a heavy hitter to restore order to the program. Richmond, still unhappy after being forced out by Clarke, needed to get back on track.

In 1980, Richmond started out as a consultant investigating the Challenger program. Everyone he talked to either tried to protect Harry Halton or was openly scornful of many of Halton's decisions. It was not easy for him to get a balanced perspective. Richmond was also asked to assess the commonality issue, the basis of the 610 design. Was it possible to stretch the Challenger into a new aircraft with few changes? Richmond had his doubts.

"Why do you want to sell three aircraft at a time?" Richmond asked Kearns. He thought Canadair had enough trouble just getting one model out the door. Nevertheless, Richmond looked into the issue. He found only a few people working on the project. They were led by Saul Bernstein, a structural engineer rather than an aerodynamicist. Bernstein had a reputation as a versatile all-around design engineer after successful stints in the jet trainer, missile and water bomber programs, but Richmond was concerned by the lack of activity. Richmond looked through the 600 flight test data, looked at what was being proposed for the 610 version and concluded that Kearns should scrap the whole idea right away. In Richmond's opinion, it wouldn't work. The 610 was becoming a new aircraft rather than a stretch. It would cost plenty to develop it, and Richmond knew Canadair couldn't afford to do it.

In spring 1981 Richmond's suspicions were confirmed. Given the 600's weight problem, the 610 would have been much too heavy, so heavy that it would have required very long runways available to get off the ground. At first the engineers thought they could finesse this problem by increasing wing area and introducing a new type of wing flap. It became apparent this solution wouldn't be enough. Two more solutions were proposed: more powerful flaps and more powerful engines.

When Canadair called GE to find out how much modifications to upgrade the engines would cost, it was shocked to learn that the price tag would be more than $150 million. GE suggested it could provide an automatic power recovery system (APR) on the existing engine at a more modest price. The APR would, in the event of one engine dropping below a certain power level during takeoff, automatically increase the power of the other engine beyond its normal maximum takeoff rating. The concept was innovative for the time and presented potential certification problems. The regulatory agencies let it be known that an APR would not necessarily receive quick approval. The last thing Canadair wanted was another certification problem. The weight problem and the lack of solutions confirmed to Canadair's management that the 610 was impossible.

A special meeting of Canadair's top management was called during the summer vacation, in July 1981. Kearns and the others stewed over what to do next. Richmond argued that it was time to put the 610 in the can, get on with fixing the 600, and speed up work on the 601. Taylor agreed. When Kearns asked Taylor what he thought should be done about the 76 orders for the 610, Taylor suggested they be converted into positions for the 601 with an incentive of $1 million off list price. And this is how Taylor finally got what he wanted, a GE-powered Challenger.

In August, sixteen months after go-ahead, Kearns was forced to shelve the 610 program. It was an embarrassing development. The gambit cost the company millions of dollars, and it made Canadair look foolish. The lost 610 development costs were rolled over into the Challenger's overall development costs, consistent with the management decision that Canadair should continue with its aggressive accounting practices. Company morale, already low due to the crash, delays and day-to-day emergencies, hit new depths. Canadair's credibility in the industry, already dubious, was worse.

The 76 orders for the stretched airplane were mainly from three customers: TAG, a U.S. charter outfit called Executive Air Fleet, and Federal Express. Peter Aird was one of the people who had to tell the 610 customers that the program was dead, and it was the worst moment of his career. "We had by now let so many people down it was almost unbearable," Aird said later.

TAG, which had ordered 35 of the 610s, immediately sent in a consulting firm to check out the numbers to make sure Canadair was playing straight with them. (The numbers checked out.) GE, the supplier of the engines, also sent in the experts to examine the situation. Canadair had failed to directly notify GE's top people of the program suspension. Brian Rowe, president of GE, heard about it from his own people instead of from Canadair. He was furious. Then Canadair, despite having made a commitment to GE for the engines, issued a graceless press release announcing the shelving of the program in such a way as to offend GE; it deflected blame from Canadair and targeted instead GE's inability to provide a powerful enough engine. At this point, GE was genuinely fed up with Canadair.

Canadair's board of directors was also unhappy. The 610, Kearns's hope for the future, was a major screwup. And the Challenger 600 situation continued to deteriorate. Kearns's faith in Harry Halton was severely tested in those days. Some of his senior people reminded Kearns that if he didn't soon make a change in the program's management, the board would likely make the changes for him. In other words, the Challenger program was about to be taken away from Halton.

A few months before Richmond was confirmed as a Canadair vice president, Fred Kearns had called Canadair's vice president of manufacturing, Andy Throner, into his office. "Dick Richmond is coming in to help us out," Kearns told him. Throner was shocked. He saw right away that a major shift in program management was coming. "Have you lost confidence in us, Fred?" Throner asked. Kearns skated past the question but Throner persisted. Finally Kearns took off his glasses and his face began to twitch, something it did with increasing regularity. "Let it ride, Andy," he said. "We really need some help around here."

In February 1981 Richmond was made vice president, operations. After a meeting with Richmond a few weeks later, Throner was left with the chilling impression that senior management was planning further changes. That night Throner told his wife to prepare for the worst. It didn't happen. Instead Throner was promoted out of the way and his second in charge, Vince Ambrico, took over Challenger manufacturing. Throner thought it would be just a matter of time before Halton got the same treatment.

Richmond didn't hide his intentions about or his opinions of the Challenger program. His criticisms of what had gone on at Canadair were seen even by Kearns as heavy-handed. And Richmond didn't confine his criticisms to Canadair. While working as a consultant for

Kearns, Richmond went down to Avco Lycoming to check out their promise that they were going to ship out 50 percent of their schedule in the coming months. As he had suspected, the promise was misleading. Avco Lycoming was going to ship 50 percent of its total schedule, but that didn't mean Canadair was going to see 50 percent of its orders. Other customers, mainly the military, were to get more than half their schedule, while Canadair would get less. He told Kearns what was happening when he returned, but Kearns wouldn't believe it; Richmond was stunned by Kearns's refusal to deal with reality. Richmond understood the operational side of the engine business from his days at Pratt & Whitney, and knew Avco Lycoming's scheduling to be an irrefutable fact. Kearns got angry with Richmond and warned him not to be such an alarmist.

Richmond's investigations continued. During a luncheon with company executives, Richmond told Kearns that it had been necessary to replace the skin sections on a number of airplanes because a worker had been using a saw to finish the installation of a part and had inadvertently sliced into the skins. Kearns was upset that the story came out so publicly in front of other executives. Later he pulled Richmond into his office and lit into him for his indiscretion. Richmond wasn't moved.

"Look, Fred, I think it's time we start acting like big boys!"

Kearns may have had reservations about this forthright engineer coming in and making waves, but he had no choice: sooner or later he would have to take the program completely away from his longtime friend, Harry Halton. Meanwhile Canadair had two executive vice presidents who ignored each other save for necessary communication in corporate meetings. It was an absurd situation for a company in serious trouble, and to some degree it reflected Kearns's lack of courage to tell his chief engineer that he had lost confidence in him. Worse, Kearns made Halton, by implication, the scapegoat for many of the Challenger's problems. People who held Halton in high regard thought Kearns was making a fool of their friend.

Halton continued to operate as though he had the full confidence of the other senior officers, but he could sense that all was not well. One day he went into Peter Aird's office and confronted him directly. "Have you and the others lost confidence in my abilities,

Peter?" Aird wasn't about to step in where Kearns feared to tread, so he reassured Halton. Halton believed him.

Finally, in February 1982, in a special meeting for all the senior engineering staff, it was announced that Dick Richmond would assume total control of the Challenger program. Halton was to begin conducting an audit of Canadair's other programs. "This is an important task!" Halton declared, as if to deflect the sorrow of the moment. It was the painful end of a difficult era in the company's history.

While Halton worked on an audit of Canadair's programs, Richmond was assessing the Challenger program to figure out the future. The more Richmond delved into the program, the more he suspected that any bad news was not getting to management, since Richmond found it difficult to get reliable information. He discovered that nobody in top management had a real grasp of what was going on.

The flood of changes to the aircraft had bogged down the processes of costing, scheduling, and even definition. And because cost and schedule information had been arbitrarily reduced and shortened in the past to keep the program moving, Richmond found the engineering staff reluctant to generate the information he needed.

Richmond's challenge was to find out the status of the engineering changes which were overtaking the program and causing confusion right down to the factory floor. The mountain of changes had produced a confusing, disorganized working environment. Tradesmen were asked to deal with ever increasing batches of parts for modification, in addition to regular production batches, all of which competed for priorities and resources. Work completed at one stage of the assembly line was being taken apart at the next stage to incorporate changes, with the process being repeated again further down the line. Shop floor managers were swimming in paper work, data and action requests. To meet revised recovery schedules, corners were cut and the addition of green workers to fill manpower gaps hurt the quality and raised factory costs. Design deficiencies and marketing demands used up precious resources while basic drawing and tooling problems went unattended. It was a mess.

In the assembly areas Richmond took a close look at the schedules tacked to the walls. They showed jobs by shift and how far each shift

had progressed on a particular job. The first thing he noticed was that
the schedules were out of date. He knew that Canadair middle
management was still consulting these schedules for their reports to
senior management, so the managers couldn't possibly know what
was really going on. He also looked at the master schedule, which
was labeled Schedule #13. It was in reality schedule 16 or 17, because
management had begun to denote schedule 13-A, 13-B and so on.
Richmond was baffled by the numbering system but found that the
confusion was caused by the legal department, which insisted that
the schedules denote numbers current with signed production agreements; while schedules changed, the production agreements did not.

By this time there was only one rule being followed in the production schedule: get it done and get it out. Scheduling depended on
who had the most influence to marshall people and resources to get a
particular job done. It was no wonder that top management didn't
have a clue about the true status of any particular job.

One day Richmond pulled aside the head of schedules, Tony
Natlacen. "Tony, tell me the truth. We haven't got the foggiest idea
of the real status of any single job going on in this plant, have we?"

Natlacen was embarrassed. He shook his head and said, "Dick,
you have no idea how many problems we've got right now. It's simply
more than we can handle."

Part of the problem was that Canadair didn't have a modern
system for tracking production. Canadair's production control and
factory systems had, over the years, evolved into a convoluted
mélange handed down from Douglas, Boeing, North American
Rockwell and Lockheed. Another problem was the production control meetings. They were attended by more than 40 people, and they
accomplished little. Richmond stopped the large meetings and got
Natlacen to look at a new planning chart that would give a better
view of the program.

Natlacen returned with a snapshot of the current state of the
Challenger program, and it wasn't a pretty sight. More than a dozen
airplanes, each unique, each in varying degrees of dress and undress.
There was still a ferocious flow of engineering change traffic. Special
audits were being conducted to make sure the right parts got into the
right airplane. In an attempt to meet delivery dates, some of them

nearly two years behind schedule, airplanes were still being sent out the door with a host of modifications to be done at considerable expense at aircraft completion centers.

Because the factory was in disarray, quality declined. Richmond's story of the employee who used the wrong tool to finish a component and cut the skins on a number of airplanes was a typical example of the quality problem. For one reason or another, workers sometimes had the wrong tools for the job. To meet the urgent schedule, they tried to cut corners. Canadair often lost more time than it gained by rushing because it had to go back and rework all the quality problems. And the stress of the Challenger program was having its effect on the quality of other programs, as well. In January 1981 Boeing sent up a team of engineers to find out why the first delivery of a component for their 767 program was incomplete.

"It was really a matter of bringing the fundamentals back to the shop floor," Richmond would say later. "We had to ensure that the workers understood their task, had the right tools and the right parts."

Several months after Richmond took over there was a visible change on the shop floor. Stations along the production route were beginning to catch up. Batches were cleared of mixes. There was more order, and because of Richmond Rule #1 — nobody touches the schedule — there was a clearer sense of the progress the program was making. By aircraft number 68 the factory began to operate on schedule. Once delivered, however, the airplanes showed equipment reliability problems. Richmond struck a new engineering and procurement task force to examine the equipment problems. He concluded that equipment had been selected with inadequate concern for aircraft requirements; rather, the specifications appeared to have been written largely on the basis of what the supplier had available. For Richmond, this was another example of trying to do things too quickly.

Richmond also had strong opinions on the role of marketing in the company's woes. He felt it had demanded an airplane that simply couldn't be built, then withdrawn its support for the airplane when it finally came off the line. Marketing was also after Canadair management to make endless modifications at a time when manufacturing couldn't handle the mandatory changes to fulfill contracts. He'd heard the industry jokes that at Canadair the laws of physics didn't apply while the laws of marketing did. When Richmond came on board, he did his best to blunt marketing's influence in the management of the program.

With scheduling and quality coming under control, Richmond moved on to the program's other desperate problem: program costs. It was clear to everyone at the executive level that no one had a clue what anything cost anymore. Richmond wanted to establish the costs of airplane equipment and worker-hours. To do that he needed industrial engineers (IEs) to monitor the shop. When Richmond arrived at Canadair the company had one IE to every 50 assembly people; Richmond wanted one IE to every 20 assembly people. It was a difficult thing to ask for when Canadair was cutting back on staff. Richmond had to overcome Kearns's fierce objections to hiring new people. He told Kearns he had no choice—the reporting task of the job was too much for the few IEs they had. When the reports started to come in from the new IEs, Canadair's management began to appreciate just how serious the cost situation had become: because of the number of changes, equipment costs (a large part of the airplane cost) were going through the roof. The program's breakeven point receded further into the future.

While Richmond continued to struggle with the modifications, he was still without engines. To keep to the schedule Canadair was forced to borrow, or "slave," engines from airplanes waiting for modifications at completion centers. This caused concern in marketing, since the customers were not happy. Customers were also worried about the engine's reliability. Several engine incidents occurred in 1981, and there was genuine concern that it would only be a matter of time before a serious accident occurred. A federal Cabinet minister had had the scare of his life when a turbine blade let loose and sliced off a piece of the engine tail pipe on a Challenger he was flying in. While it was not a life-threatening incident, rumors of it spread through the market. Some people began questioning the safety of the airplane; some refused to fly in it.

In a meeting with Kearns, it was decided that Richmond and his chief of procurement, Frank Francis, would fly down to Stratford to see what could be done to bring some control to the engine program. In Stratford they got what Richmond called the usual whitewash, but later, in a meeting back in Montreal with Avco Lycoming's general manager, John Myers, Fred Kearns asked if he could send someone down to track engine deliveries. Myers agreed.

Francis was sent to Stratford to manage the order. Francis was an engineer who had been overlooked by Challenger program management and was brought in by Richmond, who gave him responsibility for procurement. Francis had considerable senior Canadair experience in manufacturing and project management, but he also had a tough demeanor that made him one of the least-liked vice presidents in the company. He was very supportive of Richmond: Canadair was no longer going to get pushed around by suppliers, especially Avco Lycoming.

Francis began by setting up a production control system to keep track of the 2,000 or so parts that went into the engine. He would monitor quality levels, and he could also make sure parts didn't get sidetracked to other Avco Lycoming customers. In the first half of 1981 six of the 18 engines delivered had to be returned due to mechanical problems. In discussion with Myers it was determined that Avco Lycoming's tooling was in poor shape. Engine parts had to be precision tooled to very high tolerances if consistently good parts are to be produced, and Avco Lycoming wasn't meeting those tolerances. The similarity between Canadair and Avco Lycoming struck Richmond at that point. They were both doing too much too soon. "They still had two years of development work on that engine," he said. "In the same way, Canadair still had development work to do on the Challenger."

Two years later, however, the situation was no better. The Challenger 600 continued to be hampered by an unreliable engine from a troubled supplier. Richmond decided to play hardball. He had already suffered the bitching of a number of customers who were unhappy with the reliability of the Avco Lycoming engines. When Russ Harrison, chairman of the Canadian Imperial Bank of Commerce, told Richmond that his people had begun refusing to fly on the Challenger, Richmond asked Harrison if he would tell the same story to Avco Lycoming's new chairman, Don Farrar. Harrison agreed, and a meeting was set up with Farrar in Toronto.

Harrison's comments, plus the comments of another Canadian owner, Conrad Black, had a tremendous impact on Farrar. This was corporate Canada talking. Farrar immediately agreed to monthly meetings to review the problem and instructed Myers to pull out the stops to find fixes for the reliability problems. Canadair's people were happy with this turn in events until it was revealed that Avco Lycoming had had fixes for the engines but had never told them. News of this stunned Canadair's executives. Canadair's faith in Avco Lycoming was obliterated, and many in the company felt the time had come to sue Avco Lycoming.

After Fred Kearns shelved the 610 program in the summer of 1981, he got his engineers to speed up the project to introduce a GE-powered Challenger, the CL-601. That autumn Jim Taylor, Richmond and a few other senior executives flew with Kearns to GE's offices in Lynn, Massachusetts, for a two-day marathon meeting with GE president Brian Rowe. They were there to discuss the delivery schedule of the 100 GE engines for the suspended 610 program. Canadair intended to use the engines on the executive model, the 601, but wanted to change the schedule, since there were very few orders for the 601. The price had already been negotiated, and Canadair felt the matter had been settled. Then the roof came down.

"We want out of the contract," Rowe said to open the meeting. "You guys broke the contract by shelving the 610 and frankly we don't see the same market for the 601. We want a minimum order for 200 engines at a 20 percent higher unit price and a new payment schedule whereby you pay us the $35 million refundable development costs up front."

The people from Canadair were stunned. They met in private, except for Taylor, whom Kearns considered less than impartial in the matter. They looked at their options. Was there hope of Avco Lycoming coming out of their problems? Would it happen in time? Could the Challenger program survive any more engine problems?

Were they willing to scrap the 601? In the end they realized they didn't have any choice. They had to go with GE at any price.

Not only did Kearns have to swallow a price he didn't like, he had to agree to a delivery schedule far faster than what he wanted. Canadair was committed to the new Challenger, the GE-powered 601, in a big way.

With a speed that amazed even Jim Taylor, Canadair took a Challenger 600, chopped off the rear fuselage, put on a new back end with GE engines and began flight testing the next Challenger model. Taylor's battle for the GE engine was over, but Kearns's battle for his professional life was about to begin.

10

Shareholders' revolt

A year after the Challenger 600 was certified, only about two dozen airplanes had been delivered to customers. Revenues were flowing into the company, but not fast enough. The company had planned by this point to be producing airplanes at a rate of 75 a year but, because of the engine problems and the post-development modifications, they were delivering only 25. The expected flow of revenues was a trickle that came nowhere close to solving the company's cash flow crisis.

Canadair had consumed money voraciously, and there were many lenders to satisfy the company's appetite. Bankers love a new airplane program when the government owns the company. As program costs continued to overshoot projected levels, vice president of finance Peter Aird had easily found more sources of credit. The $20 million line of credit Canadair had at the start of the program had been expanded to $120 million. A letter of comfort was obtained for a line of credit with Canadair's bankers, the CIBC and the National Bank; and hundreds of millions were borrowed on this line. A friend of Aird's at Credit Suisse/First Boston in London introduced Aird to a banker from the Fuji Bank; they were touched for $40 million, then another $30 million based on a letter of comfort. The Credit Suisse/First Boston provided funds, a $20 million loan, also based on a letter of comfort. Borrowing went up and up: in 1978, $162 million; in 1979, $296 million; in 1980, $479 million. By 1981 letters of comfort had been issued covering more than $500 million in short- and long-term loans, and the interest costs were adding up.

Despite the blocked flow of information, ITC Minister Herb Gray
and his colleagues had been hearing discouraging words about Canadair. Jean-Pierre Goyer, a close friend of Trudeau and a former
Cabinet minister who had been appointed to Canadair's board after
resigning his seat, had gone to Don Johnston in Treasury and Herb
Gray in ITC in early 1981 to complain about Kearns's mismanagement of the program. When Kearns learned of this, he instructed his
people not to communicate with Goyer, even though he sat on
Canadair's board. Goyer let it be known that he wanted a permanent
office at Canadair, the chairman's chair and a share of the CEO
duties. He eventually went to Trudeau and threatened to resign from
the board if something wasn't done. Nothing was done. At the time
there was an intense rivalry for Trudeau's attention between Goyer
and chairman of Quebec Liberal Caucus, Marc Lalonde, another
friend of Trudeau. When Goyer pressed for an investigation of
Canadair, Lalonde opposed the idea. Trudeau told Goyer to take up
the matter with Michael Pitfield, Trudeau's principal secretary and
Clerk of the Privy Council. Pitfield listened to Goyer's request for an
investigation, but discovered there was already an interdepartmental
task force looking into Canadair.

Don Johnston's people in Treasury had initiated the task force.
During a review of Crown corporations several months earlier, Treasury had come across the letters of comfort that had created a
multimillion dollar liability for the government; they also noted that
Canadair was still consuming funds. Treasury was less sanguine than
Finance had been about the letters of comfort because, although the
letters did not create a debt, they did represent a contingent liability.
When Treasury realized that this liability had been created with
letters from the minister that had not been approved by Cabinet, its
legal people changed the procedure; in future Cabinet would have to
approve all letters. At the same time Treasury urged Martin Brennan,
the ITC director general of the steering committee overseeing Canadair, to examine the company's financial situation.

In early 1981 the steering committee set up an interdepartmental
task force. It was made up of Bob Silver, a junior director from
Finance; Harvey Cox, a tough-minded ex-Navy commander from
Treasury who would write the report; and Martin Brennan from
Industry Trade and Commerce. For nearly a year they and about a
dozen other government officials combed through the program's

financial history. In February 1982 the report was delivered to Cabinet.

The first red flag went up. If the program failed, the report said, losses would be significant. To quote the report, "There should be no sense of security by the small reported profits or minimal losses since acquisition; if insufficient aircraft are sold to achieve break even, a cash shortfall will occur and this shortfall will have to be met by the Government of Canada." This begged the question, Would Canadair break even on the Challenger program? The report was decidedly optimistic on this matter, thanks mainly to Kearns, who had done his best to influence the final version. He had told his people to put up with the process and make sure the task force saw the positive side of everything. Kearns and his staff responded to the task force's queries about any problem by saying, "It'll soon be fixed." The bureaucrats heard a lot of that enthusiasm and optimism, and accepted it. Kearns was so successful that the task force's forecast for annual sales turned out to be more bullish than Canadair's.

The task force did not give Kearns a clean bill of health, however. While the report was bullish on the Challenger, it was bearish on management. In a section called Management Effectiveness, the report questioned Canadair management's forthrightness with the board of directors. In particular it questioned the handling of the 610. Management had made the decision to shelve the program during plant shutdown, a time when most directors were on vacation. Most board members were informed about the decision after the fact by telephone. This, the report suggested, hardly gave the board the opportunity to assess the impact of the decision on the company and to prepare an intelligent response. The task force also found no evidence that the board had been fully informed about renegotiations on the General Electric engine order. The task force estimated the cost of the renegotiated GE order would be in excess of $200 million. "It seems unusual that corporate management should have agreed to contractual price changes of such significance without having the prior approval of the board of directors," the report said.

Kearns read a copy of the report after it had gone to Herb Gray at ITC. He became concerned about Canadair's credibility with the government. The report painted the picture of a management group with its board of directors in its pocket, running a program besieged by problems caused by optimism about opportunities and under-estimation of difficulties. It was true that Kearns tended to treat the board as a rubber stamp and was not forthcoming about problems, but he did not try to deceive the board with wholesale lies. Kearns hastily drafted a rebuttal. Even though the report was classified, a leak was always a possibility, and Kearns feared the consequences.

"The Challenger Aircraft is an accomplishment of which we as Canadians should now be extremely proud," Kearns wrote to Gray. "In the interim, we are running into the usual Canadian practice, particularly by the media, of searching for the negative aspects."

Cabinet digested the report, then decided that the government would have to limit Canadair's debt financing. After meeting with Kearns, Herb Gray settled on the figure of $1.35 billion as the absolute limit. Just before St. Valentine's Day, in 1982, Gray flew down to Canadair and signed an agreement stating that Canadair would live within that limit. But because of the 610 incident, Kearns would also have to submit to closer government scrutiny until such time as conditions improved. Kearns complained to a friend, Treasury Minister Don Johnston, of this interference, but by this point Kearns had few allies in Ottawa.

In writing to Gray to confirm the details of the new agreement, Kearns said, "We feel that the most important elements affecting program control and costs are stable and predictable." They weren't. In fact, they got much worse.

As economists talked of modest gains in the economy due to declining inflation in 1982, a recession careened out of nowhere and destroyed Canadair's hopes for a speedy recovery from its load of debt. Interest rates soared and the Canadian dollar plummeted, playing havoc with costs and revenues. The business community, reeling under the recession, began canceling orders for business jets. Canadair went deeper into a fiscal crisis as Ottawa capped the company's borrowing. All Canadair's planning charts had a bold line running across the top with $1.35 billion marked beside it. Kearns fought in vain to stay under the limit, knowing the consequences would be severe if he failed.

Canadair was desperate. It borrowed money from its own employees by withholding salaries; five percent was deducted from salaried people, ten percent from senior executives. The company also renegotiated some of its manufacturing agreements, where it was subcontractor, to generate more cash flow. In one case, it agreed to lower its price if the customer would pay Canadair's nonrecurring costs up front instead of later, as is usually done.

Peter Aird was spending all his time looking for more money. With the recession, credit was harder to find and a lot more expensive. In early 1982 Aird went to the Eurobond market for a public loan of $120 million, but he found that conditions had changed there, as well. Interest rates had risen from 8 ½ percent to 12 ½ percent. Back home, the letters of comfort were falling out of favor with Canadian lenders, in particular Russ Harrison, chairman of the Canadian Imperial Bank of Commerce. The CIBC was Canadair's principal banker and also one of the banks with a significant exposure in the Dome Petroleum fiasco. Harrison let it be known that if Canadair wanted more credit, nothing less than a government guarantee would be accepted.

In mid-1982, there was another cash crisis. Aird didn't have time to get Parliamentary guarantees, so he contacted a friend at Morgan Guaranty. He pleaded with the friend to take the letter of comfort. Morgan Guaranty accepted what turned out to be the last letter of comfort for Canadair.

As part of its St. Valentine's Day agreement with Gray, Canadair submitted a five-year operating plan, which Kearns insisted should show a business-as-usual view of the world. But it was far from business as usual in 1982. The recession forced Canadair to take back orders from cost-conscious company presidents who no longer saw a company jet in their future. (Though the orders had been taken back, the airplanes remained as "orders" on government reports, although Canadair was the owner.) There were few prospects to pick up these canceled orders, and the order book contained more and more Canadair-held orders. Recessionary cost-cutting measures flooded the market with used business jets that cost much less than the Challenger. As the recession dragged on, heated arguments broke out in Mahogany Row over the sales forecasts. Jim Taylor reminded everyone that Canadair hadn't seen a new order in nearly two years and that a third of the orders he did have were soft. Still, sales forecasts for the five-year plan remained optimistic, and Taylor, who

knew what the recession was doing to corporate America, felt that
Kearns was setting the forecasts way too high.

Kearns remained doggedly optimistic because he had found a new
market. Half the small jets owned by the U.S. military were more than
two decades old, ready for replacement. But Canadair had yet to sell
a single airplane into that market. Fred Kearns decided it was time to
make a concerted effort to change that. He opened a Washington
office and went looking for a sales staff.

Lt. Col. Charlie Gray was a military pilot who had spent the past
four years working for the Pentagon. When he heard that Canadair
was looking for people, Gray applied and was hired. He went to
Montreal and met with Kearns over lunch in the executive dining
room, and when the lunch was over the purpose of the meeting
became clear.

"Now, Charles," Kearns said as he put his knife and fork down and
dabbed his mouth with a napkin. "This is the message I want to give
to you. Your first priority is to go after the JetStars used by the Air
Force and get them replaced with Challengers. I want you to spare
nothing in your effort to make this come about. Is that understood?"

Gray understood. When he got back to Washington he began to
lobby the military on the need for the acquisition of new executive
aircraft. Gulfstream was also after this market, and pretty soon the
military, which recognized the need to replace the aging JetStars, put
out a request for proposals (RFP) for the acquisition of 20 executive
jets for a Special Air Mission, or C-SAM, as it was designated.

Gray learned early on that Canadair was in for an uphill battle. The
"special air mission" was to fly the president and his senior people
around the country. Therefore, the preference of the president's
pilot would factor heavily in the Air Force's selection of an aircraft.
Both Canadair and Gulfstream put their aircraft at the disposal of the
president's pilot, who came down unequivocally in favor of
Gulfstream's latest offering, the G-III, principally because it could
zoom to 45,000 feet and fly nonstop from Washington to the
president's home in California; the Challenger couldn't do that.

Undaunted, Gray waged a campaign in the House of Representatives to try to keep the Challenger a contender. While Gulfstream
lobbied its contacts in the Senate, Gray flew three key House of
Representative politicians—Speaker Tip O'Neill, Bill Chapel of the

Armed Services Committee and Dan Daniel of the House Appropriations Committee—around in a Challenger. Gulfstream chairman
Allen Paulsen, whose company was located in Georgia, countered by
using his influence as a big financial supporter of one of the state's
two senators, Matt Mattingly, a powerful Republican fund-raiser
and member of the exclusive Republican Eagles Club. Many people
believe that it was as a result of Mattingly's efforts that the Senate
Appropriations Committee report attached a condition to the aircraft acquisition funding bill stating that "the aircraft selected to
perform this mission be manufactured in the United States by a U.S.
firm." If Gray couldn't get that wording changed in the House, the
Challenger wouldn't have a chance.

Canadair went ahead with its proposal, an immense undertaking.
The RFP called for an executive jet to be fitted out with special
communications and other electronic equipment, all of it heavily
classified and secret. Because of the security surrounding the electronics in the aircraft, the RFP stipulated that the prime contractor
had to be a U.S. company with security clearance, but the Air Force
added that this did not necessarily exclude a foreign-built aircraft.
Canadair was advised that it could get around this issue by teaming
up with a U.S. company that would be the prime contractor. This
Canadair did, joining with Rockwell's electronics division and coming in as the subcontractor.

In Montreal, Canadair placed its hopes on C-SAM as the savior of
the program. Even though the company had no money to spare, a
million dollars was earmarked for C-SAM and a special team was set
up under Jess Munro to prepare the bid. Canadair had never made
such a proposal for the Challenger, and the team of some two dozen
specialists worked feverishly over a three-month period to prepare a
bid that would cover all the bases.

Meanwhile, Kearns's new initiatives were still not much more than
that—initiatives—and not surprisingly Herb Gray rejected the rosy
five-year plan proposed by Canadair. The new monitoring process of
Canadair produced a quarterly review for 1982 showing a massive
deterioration in sales and revenue. The Minister wrote to Canadair's
chairman of the board, Guy Desmarais, and said the company must

come up with a more realistic operating plan. Gray also reminded
Desmarais that if Canadair could not live within the $1.35 billion
limit, the government would give "full consideration of all the alternatives open to the government to protect its interest as share-
holder." The fact that the minister had written to Desmarais alarmed
Kearns, but the comment, "full consideration of all the alternatives,"
made him shudder.

In October 1982, Peter Aird began to realize that the program was
not going to make it through the year without a loss. The combination of a sinking Canadian dollar (nearly all aspects of the program
were calculated in U.S. dollars), creeping inflation, stratospheric
interest rates, program cost overruns and a depressed market for the
Challenger had smashed Canadair's elegant forecasts to smithereens.
He came to this conclusion while preparing the prospectus for a $150
million Eurobond issue. Aird had gone to the European bond market
twice before, and this time he was concerned that Canadair might
have a credibility problem, not with the market, but with Canadair's
lenders. The balance sheet showed total program revenues of a little
more than $650 million and total program costs of more than $1.8
billion, a difference of $1.15 billion. In the short term Aird saw a
continuing increase in negative cash flow. The long term was still
anybody's guess. To maintain some credibility with lenders, Aird felt
that Canadair should disclose the possibility of a loss. But he would
have a hard time convincing Kearns of this, because it would certainly
mean trouble with the government.

Aird took his papers into Kearns's office. There was that sign on
Fred's desk: Stop crying and start trying. He knew Kearns didn't want
to hear what he had to say. Right from the start of the program
Kearns had said the program could not and would not lose any
money. If the program cost a little more than anticipated, then those
costs would be spread out over a greater number of airplanes sold.
But costs had risen so much they were being spread out over an
unrealistic number of airplanes.

"Fred, I think we might have to consider a writedown," Aird said.

Kearns was silent. To admit a loss would invite the wrath of the
government. The loss would become public, and Kearns would
forever be associated with it. He was still clinging to the hope that the
program could pull out of its slump. They were still in the running for
the C-SAM bid. As bad as the situation was—and in September 1982

it was desperate—he refused to give up hope and face the harsh reality of a loss.

"Peter, deep down in your heart of hearts, do you really believe we're not going to make it without a loss?"

"It's a real possibility."

Kearns reluctantly agreed to Aird's recommendation. Attached to the November Eurobond Ex-tel card Aird placed a warning: "The value of the inventory of the Challenger program may require significant adjustment." He had let the market know that since most of Canadair's inventory consisted of unamortized development costs, interest charges and other soft items, the value of the inventory depended entirely on Canadair's ability to sell lots and lots of airplanes, which it wasn't likely to do in the near future. The warning shot had been fired.

Kearns didn't know it, but it was already too late. Since April Canadair had borrowed more than $300 million, most of it to cover past borrowing, and Aird's November visit to the European bond market would put Canadair over a $1.35 billion cap on borrowing. Earlier that week Kearns had written ITC Minister Herb Gray, informing him that Canadair was about to exceed its borrowing limit. Kearns wrote that letter confident his friends in Ottawa would not abandon him. He was wrong.

It was nearly three weeks before the government replied. When the letter arrived, Kearns was stunned. For one thing, the letter was signed by a new minister, Ed Lumley. Gray was out.

The letter stated that the minister would effectively take all major decision-making powers away from Kearns. He couldn't change production rates, he couldn't buy new equipment, he couldn't set terms for sales, he couldn't make deals with distributors, he couldn't do anything without the minister's permission.

The letter from Lumley also stated that Kearns would have to go through Parliament rather than Cabinet to seek guarantees for future loans. This was a new twist. The days of cozy negotiations in the executive dining room and easy securing of hundreds of millions of dollars were definitely over. Now Ottawa demanded that Canadair present itself before a Parliamentary committee if the company wanted any more money.

Kearns couldn't let this bother him. His first concern was to keep the program running. He would have to convince the Parliamentary committee the same way he had convinced everyone else—there were no problems without a solution, and everything was going to be fine just as soon as they got around the next corner. Kearns was not crying, he was trying, desperately.

Long hours went into the preparation for the November 1982 hearing before the public accounts committee. Kearns and Aird drafted a request for $200 million in equity, the first official request for equity since the program was started. The $200 million figure was an arbitrary one since nobody had a clue how much was needed to keep going. They went over every possible issue that might arise in the hearings. Kearns was in control. It would be his presentation, and everyone knew there would be no letting down of appearances. The message: The problems are behind us now and the program is going to make it.

On the day he went to Ottawa he got a call from Charlie Gray in Washington about his last hope for turning around the sales figures, the C-SAM.

With about two weeks to go before the formal bid submission, Gray had run into serious trouble on Capitol Hill. After an intense bit of lobbying, Gray had managed to get his key contacts on the House subcommittees to amend the requirement on their version of the acquisition bill that the aircraft be built in the United States. But when it came time for a vote, he found that his contacts were about to trade away the wording that would save the Challenger for a vote on another issue. The fabulously expensive MX missile program was in the works, and powerful lobbyists worked the Congresspeople to get the bill on the MX passed. In all the horse trading that ensued, Gray's contacts gave up their support for the change in wording, and the Challenger lost the battle.

In Canadair's Washington office, Gray stewed while he thought what he would do next. It was clear that, once the bill passed, no one would challenge Congress by selecting a non-American aircraft. Gray called Kearns and suggested that Canadair immediately pull out of the competition.

It came as a terrible blow to Kearns. Six months of hard work and about a million precious dollars the company could ill afford to waste were doomed by the Challenger's native roots. Everywhere Kearns turned to find a solution to his problems, he was stymied. That day, as he rehearsed his upbeat and optimistic presentation for the bureaucrats, his mood was bleak. He was running out of solutions, and as he prepared to make his trip to Ottawa, it appeared he had also run out of time.

A Canadair limousine was brought around and Kearns, Aird and comptroller John Mackenzie set off for Ottawa for the last defense of their program.

Concern in Cabinet about Canadair had been mounting since Kearns's letter to Gray saying Canadair would exceed the $1.35 billion borrowing limit, and his presentation in Ottawa made the Trudeau Cabinet extremely nervous. The Cabinet had good reason to be nervous. Immediately after the letter from Kearns arrived, Michael Pitfield was told to get an outsider and find out what was really going on in Canadair. Pitfield called for the Gunslinger. People in investment circles called Terry Godsell the Gunslinger because he liked to shoot from the hip. The analyst from Shieldings Investments, a venture capital division of Richardson Greenshields, had gone in to find out where Canadair's debt situation was heading. He came out with a report that was a scathing indictment of Kearns, Canadair and the airplane. It produced the famous line, "The Challenger is another airplane the world could do without."

Godsell's slant on Canadair's problems was completely different from the government reports of February 1982. Beside the pop-gun task force report, it was a cannon that blew away the facade of Kearns's optimism and enthusiasm.

A few weeks after the November hearing in Ottawa, Kearns received a call from ITC's Ed Lumley. The game was up. The government was coming in to take over the company.

A week after Fred Kearns's testimony before the Parliamentary committee in November 1982 an urgent meeting of Trudeau's inner Cabinet had been called to decide what to do about the rapidly deteriorating situation at Canadair. With the Challenger program looking more and more like a cost fiasco, it appeared that the government's industrial development strategy had gone right off the rails.

The shock of realizing just how bad the Canadair situation was, and how the government had been misled by its own bureaucratic managers who were to keep a close watch on the company, forced Cabinet to make major changes to its industrial development strategy sooner rather than later. The first step was a sweep of Industry Trade and Commerce, the powerful development ministry responsible for Canadair, de Havilland and other government-owned companies. A group of senior bureaucrats from the Ministry of State for Economic Regional Development (MSERD), led by Gordon Ritchie, came into ITC and purged senior officials. No one was fired but many were exiled. One exception was ITC's assistant deputy minister responsible for Canadair, Antoine Guerin, who had seen the writing on the wall a year earlier and convinced Canadair's board to hire him. The two ministries—ITC and MSERD—were united, and ITC lost most of its power over economic development. Many ITC people blamed Canadair for this.

Then responsibility for Canadair was taken from ITC and placed in the hands of the still unconstituted Canada Development Investment Corporation. The CDIC was to be a government holding company that would manage some of the country's publicly owned corporations. Companies other than Canadair were taking a beating in the recession, and Cabinet wanted a corporate tool to carry out quick fixes for ailing Crown companies. When the CDIC was first discussed in 1981, it had been clear that the strategy of buying companies in the public interest, then pumping them with money to fatten them for privatization hadn't been working out very well. By 1982, things were much worse. Massey-Ferguson was about to declare the second-largest corporate loss in Canadian history, $413 million; Eldorado Nuclear was facing a declining demand for uranium-related fuels despite government efforts to create a cartel; and de Havilland's sales of the DASH-7 commuter aircraft were being hammered by the August 1982 air traffic controllers' strike. The only bright lights were Teleglobe Canada, an overseas telecommunications monopoly that was making money, and Canadair, which appeared to have great expectations in the Challenger even though it was spending money like crazy. Until November Canadair was still declaring a modest annual profit, and the government had had no reason to doubt it. Once the bad news about Canadair became known, Pitfield prepared a package containing various reports on Canadair's crisis and sent it to Joel Bell, then vice president of Petro-Canada. The CDIC was about to be put to work.

Bell, a McGill-Harvard alumnus in law and economics, had worked as a high-level consultant in Ottawa for nearly 10 years on combines investigation, foreign investment review, labor and employment and energy policy. After a two-year stint as an economic adviser to Trudeau, Bell was appointed senior vice president of Petro-Canada in 1976. Pitfield sent the documents to get more than Bell's comments. The government wanted Bell to take the presidency of the new CDIC and lead the effort to rescue Canadair.

In late November the three people most responsible for shaping Canada's economic policy of state interventionism—Senator Jack Austin, Joel Bell and Maurice Strong, Trudeau's favorite businessman—met to draft the bare bones of the new holding company that would report directly to the inner Cabinet. Before the birth of the CDIC, various members of this team had been involved with the creation of such diverse projects as Canada Development Corporation, Petro-Canada, the Foreign Investment Review Agency and the uranium cartel. On November 23, Cabinet passed eight orders-in-council putting as much flesh as possible on the bones of CDIC. Reporting to Austin, the Minister of State for Social Development, CDIC had a chairman (Strong), a CEO (Bell) and a $500,000 budget, the maximum allowable without going to Parliament but not enough to cover operating expenses. Once the company was up and running, the CDIC would live off the fees it charged to the companies it managed.

The next day Ed Lumley called Fred Kearns at Canadair and told him that responsibility for Canadair had been passed entirely into the hands of a new holding company, the CDIC, and that he, Lumley, was no longer responsible for Canadair.

It was the start of a long winter for Canadair. In early December Canadair's new "owner" arrived. A team of four from CDIC and Peat Marwick, led by Joel Bell, came to the Montreal head office to act as trustee. Canadair had become used to this kind of intrusion. For nearly two years the company had played host to auditors, lawyers and consultants from one investigative group after another. By the time Bell and his group arrived Canadair management was exhausted. Daily problems had to be managed while the managers also met the demands of people who wanted to know what they'd done, what they were doing and what they were going to do. Nerves along Mahogany Row were frayed.

Bell's group replaced another from ITC, which had been conducting a task force update in response to Kearns's announcement that Canadair would pass the $1.35 billion borrowing limit. Once Canadair was handed over to CDIC, the update task force's mandate was canceled. One group out, a new one in. But the new one was different. It included Jim Baillie, the former Ontario securities commission chief and senior partner with the Bay Street law firm Tory Tory, and two months later lawyer Gil Bennett, friend of Michael Pitfield, joined the team. Kearns didn't know it, but CDIC was not at Canadair just to make reports. CDIC was there to make changes.

Bell and his group had two immediate tasks. First, to determine if the Challenger could ever make money. Second, to assess the corporation and find out if it could be saved. If the company was salvageable, the CDIC was to do a thorough assessment of all aspects, including management, and do what was necessary to get Canadair operating in accordance with sound business principles. Once CDIC had the company back on track, it would be sold.

In the early days, the CDIC's accountants climbed over a mountain of documents trying to find out where the money was going, while Bell and Bennett conducted interviews with management. While an impassioned Bell probed for details of management's decisions, the cool Bennett maintained his sangfroid, though this was hardly reassuring. Bell asked pointed questions and management bristled in reply, with the exception of the unflappable gentleman Peter Aird.

Bell and the other CDIC members quickly grasped the fact that the weight, engine and certification problems had fed on each other and that the failure to freeze the design and management deficiencies had combined to consume most of the money; interest payments—the price of the government's debt financing policy—ate up the rest. This was the simple explanation to where all the money went.

The engine issue continued to be very sensitive, since Avco Lycoming was still Canadair's principal supplier. CDIC took up Canadair's cause with Avco Lycoming and began to repair the relationship with GE. Once they had completed their initial review, CDIC's representatives were convinced that technically, the Challenger was a winner and they wanted to ensure that production would continue. Their assessment of the Challenger's managers was not as positive.

The biggest failure laid at management's and Kearns's door involved the sales projections and contracts. Bell was amazed at the number of soft orders being figured into projections as firm orders. But what got Bell upset were the terms and conditions of many of the actual deals. "A contract is a contract!" Bell repeatedly responded when confronted by the list of modifications attached to yet another Challenger contract. "What is this crap you guys promised? Couldn't you guys just once sell an airplane with no strings attached?"

The contract that got under Bell's skin was the distribution contract signed with TAG, Akram Ojjeh's trading company. TAG had the most orders for Challengers with the most modifications promised, and as far as Bell could see, TAG was the a big reason why Canadair's sales forecasts, even if they were realized, would not lead to profitability:the modifications specified in TAG's contracts were so costly that money would be lost on every delivery.

By this time relations between TAG and Canadair had became strained. TAG had taken delivery of only three of thirty-six aircraft, and had sold only one. TAG had argued that the 1979 decision of the Clark government to move the Canadian embassy in Israel to Jerusalem had provoked a serious anti-Canadian backlash within the Arab community, and that this had hurt their prospects.

Bell did not buy this argument. He concluded, correctly, that TAG was not taking delivery of its aircraft because, although it was sole distributor, it wasn't that interested in selling the aircraft. TAG was also distributor for the French-built Dassault Falcon aircraft, one of the Challenger's competitors. The Dassault was preferred by TAG's Arab customers for, among other things, its superior field performance compared to the Challenger; specifically, the Falcon was a better aircraft in hot, dry desert conditions. Given the ruinously expensive contracts with TAG, Bell concluded that Canadiar would be better off if TAG didn't take delivery, and was determined to cancel their contracts if he could not re-negotiate them.

Canadair under CDIC had other problems to deal with. In 1983, three days into the new year, a Challenger crashed, killing its two pilots. Henry Cook, 58, and Chester Wesolek, 57, had been flying the Challenger 600 for their company, A.E. Staley Manufacturing Company Inc. of Illinois. On January 3 the two pilots, who had a total of 34,000 flying hours between them, set out from Illinois to pick up the owner of Staley at Sun Valley Airport in Idaho.

At about nine in the morning, Cook began his descent toward Sun Valley. He was looking for Bellevue, a small town often used as a visual checkpoint by pilots for their approach into Sun Valley. Cook broke under the cloud ceiling at 1,500 feet, lowered his flaps and landing gear and spotted Bellevue. But what he took for Bellevue was in fact Hailey, a town two and a half miles north of Bellevue. Suddenly Cook was lost. He began rocking his wing to get a better look at the ground beneath him, but he could not get his visual bearing. Sun Valley was surrounded by mountains, and the cloud obscured most of them. Cook banked to the right, hoping to see the airport. Instead he headed into low cloud north of the airport, and behind the clouds was a wall of mountain. The altimeters went crazy. Recognizing what he had done, Cook immediately throttled the engines up and tried to climb out. It was too late.

The airplane struck just below the crest of a slight ridge, slid along the ground about 55 feet to the crest then became airborne. It broke into eight major pieces and, without the wings, the fuselage traveled 500 feet in the air, struck the ground again then slid down the mountain slope. As crash investigation officials would say, it was an unsurvivable accident.

The second fatal crash of a Challenger didn't generate much fear along Mahogany Row. There was some concern among Canadair accident investigation officials that a faulty flap vane may have figured in the crash; the separation of a flap vane support had nearly caused the crash of another Challenger months earlier. These fears were put aside when the crash recovery team located the flap vane support in one piece. Nevertheless CDIC people had some concerns about the safety and therefore the future of the airplane. Although convinced that the plane was technically sound, Gil Bennett was going to withhold his final judgment until the National Transportation Safety Board (NTSB) produced its report on the crash. The Challenger's credibility was at an all-time low in the marketplace. Even before the report came out, Staley, the company that owned the lost Challenger, said it was going to buy a Falcon to replace it.

In January 1983 Canadair and the Challenger program hung in limbo. As they waited for the report on the Sun Valley crash, senior Canadair executives also waited for the shoe to drop as far as the executive firings were concerned. Employees waited for production cutbacks to take effect on the shop floor. And Challenger owners waited to see if their aircraft would become orphans. To some observers outside the company, the CDIC shake-up at Canadair sounded more like a death rattle.

11

The fifth estate

W hile it was apparent that costs had spiraled out of control, investigators at Canadair tried to keep details of the massive corporate loss confidential until the assessment was completed and recommendations could be made. By the end of 1982 there were three documents that outlined the details of Canadair's financial problems to Cabinet, and they were treated with an extraordinary degree of security. The master copy of one document was secretly coded so that any leaked copies could be identified. It was circulated only on a need-to-know basis. It was carried into Cabinet, and although the full Cabinet rubber-stamped Canadair's latest request for $200 million in equity, the details of the decision were discussed in an ad-hoc Cabinet committee chaired by Marc Lalonde, chairman of the Quebec caucus.

Despite the elaborate precautions, the facade of normalcy could not hold forever. Word of severe problems at Canadair began to circulate within the bureaucracy. It wasn't long before some of the details reached CBC television reporter Eric Malling.

Malling had smiling boyish looks that belied a scrappy demeanor. His background came through in his cynicism and a sense of outrage that bordered on stridency. These qualities made him an enduring cohost of *the fifth estate*, a program started in 1976 at the height of the investigative journalism fad that followed Watergate. His passion fueled stories involving political patronage, Canadian involvement with Pakistani nuclear bombs or South Africa arms dealing, industrial pollution and squandered public money. By the time the Canadair story came into Malling's life, he was a seasoned pro, having won a 1979 ACTRA award and the Gordon Sinclair Award for outspoken opinion and integrity in broadcasting.

In late 1982 Malling took in a Toronto football game with a buddy of his from Ottawa and the subject of Canadair came up. It wasn't the first time Malling had thought of Canadair. Two years earlier he and his producer, Mike Lavoie, had considered Canadair for a success-story segment. It wasn't the season for success stories, and the idea was shelved. But Malling's pal at the football game didn't have a success story in mind. He told Malling to check out Canadair because they were in real trouble.

Malling forgot about the football game as his friend told his tale. He had been at a table in a coffee shop in a building that housed the ITC when a group from the ministry sat down near him. The major shake-up at ITC, which saw it subordinated to the Ministry of State for Economic Regional Expansion, was underway, and responsibility for Canadair had been handed over to CDIC. Feelings were running high, and a number of bureaucrats felt that Canadair had betrayed them. Malling's friend had listened as they discussed Canadair's business. One member seemed familiar with the contents of the reports and gave an elaborate picture of Canadair screw-ups. He added some levity: "They say the Challenger might fly the Atlantic if the pilots don't wear socks!" The story of Canadair's problems had been leaked.

Malling took out a pack of matches and scratched down a few key words. Airplane. Sales. Cost. Politics. These words became the structure for the story of his career. Malling went to Lavoie and told him what he had heard. Lavoie and Malling needed one more story to close the regular season. Lavoie knew Malling's friend and thought he was a credible source. He decided they would look into Canadair as soon as they had wrapped up their current story.

On St. Valentine's Day, 1983, Malling and Lavoie met with executive producer Robin Taylor, the show's founding senior producer Ron Haggart, and researcher Maxine Siddran to talk about Canadair. They had done some preliminary work and there was no question they had a story here. The CDIC had taken over, the company was having problems delivering its planes, and it looked like the public was going to get stuck with the bill. The difficulty of doing the piece was timing: *the fifth estate* was short on time and money, and the story was leaking fast. They would have to move quickly or risk losing it.

"If Canadair is smart, they might release a bunch of statements to control the damage," one of the producers noted.

They were betting on Canadair not being so smart. (In fact, with Ottawa in charge, Canadair had already lost control and couldn't have released any statements, even if it had wanted to.) The television crew decided to do a rush job and produce the show in two months—a very short time for a production. They assumed that revelations from sources besides Canadair were bound to come out now that the government was involved.

The group considered their strategy. The obvious approach would be a simple business story. Take the early glowing reports. Take Fred Kearns's optimistic presentation before the Parliamentary committee in November 1982. And then shoot down the works with the details of airplane shortcomings, sales failures, cost overruns and political and corporate mismanagement.

The first thing they needed was film from inside Canadair. The following week Lavoie contacted Canadair PR man Ken Romain and described in vague terms the purpose of the story: a business profile about the difficult art of making airplanes. A date was set for a meeting, and Lavoie and Siddran showed up at Canadair with a film crew. While Lavoie and the crew went through the plant, Siddran asked Romain who would be the best person to talk to about the Challenger. "Harry Halton is your man," Romain replied, and Siddran was taken to meet him.

Halton thought it was a curious interview. Siddran asked a few questions about the buy-back deal with Federal Express. Puzzled that Siddran should want to talk to the chief engineer about a sales deal, Halton nonetheless obliged her with an extensive explanation of the deal as he understood it. Siddran took few notes. For the researcher, the story wasn't Halton and his problems of building the airplane, even though Halton was directly responsible for many of the cost and delivery problems. The principal reason for the visit was to get enough film in the can before Canadair caught on to the story's main thrust. When Lavoie and the crew had about three thousand feet of film, they returned to collect Siddran. It was agreed with

Romain that a date would be set up to interview Fred Kearns, then they left.

Slowly the story began to take shape. Lavoie went to the thin file he had opened two years earlier, when the good-news story was considered. As he flipped through the glowing reports, he wondered how much trouble the company had been in then. Siddran went to check out Fred Kearns's claims before the Parliamentary committee. She researched how the industry worked then started contacting all known Challenger owners, brokers, completion centers and competitors. As she traced the owners she found out about Challenger aircraft sitting in completion centers.

Siddran and Malling worked the telephones. They covered their office walls with hundreds of sheets of paper listing names, places and engineering terms. Only one wall, the one with a poster of a Concorde cockpit, was spared. Often the researchers sat and stared at the walls: it was as far as they were getting. Everywhere they turned, they ran into walls of silence.

Malling and his team were asking the sort of questions nobody wanted to answer on the record. They were probing, prickly questions with answers that could cost people their jobs.

More than jobs were at stake, however. Owners and brokers didn't want to talk because they feared an exposé would hurt the resale value of their multimillion-dollar airplanes. Malling and Siddran contacted hundreds of people, but nobody would talk on the record.

By this time the CDIC had begun to take control of Canadair's public relations. Canadair PR referred Malling to David Crane, director of public relations for CDIC, instead of answering his questions. Malling and Crane were old friends. Crane had been a journalist at the *Toronto Star* before he went to CDIC. When Crane took Malling's call and agreed to meet for dinner, he accepted Malling as a friend and former colleague.

At dinner Malling got right down to business. Just how bad were things at Canadair? he asked Crane. Crane shifted in his seat and tried to explain the situation without saying very much. He finally agreed to work from a list of questions. Malling would draft the list and Crane would get answers from Canadair by a certain deadline. Malling decided to play things safe and do a lot more research before coming up with the questions.

It wasn't easy. Malling and the team had a lot of suspicions but little hard information to back up the story that was beginning to take shape—a tale of Canadair mismanagement. The mood in the CBC office was tense as time ran out. The more denials they heard, the more the journalists were convinced there was a huge cover-up. Malling fired a series of questions to an ITC deputy minister, and his silence spoke volumes. Malling was certain they were on to something.

Still, they didn't have anything to call a story, just a lot of teasers that drove them crazy. "Yes, I know what went on, it was a real mess, but I can't talk to you." They heard this more than once. Another teaser was, "I'll call you back." Team researcher Marlene Perry called Ross Chafin, president of one completion center, Page-Avjet in San Antonio. Page-Avjet was responsible for modifications to some of the aircraft. Chafin was out of town and his assistant, Terry Baker, took the call. "Hell, yes, we had to rebuild that airplane from the ground up!" Baker said. Perry picked up on this and started to move in on Baker, who panicked.

"Look, I got to check this out with Canadair before I talk further." He never called back. He did call Canadair, though, and warned another PR man, Justin Battle, that the researcher meant trouble. "I hope you guys come through okay," Baker told Battle. "This sort of thing doesn't do anyone any good."

Canadair did have friends. Dick Van Gemert of Xerox was not afraid to talk, and he was very discreet and diplomatic, never emphasizing the negative aspects in the face of an increasing barrage of negative questions. But after six years of stress and frustration from trying to do the impossible, Canadair had also developed a number of enemies, and they were happy to talk. One was a former Canadair sales executive who had left the company in 1981. He told Malling, "I didn't know if I had principles until I saw the shit that went down at Canadair." Another was a Challenger customer who was dying of cancer and thought nothing of spilling all the woes his plane had caused. Ministerial aides told of close calls as a Challenger aircraft flamed out in flight with their ministerial baggage; a Department of Transport pilot who flew the ministers told Malling that the airplane had a lot of limitations. There was even a Canadair director who complained that management had been playing games with the board.

By the beginning of March, three weeks after starting out, Malling and his team had enough information to ask some tough questions about Canadair and the Challenger. Malling delivered 31 questions to Crane, who passed them on to Canadair management. The reaction was swift. The questions gave CDIC and Canadair an idea of the tone of the CBC's investigation, and both went into a reactive mode. CDIC ruled out the possibility of an interview with Kearns and clamped down on information coming out of Canadair.

Canadair tracked down anyone who might have been interviewed by the television team and started building a case to challenge the implications of the 31 questions. They carefully drafted answers that explained the problems in terms of the solutions underway and the prospects for the future. But when Canadair's answers were passed to Malling through CDIC, Crane and Bell reviewed them with a skeptical eye. Bell and his group were accountable to Parliament not only for decisions at Canadair but also for any information that was released. They felt the sales forecasts were over-optimistic and while CDIC would confirm the technical excellence of the Challenger, they had no intention of defending the sales projections.

The *fifth estate* team had a fairly good idea of what their story was, but still missing was the total cost of this fiasco. Then Malling came to the office one day with a copy of the Treasury Board report on Canadair. Malling read out loud the passage that said the government's total exposure on Canadair was more than $2 billion, and there was a collective gasp from the team. Their research had uncovered only the sale price of the company and projected development costs of the program, which put the government's exposure at a few hundred million. Lavoie said the information was so explosive the report would have to be checked for authenticity. He went to Ottawa to talk to a source who would have had access to such a report. The source was very nervous.

"Look, don't come here to my office," he said. "Meet me at my house tonight."

That night, just to make sure his source was giving him the right information, Lavoie included some false numbers in his questioning. The source identified them right away, and Lavoie had Malling's document confirmed.

The CBC producer soon became fascinated with the way the $2 billion liability had been accumulated—the letters of comfort. He discovered one such letter in the orders-in-council which stated, as the later ones did, that the minister would endeavor to secure a formal guarantee from Parliament "as soon as possible." The letters of comfort Lavoie found included one dated 1977, nearly five years earlier. Surely there had been time to seek Parliamentary approval since then? Meanwhile, the government had issued letters covering hundreds of millions of dollars, and Parliament didn't know a thing about it. It was a political time bomb. Here was a company, not even a Crown corporation, with a billion dollars of debt guaranteed by the government of Canada. As Canadair's chief financial officer would later admit, Canadair had been able to be as sporty as any other aircraft company only because it had a silent partner with very deep pockets—the public.

By mid-March Malling and the team had the four subjects he had scratched on the matchbook cover fairly well developed. They had a story about a company run by honorable, ambitious and obsessed men apparently out of touch with reality because of their government-guaranteed line of credit. The company's airplane was unreliable if not unsafe. Sales were falling apart, and the costs were out of control. And the politics that kept the whole mess together were explosive. The time had come to pull a show together.

By now there was a growing awareness in the industry that their story was going to be far from positive, and the *fifth estate* crew was unable to get any more interviews, much less a chance to film. All they had for visuals were the shots from inside Canadair. They faced a television producer's nightmare: a dynamite story for TV—and no film footage. They decided to visit the completion centers.

First they flew to San Antonio, where the assistant president of Page-Avjet Terry Baker had been so voluble. He'd even asked them to visit. While the team checked in at the front desk at Page-Avjet, Malling took a stroll into the factory to see if there were any Challengers. He saw some and took down their numbers before he was spotted and escorted out of the area. Soon the whole team was escorted off the grounds. There would be no filming at Page-Avjet. The team went to Houston, to Clinton Aviation, another completion center. There they were met with open arms by aviation department manager Denis Blackburn, who had a Challenger all polished for show. He was trying to sell the aircraft and hoped for some free publicity. (After Blackburn saw a tape of the show, he was furious.

"They said there was gold everywhere inside that airplane," he told
Justin Battle at Canadair. "It was brass! That really pissed us off!")
The film crew went to Connecticut, hoping to film inside Avco
Lycoming, but the facility was on a military security list, and the team
was hustled off the grounds by local police.

Nobody in Ottawa would speak on the record about Canadair.
Herb Gray, whom the journalists took to calling "Gray Herb,"
refused to talk since he was no longer the minister responsible, a
defense he also used when he was asked to appear before a Parliamentary committee investigating Canadair. Malling and his crew
decided to hit on Jean Chrétien who had been president of the
Treasury Board when the program got the go-ahead in 1976. They
hung around his office hoping to catch him, and Malling was psyched
up for the interview. He knew that Chrétien would try to give him the
same brush-off Gray had used, and he was prepared for a scrap.
Finally Chrétien came out of his office, and Malling did his best to
surround him.

"Mr. Chrétien, I would like to ask you some questions about
Canadair."

"Hey, I'm not the minister for that. You've got to talk to Senator
Austin now," Chrétien replied.

"Yeah, but you were one of the ministers who gave the okay for
this $1.5 billion airplane. If you thought it was such a great idea then,
why don't you have the guts to stand up and say something about this
now?"

Chrétien stopped. Malling was baiting him, and it worked. Not
one to shy away from a challenge, Chrétien agreed to do the interview. If nothing else, it confirmed to Malling that Chrétien had guts.

The final week was a terror for the producers. Some 15,000 feet of
film had to be edited, and there were still important film clips
missing. Lavoie got the rights to the NFB film *Canadair, the Industrial Romance* and used parts of it. A crew went to Toronto International Airport to capture a Federal Express airplane on film. Finally
Lavoie and the crew went for another shoot at Canadair. This time
the atmosphere was very tense. No interviews were granted, and the
crew was rushed out as soon as they had finished filming. Still there
wasn't enough usable film. Producers racked their brains for ideas to
get more film into the broadcast. The stress was tremendous as time

ran out, and in the first week of April they had to take what they had and piece it together as best they could.

In the end, they had 52 minutes of television that broke all the rules as far as visuals were concerned. There were too many links, too many stock shots, and it wasn't pretty. But the litany of troubles at Canadair packed a wallop. It was journalism that could be best described as sensationalist.

On April 7 Don Macdonald, the head of current affairs programming at CBC, was given a screening. It was unusual but not unheard of for the head of current affairs to screen a program. CBC's top people knew what was in the works and were aware of the impact the program would have. As Malling read from his text and the video monitor displayed the shots and images, Macdonald sat impassively. When it was over, he got up, said, "Good show," and left.

Another screening was done for the corporation's lawyers, who concluded that Canadair wouldn't dare sue the CBC. A week later the show went to air.

On Wednesday, April 13, 1983, Canadair's top management and CDIC executives gathered in the main dining room on Mahogany Row for a dinner of roast beef with wine. After dinner they would watch the Canadair Challenger story on prime time television. Jacques Ouellet, Canadair's vice president responsible for the company's public relations, knew it was going to be rough. During the meal he tried to brief everyone so they would know what to expect, but he had no idea how rough it would be. Even though the journalists had asked some tough questions during the preparation of the program, positive responses had been provided, and most people hoped the show would include the usual media hype. Joel Bell and others from CDIC also had a better idea of what the show might contain. Bell had already arranged to be in Ottawa the next day to handle any aftershocks.

The executives were settled down with their glasses of port at eight o'clock sharp. The lights went down and the program came on. Within the first minute everyone in the room knew what was about to happen: Canadair was going to get the business end of a hatchet job.

"Taxpayers are all shareholders in Canadair, and our investment in the Challenger jet is on average $150 each. We're subsidizing the very rich people who have been able to buy these planes for much less than it cost to make them."

That was just the prologue; the program that followed was relentless. For 52 minutes Malling enumerated the Challenger's problems and tallied up the extraordinary costs of the program, highlighting the attempts of the government and the company to downplay any problems and the overoptimism of Canadair's management. The government believed in Canadair and Canadair blew it. Everyone watched in stunned silence, along with a million and a half other Canadians.

Given the complex nature of the aircraft program—the mass of technical details, the span of seven years, the many interests involved—the *fifth estate* program could hardly be called balanced journalism. The story was intricate, and 52 minutes allowed little room for a full treatment. And since Malling and his team had been given more problems than explanations, the details they did have made a devastating and merciless portrait of an aircraft program gone terribly wrong. The show was an entirely negative document.

It was also inaccurate in places, due to the lack of time and information. The claim that the Challenger needed a longer runway than a DC-10 was false. The details of the aircraft's limitations were based on a Department of Transport pilot's comments, and DoT operated the aircraft under much tougher FAA airliner rules rather than FAA business jet rules. Other details such as engine prices, performance capabilities and the number of modifications—CBC's number was too low!—were either wrong or misleading. But it wasn't the errors that bothered everyone in the Canadair boardroom as they watched their company and their program publicly humiliated. What bothered them was the tone. It was anti-Canadair, anti-aerospace industry; it was even anti-Canadian. There was no scandal, no wrongdoing. *The fifth estate* took all the mistakes they'd ever made in a high-stakes game and viewed them all under the worst possible light. When it was over, Ouellet turned to look at his boss, Fred Kearns, who was ashen and visibly shaken.

"This is devastating, absolutely devastating," Kearns said.

When the lights went on in the hushed Canadair dining room, Joel Bell stood up and said that from now on CDIC would take full control of Canadair's media relations. It was assumed that what they had just seen was going to cause a political crisis the next day in Parliament.

"No interviews, no camera crews, nothing is said or done publicly by Canadair without David Crane and myself knowing about it," Bell said emphatically.

The executives of the company were livid. They were going to get the blame for all the problems, and they didn't want to let the CBC get away with it. They wanted to sue. Bell opposed the idea of a suit but immediately wrote to Malling and his boss, Pierre Juneau, sharply criticizing the program and citing its inaccuracies. He then went public with his defence of the Challenger jet.

The next day the company was in a state of shock and grief. Employees were crying. They were exhausted by the events of the past seven years, and their faith in the Challenger program and their desire to continue to work hard were severely shaken. Absenteeism shot up in the weeks that followed. Employee booster meetings were called in the theater to try to keep the morale from sinking. Many of those who came to the meetings were angry. They had heard more about Canadair from *the fifth estate* than they had heard from their own management, and they felt betrayed.

The story made front-page headlines across the country, and the market saw them. IBM had planned to buy four Challengers but called Canadair to cancel the order after the segment aired. Other customers began to have second thoughts about taking delivery of their long-awaited aircraft. Once again, just when it looked like things were about to turn around for the Challenger program, everything turned to ashes.

One company that benefited from the exposé was Gulfstream, Canadair's principal competitor. Allen Paulsen, the flamboyant entrepreneur who ran Gulfstream, was ecstatic after he saw a tape of the *fifth estate* program. He had hundreds of copies made for distribution to Gulfstream owners. The show was a vindication for Paulsen; it confirmed all the criticisms and doubts he had leveled against Canadair from the beginning. He also sent a copy of the tape to the Gulfstream factory, where it was shown regularly to employees as a no-cost morale booster. Gulfstream salespeople carried copies and began sales sessions with "a word from the competition." Paulsen milked it for all it was worth. When Canadair later tried another bid on a U.S. government aircraft acquisition program, Paulsen sent copies of the tape to key personnel with a note saying that selecting a Canadian-government-subsidized Challenger over a private-enter-prise-built Gulfstream wouldn't be fair.

Canadair employees did have a few defenders. FSI, the Mojave subcontractor on the flight test program, spoke up on their behalf. An FSI employee wrote a letter to the Montreal *Gazette,* which said in part, "No matter what the Canadian media say about the Chal-lenger program, the facts are that they do not and never will know of the personal sacrifices (blood, sweat, and tears, to quote a cliché) all of us, Canadian and American alike, put into this, the most tech-nologically advanced, safest, most economical and the most beau-tiful business jet aircraft ever produced."

Such praise was lost in the din of criticism that followed the *fifth estate* program. The government, the opposition, the bureaucracy and the business community were all out for blood. While CDIC continued to insist that no action be taken without careful assess-ment, the pressure to do something soon increased enormously.

Exactly one month after the program aired, on Friday, May 13, Canadair's board of directors convened for its monthly meeting. The company's executives were asked to leave while the board met in private. It wasn't the first time this had happened; since the arrival of CDIC six months earlier there had been many such meetings. The "turnaround committee" that had been formed met weekly and reported to the board fully on all findings and actions taken. But this was the first board meeting since the television show, and it was obvious something was going to happen. Kearns, Aird, Halton, Mackenzie and other executives waited outside the boardroom for nearly three hours. They all suspected that the ax was about to fall.

Around noon Charles Rathgeb came out of the boardroom and pointed to Kearns. Rathgeb had been a Canadair director since the days of General Dynamics. Rathgeb and Kearns knew each other very well, but it had been an uneasy relationship. Rathgeb was a blue-chip member of the Canadian Establishment, listed in *Who's Who* as a construction executive, but he was much more than that. He was a wealthy adventure seeker and jet-setter. Kearns considered Rathgeb to be an outsider and would often speak to him in patronizing tones. Rathgeb was never included in the group of directors Kearns consid-ered to be his key allies.

"We have to talk for a minute," Rathgeb said. "Alone."

When they were in Fred's office Rathgeb said, "Fred, I'm speaking to you now as a friend, not as a director. I think it would be best for you at this point to resign voluntarily, and if you do, you will be generously compensated."

Kearns was stunned. If the board had plans to fire him, Rathgeb wouldn't say. Early retirement wasn't mentioned. If Kearns didn't resign, he might be fired before he could take early retirement. Rathgeb said he needed an answer right away. Kearns agreed to resign.

As Harry Halton noted afterward, Kearns was shocked. "He still didn't believe that it could have happened, that after running this company single-handedly for nearly twenty years he could be asked by his own board to resign."

It was over in a few minutes. Kearns went to his office, drafted a resignation effective immediately and made one last tour of the executive offices along Mahogany Row. Quietly and with few words he informed his people of what had just happened.

Six months after the arrival of CDIC the first head had rolled.

12

Days of reckoning

I n early 1983 CDIC had ordered Avco Lycoming to come to Canadair and prove that they had met the engine specifications. Avco Lycoming made their presentation, but when Canadair analyzed it they found that Avco Lycoming again introduced unrealistic numbers. This was the last straw.

Back in 1981, when management had found out that Avco Lycoming was less than forthright in providing solutions to their problems, the board of directors had strongly urged management to launch a suit for damages. Kearns had objected. It wasn't his style, for one thing, and for another, he was having enough problems with Avco Lycoming; he didn't need a legal fight to complicate matters. The idea of suing Avco Lycoming was never completely shelved, however. The contract contained a clause that limited the amount of time Canadair had to launch a suit, and that time was running out. Canadair hadn't received all the engines for the 600s, but the company would have to decide whether to go after its supplier.

Dick Richmond thought the Lycoming-powered Challenger 600 didn't have a future; the success of the 601 made it expendable. Some 238 Canadair service bulletins had been issued since the airplane was launched, along with nearly 40 DoT and FAA airworthiness directives, a number of them relating to the ALF-502 engines.

Canadair finally decided to sue Avco Lycoming in the summer of 1983. During the Paris Air Show, Richmond was invited into the chalet run by Avco Lycoming to chat with their chairman, Don Farrar. He wasn't sure what the topic of discussion would be. Canadair and the engine manufacturer were already negotiating a settlement for $120 million in damages, but Avco Lycoming was negotiating on the assumption that once the settlement had been reached, it would be business as usual. Richmond knew it was far from a sure thing.

The current negotiations included an extension of the time clause limiting the opportunity for damage claims. As Richmond and Farrar chatted amiably, Canadair and Avco Lycoming lawyers couldn't agree on waiving the time clause. That night Richmond called head office to find out what had happened.

"We haven't got a deal on the time clause," Richmond was told by Bob Wohl, Canadair's chief counsel. "Avco's lawyer won't go for it. Maybe we'll have to sue them."

It sounded noncommittal enough to Richmond. But the next day Farrar confronted Richmond.

"Are you some kind of coward, Richmond?" Farrar blurted. "You small talk me in the chalet yesterday about how swell things are while your guys back home decide to sue us!"

Canadair had made the decision to sue but had not informed Richmond. Canadair filed its suit against Avco Lycoming for $109 million U.S. The suit meant, among other things, that the Challenger 600 was dead. Canadair told Lycoming it wouldn't reorder ALF-502 engines because it was ending the 600 model. Avco Lycoming filed a countersuit for breach of contract for failing to reorder and claimed $100 million U.S. in damages.

Soon after the legal papers had been deposited in the courts Avco Lycoming came to Canadair with a proposal. It wanted to keep the Challenger 600 program alive and it offered to sell additional engines for next to nothing if Canadair would relaunch the 600 model. But the relaunch would have cost Canadair more money. It had been decided that the 600 would be sacrificed; by ending the 600 program, Canadair could appear to be breaking with the past and its problems. All hopes were pinned on the future and the GE-powered 601. Canadair turned down Avco Lycoming's proposal.

It was perhaps an unfortunate decision. By the time Canadair delivered its verdict on the future of the Challenger program, the 600 model was finally beginning to take its place in the market. Jim Taylor's product support group successfully overcame its early response-time problems, and by 1983 had a well-oiled operation working overtime to restore confidence in the airplane. A 1983 magazine survey of Challenger 600 operators showed, despite all the early problems, an extremely high degree of satisfaction with the airplane. Jim Taylor's arguments to the contrary appeared to have been unfounded.

"They [the owners] contend that for their requirements, in terms of initial cost and superb factory support, the Challenger is the best buy on the market today," wrote Robert Parrish in the magazine *Business and Commercial Aviation.* "Some claim, in fact, that the CL-600 represents new standards in excellence which will culminate in an explosive rebirth in popularity (and consequently in production) when the present wave of mainly unearned, uninformed critical innuendo subsides." While another aircraft manufacturer might very well have plastered these comments in full-page ads in the trade publications, the new Canadair managers ignored the praise. The 600 was dead, it was history. That was how they dealt with the wave of innuendo.

About this time CDIC's president, Joel Bell, decided it was time to deal with TAG. TAG was still not taking delivery of the airplanes it had ordered, and the matter of re-negotiating or cancelling the TAG contracts was still unresolved. Bell was at the Paris Air Show with Richmond and the marketing group. Ojjeh's sons, Aziz and Mansour, dropped by the Canadair chalet and made arrangements to join Hurley and Juvonen for dinner at a small restaurant.

Bell decided to stop by the restaurant later. He had received an ultimatum from Akram Ojjeh concerning the settlement of the contract dispute. At the restaurant, he asked Akram's sons to give their father a message. To keep the issue confidential, Bell spoke to the brothers in French. Juvonen was stunned. "Hey, Joel, talk in English for the rest of us," Juvonen asked.

Bell turned to face him and said, "Stay out of this, Juvonen. You're better off out of this situation."

An angry Juvonen got up and went to the bar while Bell sent his message. When Bell had finished with Mansour, he went over to the bar and apologized to Juvonen.

Juvonen, twice the size of Bell, was furious. "I don't like your style of conducting business," he hissed, and left.

"I'm sorry about that, but I've got to play hardball with these guys and I didn't mean to take it out on you," Bell said.

A week later TAG launched a $135 million damage claim against Canadair.

"You know, I love Fred Kearns and I wouldn't be doing this to Canadair but I have already lost face in the Arab world because of the aircraft and I have lost money," Akram told a Canadair vice president. "I don't need this personal aggravation as well." TAG and Canadair eventually settled their differences by agreeing to swap four 600s for four 601s.

By the end of the summer of 1983 Canadair seemed to have hit bottom. The company had a government bankruptcy trustee running the business; it had a reduced rate of production, a paralyzed senior management, nearly $250 million in legal suits from its engine supplier and its number-one customer, a crushing billion-dollar debt and few new orders. Nothing short of an explosive rebirth in popularity could save the whole Challenger program. Canadair people started to prepare for the worst. They were especially worried because the government was involved, and the government's record in business enterprises was not encouraging. A failure in government nerve had led to the overnight demise of the Velvet Glove missile in 1956. A government had wiped out A.V. Roe Canada Ltd., makers of the Avro Arrow, in 1959. A government had ended the development of the Bras d'Or hydrofoil (1971), the magnetic urban transit railway (1974) and the Bricklin automobile (1975). Many people at Canadair wondered if the Challenger might be next.

The Canadian aviation trade press tried to rally to the Challenger's cause. "Requiem for the Challenger" was title of an essay by *Wings* publisher Larry Carbol. "The Challenger has become an ugly duckling," Carbol wrote, adding, "it would be tragic if the Challenger were to join the Avro Arrow on the scrap heap." *Canadian Aviation* magazine also rang with faint praise: "The mess at Canadair must be straightened out or a good plane will die because its maker has lost all credibility in the marketplace."

Canadair's management knew the mess would have to be straightened out soon. John Mackenzie, Canadair's vice president and comptroller and a 30-year veteran of the company, had known since Kearns left that the day of reckoning was coming for the other managers. But it still came as a surprise when he found out he was considered one of the culprits. Shortly after Kearns was forced to resign, Mackenzie had taken a call from a friend of his, a highly placed official in the government.

"John, there's a hit list of Canadair executives slated for removal and it's going to Cabinet very soon," the friend said. "I'm afraid your name is on the list."

"Don't worry, John, they won't get rid of you," Harry Halton said when Mackenzie confided in him about the call. "It's us they want. They just made a mistake."

Unknown to Mackenzie, those in government had no say in the final decision on who left and who stayed at Canadair. The responsibility rested with Gil Bennett, who was drawing up plans to downsize the company until its expenses were in line with its revenues. CDIC did not need Cabinet approval to take such action; Bennett's only obligation was to keep the Minister informed.

After nearly six months of sifting through the mountain of paperwork, in June 1983 the latest team of accountants came to the same conclusion Peter Aird had foreseen the previous December: the value of Canadair's inventory needed a write-down. When the CDIC's accountants finally calculated the bottom line, operating losses and an inventory write-down for the company in 1982 totalled nearly $1.4 billion. It was a staggering figure. By comparison, de Havilland had a profit of $2 million on sales of $450 million for 1982, albeit with modest equity infusions and loans totaling $650 million from the government. Canadair's $1.4 billion write-down on inventory and provisions for losses to come for 1982 was the biggest corporate loss in Canadian history, and fueled the outrage begun in April by *the fifth estate.*

The massive write-down and losses made the industry and the market very nervous. The public began to question whether the Challenger program would continue and nobody wanted an airplane that was a potential orphan. Who was going to honor the warranty, support the airplane and provide product improvements if the Challenger production line shut down? And who was going to pay the customer for the suddenly depressed value of their investment?

At the August 1983 Challenger operators' seminar in Montreal Gil Bennett confirmed the continuation of the program. "We're now faced with a new decision and that is, does it make sense to keep building this airplane?" Bennett told the owners and operators. "There's no doubt about it. It does."

Eric Malling had not been idle during the summer of 1983. The April show had been wildly successful, and he was anxious to do a follow-up. He caught up with Joel Bell at the National Business Aviation Association trade show in Dallas.

It was the first time Malling had seen his old friend since the devastating report on the Challenger. Malling and a film crew had gone down to Dallas to gather interviews for a second Challenger story. This time he wanted to focus on the business practices of its marketing division under Jim Taylor, and Malling hoped to catch Bell on film.

Malling asked David Crane for an interview with Bell and was invited up to the hotel room for a talk. Canadair had a lot riding on the NBAA conference; this was the first time the market had a chance to see the new General Electric-powered 601 airplane, and CDIC didn't want any more Canadair disaster stories.

"I want you, just you and not the camera people, to come up to my hotel room for a minute," Malling was told.

When Malling got there, he saw that he had walked into an ambush. Gil Bennett and Dick Richmond were with Bell, and Malling could taste the hostility in the air. This was no one-minute interview. Bell promised Malling he could have his on-camera interview back in Toronto but then the meeting became a three-hour tirade against Malling and the CBC. Malling squirmed in his seat as Richmond and Bennett droned on about how Malling and the CBC were trying to destroy a Canadian success story.

The tirade ended and Malling left without any film of Bell talking. He and the crew decided to set their own ambush. Malling and the cameras pounced when they spotted Bell at the NBAA conference center.

Bell, having promised an interview back in Toronto, was fed up with this nonsense. "Get the hell away from us!" he said angrily.

On the 18th of November *the fifth estate* aired its second damning investigative report on Canadair, and on the same day CDIC announced that a dozen Canadair executives had been fired, taken early retirement or been demoted. The group included Harry Halton and Peter Aird. John Mackenzie's name was on the demotion list.

To outsiders it appeared that conditions at Canadair were continuing to deteriorate. Hundreds of employees were being laid off. Production was cut back. Market conditions declined. Inside Canadair, there was a feeling that things were finally being brought under control.

When the second *fifth estate* episode aired, the people in the marketing group could see the writing on the wall. Since the departure of Fred Kearns, the hands-off management of Canadair's Connecticut marketing operation had come to an end. Gil Bennett had taken over, and Taylor had been kicked upstairs and out of the way. (His new title was chairman of Canadair Inc.) Taylor's contract had an expensive severance clause, and CDIC figured it was cheaper to keep him on. The U.S. subsidiary and its 80 employees had spent nearly $20 million in 1982. This included a product support group, which had rung up tremendous costs to support the aircraft in the difficult first year and a half. When Bennett and Bell calculated those costs against the revenues from the number of aircraft sold, they were aghast.

Tension between Connecticut and Montreal had been high even before *the fifth estate* struck. Dick Richmond was dead against increases to marketing expenditures. He held marketing partially responsible for the mess Canadair was in; marketing had continued to negotiate contracts promising expensive modifications. He also blamed Connecticut for the inflated sales projections, and criticised marketing expenditures based on these projections. Taylor wanted production doubled and new models announced. In the summer of 1983, Richmond and Bennett settled on a revised production rate of 15 aircraft a year instead of the projected 60 aircraft. Taylor responded in a letter to Richmond. "I must state emphatically at this time that if we cut production again we're really committing political and product suicide. Long delays will lose more sales."

Taylor was losing sales to Gulfstream. Thanks to Canadair's publicly exposed problems, Gulfstream had the big bizjet market all to itself. Taylor was fed up with hearing about yet another Challenger order canceled for a Gulfstream. In March 1983 Gulfstream had announced the launch of another new business jet, the G-IV. Within six months Gulfstream received more than 60 orders for the airplane while Canadair continued to lose prospects. Potential customers were suddenly dropping the Challenger from their list of possible buys. Taylor urged Bennett to do something, to announce improvements or new models. He bombarded Bennett with memos until Bennett decided he had had enough.

"With due respect for your many years in the industry, I would suggest that neither you nor your consultants have any conception of the likely economic outcome of your recommended course of action," Bennett wrote. "You have no real idea of the cost of designing, developing and building the new models you recommend; so far as I am aware, you have undertaken no studies to determine the number of new model aircraft which could be sold or the prices which could be charged for these models. I recall your assurance that we don't actually have to build these models; all we have to do is announce that we are considering the possibility of building new models. That assurance makes me nervous. We are suffering now as a result of Canadair's past failures in meeting express or implied promises."

Bennett concluded that, if Taylor couldn't sell Challengers without announcements of product improvements and new models, "then I suggest we need to discuss your role with the company."

Taylor was not the only target. Four months after the November *fifth estate* episode, Bennett called up Bill Juvonen, who was attending a General Electric engine seminar in Cincinnati.

"Could you come up to Montreal as soon as you can?" Bennett asked. "I've got some uncomfortable things to say that can't be said over the telephone."

Juvonen agreed to come right away. Bennett asked if Dave Hurley was there. Yes, Juvonen replied, and so was Angelo Fiataurello, the vice president of finance.

"Okay, well, all three of you better come up here right away."

By this point, the salesmen, in particular Dave Hurley, who had closed most of the Challenger sales, felt abused and betrayed by head office. The *fifth estate* episode had been a broadside at marketing that made much of an aircraft owned and operated by the salespeople but leased to Canadair. The television program made it appear that Hurley was getting some personal gain at the company's expense. The program showed Bell saying he didn't approve of the deal, and Hurley was wounded by the challenge to his integrity.

When the three got to Canadair head office in St. Laurent, they were fired. Powerless, Taylor watched as his hand-picked team of salespeople were shown the door. Taylor's arch rival, Charles Vogeley, recently retired as vice president of marketing for Gulfstream, was hired by telephone to take over Challenger marketing.

On May 10 Bennett called Taylor and asked him to stay away from the office until Vogeley had gotten his feet wet. Bennett never called Taylor in again. Four months later, Taylor sent Bennett a plea. "I have been left at loose ends for the last four months, with no knowledge of what my responsibilities or my options are. I've done my best to comply with your wishes, but I'm sure you will appreciate that the uncertainty is very difficult for me."

Taylor was offered early retirement, and he took it. He went to work for Gates Learjet. A small circle had been closed.

With Taylor gone, nearly a quarter of Canadair's top management had been given their pink slips, and hundreds of years of senior management experience in the company, and the industry, went with them. Bob Wohl and Jacques Ouellet were the only survivors of the original senior management team most closely associated with the launching of the Challenger 600, a piece of aviation history. CDIC and its managers, none of whom had any experience in the company or the industry, were in control of every aspect of a business they did not appreciate or understand. Their attempts to turn the Challenger program around proved frustrating and expensive. Insiders at Canadair were alienated, unable to believe that CDIC could do any better than their own people had.

Since there was little action in the business jet market, Canadair turned to a more familiar market, the military. However, Charlie Gray was pessimistic about sales prospects. Mindful of the C-SAM failure, Gray took an old friend of his, a major general in the U.S. Air Force, to lunch to check out the state of Canadair's image with the U.S. military. It wasn't good.

"I'm afraid you guys are showing all the classic signs of a program approaching the death rattle stage," Gray's contact admitted.

"Yeah, but look at Chrysler," Gray replied. "We're like them. We're tightening up the reins, eliminating fat, girding for the long haul."

"Sure, but Chrysler is coming out with new models and product developments. You guys are doing nothing. What have you got in development? Are you going to sell the same airplane for the foreseeable future? Moreover, you guys are financially up the creek. Nobody will buy from you because you're not a viable company over the long term."

This was certainly a problem. Despite a plea from CDIC, the Japanese government deferred their acquisition of a Challenger indefinitely because of the program's uncertain future. The German government was holding off a major decision to proceed with the CL-289 surveillance drone program because of the company's desperate financial situation. Malaysia, another potential Challenger customer, procrastinated. The government had to do something soon about Canadair's debt situation or there wouldn't be anybody interested in buying a Challenger jet.

Canadair's relationship with Canada's defense establishment wasn't much better. Its commitments to the military were met grudgingly and with the usual arrogance the military had come to know over the years. Since the launch of the Challenger, Canadair hadn't wanted to talk to the military, because it knew the military jobs involved hard work for a lower return. In 1982 Ottawa had had to twist Fred Kearns's arm to get him to accept a McDonnell Douglas subcontract to produce a small and uncomplicated component for the F-18 fighter aircraft. There was a recession and a separatist government in Quebec, and Ottawa wanted to create jobs on a no-lose subcontract for a government-owned company. But by the end of 1983 Canadair needed something substantially more than the odd contract from the government.

In early 1984 John Mackenzie put the finishing touches on a request to the Treasury Board for another equity infusion of $310 million. He was so anxious to get the proposal done that he got the English and French texts reversed on the official submission. It was the most critical request for government support ever presented by Canadair, and Mackenzie felt miserable when a Treasury Board staffer later called him and told him he had goofed.

The proposal was the first of many steps toward restructuring Canadair's massive debt. It contained two scenarios, scenario A with debt restructuring, scenario B without debt restructuring. In either case Canadair faced a desperate cash shortfall and needed some dramatic action. Over the projected 16 months, Canadair, which had a negative net worth of more than $1 billion, would need more than $200 million to cover finance costs, $69 million for customer refunds, $72 million for nonrecurring payments resulting from the production slowdown, another $72 million for inventory buildup, and finally $34 million in losses on aircraft already delivered. Canadair's previously negotiated advances on some of its subcontracts also meant a cash slowdown. Hope for early cash-flow increases depended on selling the Challenger 601. Under scenario A, there was a hope of getting to a reasonable return on costs; under scenario B, with no restructuring of the debt, there was no hope of getting a return.

Every day of delay in the restructure would cost the company millions of dollars. For each assumed CL-601 delivery in 1984 that did not take place, Canadair's cash requirement increased by approximately $12.5 million, or the equivalent of the price of the airplane. Bell and Bennett had sold the CDIC board on the debt restructuring, and they lobbied Cabinet. On February 9, 1984, Cabinet agreed to a reorganization plan. That summer, a new Canadair was created. The old Canadair kept the debt, the new Canadair kept the business. Canadair, lucky Canadair, was given a new deal.

For the first time in a decade the company was in reasonable fiscal shape. The economy picked up and the restructuring had its desired effect: financial credibility of the company was restored. The Challenger 601 was proving itself to be the aircraft Canadair had promised in 1976. With the new Canadair and the new Challenger, billions of dollars and millions of work-hours were erased from the books. And with a $200 million deal with Ottawa and the provinces for 15 water bombers, the company's balance sheet began to show some life.

After a long drought, Canadair started selling Challenger 601s. Seven went to the German Luftwaffe and nine to the Canadian military as part of a government-negotiated settlement with TAG. (Most of the aircraft that went to the Canadian government were TAG-ordered aircraft.) Corporate sales began to stir the air, as well. Things appeared to be on the upswing. But all was not well in Mahogany Row.

Canadair's future was thrown into doubt once more in the fall of 1984 when the Liberals lost the federal election and the Conservatives, who had been highly critical of Canadair during the public hearings the year before, came to power. One of the first things the new government did was fire Joel Bell (who later successfully sued the government for wrongful dismissal). Canadair president Gil Bennett was kept on but he offered to relinquish his post as a gesture to the new government. This precipitated one final indignity at Canadair: an internal battle for the president's job.

In the spring of 1985 as Dick Richmond and Gil Bennett started making plans for the Paris Air Show, Bennett told Richmond of his likely departure and said that he hoped Richmond would be his replacement. Word of this leaked out to Canadair's public relations office which issued a staff notice stating that Gil Bennett was planning to leave the company. Although the notice made no mention of Dick Richmond, many in Mahogany Row knew that, as chief operating officer of the company, he was the likeliest choice. What followed was a classic case of the two solitudes in corporate Quebec.

Jacques Ouellet, Canadair's vice president of human resources, was a Catholic French Canadian of some prominence in the community who displayed both charm and culture, and he very much believed he should be the next president of Canadair. Soon after Bennett's planned departure became public knowledge he and Dick Richmond were considered the frontrunners for the position. The French Canadian side of Canadair supported Ouellet, including the union and the growing ranks of francophone white collar employees. Richmond was considered by some to be an outsider supported by the largely anglophone engineering and senior management side of the company.

Once again there was a charged atmosphere in Canadair's beleaguered executive offices. There was certainly the sentiment among many in the company, including directors on the board, that Canadair's next president should be a francophone, and indeed Ouellet was not the only francophone vying for the job. What happened next took many by surprise. At the end of 1985 Bennett was abruptly replaced and Ottawa appointed a dark horse, Pierre Desmarais, a former City of Montreal urban community chairman, in his place. Desmarais's mandate was to get Canadair ready for sale. Shortly afterwards, the government announced it was considering a number of offers for the company.

At first there was only one serious bidder, a newly created shell company, Canadian Aerospace Technologies Ltd. (CAT), a joint venture between German aerospace executive Justus Dornier and Montreal businessman Howard Webster. But while the Conservatives liked their proposal, the Canadair management and board did not. Canadair's archrival Gulfstream was also a contender. Then Bombardier Inc. appeared on the scene. There was no question who Canadair favored as an owner.

It didn't start out that way. When Canadair's management heard that Bombardier was considering making an offer, many scoffed at the idea. Bombardier made snowmobiles and locomotives. What did they know about the airplane business? But when a contingent of Bombardier executives came to look over the facility, they dazzled the Canadair people with their sharp business sense.

Bombardier had all the markings of a successful company on the way up. It had been founded in 1942 by J. Armand Bombardier to manufacture all-terrain tracked vehicles, including the famous Ski-Doo. Under the stewardship of Bombardier president Laurent Beaudoin the company diversified into the mass transit industry with a major contract to build subway cars for the Montreal transit commission. In 1975 the Bombardier family holding company bought MLW-Worthington Ltd., a major steam locomotive manufacturer, and through a reverse takeover a new company name was created: Bombardier Inc. By the time Canadair came on the market under the Conservative government, Bombardier Inc. was a company with a half a billion dollars a year in sales and with 5,200 employees.

Canadair and Bombardier were very nearly equal in size and were at least in the same business, transportation.

The bidding was very close. The two offers differed little, but Bombardier had a distinct advantage. While CAT was a piece of paper, Bombardier was a Canadian company of substance, which had demonstrated that it could manage itself very well.

Bombardier saw that the government was offering a heck of a deal. Canadair's Challenger debt had been wiped clean, all programs were profitable, the lawsuits had been settled, the company had a $200 million contract with the federal government to produce water bombers and, to ice the cake, the government was on the verge of giving Canadair a multimillion dollar contract for systems engineering support for the CF-18. And after years of thinking of selling Cartierville Airport, the Canadian government decided to toss it into the deal. In August of 1986, Bombardier purchased Canadair for $120 million.

What pleased Canadair's board was that there was no doubt that Bombardier wanted to keep Canadair in the business of building complete airplanes. Not only was it committed to the Challenger, but it initiated plans to build a stretched Challenger, a longer version of the shelved CL-610, called the Regional Jet. Canadair's future as an airplane builder, the dream of Fred Kearns and the reason he launched the Challenger business jet program in the first place, was made secure.

EPILOGUE

As in the days with General Dynamics, Canadair is once again part of a larger corporate strategy. In the years since its acquisition of Canadair, Bombardier has acquired three more aerospace companies: Learjet Corporation, Short Brothers of Belfast, and, most recently, de Havilland of Toronto. When Bombardier bought Canadair in 1986, the company's income statements showed annual revenues of $500 million, today Bombardier has annual revenues of $3.5 billion and counts on aerospace as its single largest source of income.

The Challenger jet is a big part of Bombardier's success. In 1990/91 the business jet accounted for nearly half of the company's aerospace sales and a quarter of the profits. Last year Canadair celebrated the delivery of the 250th Challenger – no longer an airplane that the world could without. Considering its technical excellence, the Challenger will continue to be a competitive product well into the next century.

Canadair's most recent success has been in the booming market for regional airliners – the Regional Jet, based on the Challenger 610 model, has found its niche. The Global Express is a new Canadair product in development; it promises to be the longest range business jet in the world. And the CL-215 amphibian, which has re-emerged with new engines as the CL-415, is in full production.

The launch of the Challenger jet has finally paid off. Canadair has made a profitable place for itself in the world market for business and commercial aviation and justified the faith of all those who created the dream and fought to save it.

NOTES

Chapter 1

Page 9 "Who built this airplane?": Halton, interview 09/89. Page-12 "Everyone liked Fred": Robillard, interview 10/90. Page 19 "I've got warehouses": Aird, interview 06/90.

Chapter 2

Page 28 "There were two Bill Lears", page 37 "Sweetheart!", page 37 "I've got a great idea", page 39 "If this airplane is going to carry", page 40 "We've never built": Carl Ally, interview 02/90.

Chapter 3

Page 45. "Can we build it", page 48 "You guys think", page 55 "It'll give me an idea": Halton, interview 09/89. Page 56 "There's the windshield": George Turek, interview 10/90. Page 56 "I guess it's time", page 57 "I looked at", page 57 "Wind tunnel tests": Halton, interview 90/89. Page 57 "I recognized pretty soon": *Challenger History* by Harry Halton (unpublished). Page 57 "How involved": Halton, interview 10/89. Page 58 "In retrospect": Halton, interview 10/89. Page 59 "There were no new defense", page 60 "I've just spoken", page 61 "Yes, Mommy", page 61 "I know you're", page 62 "Where's Bill", page 62 "Well, Bob": Bob Wohl, interview 12/89.

Chapter 4

Page 63 "There's a fellow": Carl Ally, interview 02/90. Page 64 "The question is": Harry Halton, interview 10/89. Page 64 "The future of aviation": *Avionics News*, September 1979, (p. 32). Page 64 "The headmaster", page 65 "Go out there", page 69 "Look, Jim": Jim Taylor, interview 09/90. Page 72 "the longer sales": *Forbes Magazine*, April 1, 1972, (p. 50). Page 75 its erroneous prediction: *Forbes Magazine*, January 18, 1982, (p. 105). Page 75 "I'll be damned": *Forbes Magazine*, April 1, 1972, (p. 52). Page 76 "You know, Dwayne", page 76 "I've decided": Jim Taylor, interview 02/90.

Chapter 5

Page 80 "Your figures", page 80 "That plane's too heavy": Halton, interview 10/89. Page 81 "Look, Moya's not well": Carl Ally, interview 02/90. Page 84 "What do you mean": George Turek, interview 10/90. Page 84 "look after that man", page 88 "Listen, Lear", page 92 "This has got to be", page 96 "I didn't appreciate": Halton, interview 10/89. Page 97 "This is a sporty game": *New Yorker Magazine*, June 21, 1982, (p. 54). Page 99 "The reason you want": Jim Taylor, interview, 02/90. Page 100 "Fred, do you want to buy": Peter Aird, interview 04/90. "Go ahead and call": Jim Taylor, interview 02/90. Page 101 "All activity", page 101 "Bill, I've got a birthday present": Harry Halton, interview 10/89. Page 101 "The Canadians seemed to know": *Business Week*, February 6, 1978, (p. 64). Page 104 "Our customers", page 104 "I don't think Fred appreciated": Harry Halton, interview, 11/89. Page 107 "That leaves": *Business Week*, February 6, 1978, (p. 62). Page 112 "Personally, I feel": memo from Jim Taylor to Bob Wohl, August 24, 1976.

Chapter 6

Page 113 "We keep moving forward": Harry Halton, interview 10/89. Page 115 "He's a U.S. engineer": George Turek, 10/90. Page 116 "Enough!": Harry Halton, interview 10/89. Page 123 "Aziz, you have done", page 123 "How do you say", page 123 "They bought the house": Bill Juvonen, interview 03/90. Page 124 "I've got some good news": Bob Wohl, interview 12/89. Page 128 "I now believe that": *Challenger History* (unpublished), (p. 82). Page 129 "a too-nice set of guys": Harry Halton, 10/89. Page 130 "Sometimes Harry": George Turek, interview 10/90. Page 133 "It's obvious": Harry Halton, interview 10/89. Page 136 "We're going to get even": memo from Albert Blackburn to Jim Taylor, September 22, 1978. Page 140 "We have a serious problem": memo from Jim Taylor to Fred Kearns, August 16, 1978.

Chapter 7

Page 142 "If DoT could figure": Doug Adkins, interview 03/90. Page 143 "The man you want to talk to": Albert Blackburn, interview 02/90. Page 145 "For that year": Ron Neal, interview 06/90. Pg, 146 "Well, now that was interesting": Doug Adkins, interview 03/90. Page 149 "You can't do this": Harry Halton, interview 11/89. Page 150 "philosophy underlying the approval": *Engineering Flight Test Circular Guide for Transport Category Airplanes*, FAA Order No. 8110.8; September 26, 1974. Page 152 "You better ask Canadair": Dick Ven Gemert, interview 04/90. Page 154 "You know": Harry Halton, interview 10/89. Page 155 "Dobak confided": memo from Jim Taylor to Fred Kearns, May 23, 1979. Page 157 "I'm not looking for": memo from Harry Halton to Fred Kearns, November 28, 1979. Page 157 "I think you've got to write": Harry Halton, interview 10/89. Page 159 "Up to now": memo from Fred Kearns to Jim Kerr, August 24, 1979. Page 159 "would be about 300": letter from Harry Halton to customers, September 10, 1979. Page 161 "guilty of insubordination": memo from Fred Kearns to Jim Taylor, June 8, 1979. Page 162 "Time is running out": memo from Jim Taylor to Fred Kearns, January 24, 1980. Page 163 "We haven't been able to": Harry Halton, interview, 10/89. Page 165 "It was a lot of people": Bill Greening, interview, 12/89. Page 166 "We felt it was wrong": Doug Adkins, interview March 1990.

Chapter 8

Page 168 "We're into a deep stall": *National Transportation Safety Board Crash Investigation Report*, May 1980. Page 171 "To think that", page 172 "We didn't know where": Transcript of a presentation made to Canadair Program Management by Canadair Flight Operations, April 4, 1980. Page 173 "That's your decision": Harry Halton, interview 10/89. Page 179 "Are you sure", page 181 "Harry, you've got to": Andy Throner, interview 05/90. Page 181 "Go easy on this", page 182 "Geeze, Harry": Harry Halton, interview 10/89. Page 183 "I feel it is": letter from Fred Kearns to Canadair employees, July 24, 1979. Page 187 "This kind of unthinking": memo from Peter

Ginocchio to Jim Taylor, March 30, 1982. Page 188 "Don't do it": memo from Jim Taylor to Fred Kearns, May 26, 1981.

Chapter 9

Page 192 "A Dick Richmond": Harry Halton, interview 06/90. Page 192 "Don't you believe it", page 195 "Why do you want": Dick Richmond, interview 06/90. Page 197 "We had by now": Peter Aird, interview 06/90. Page 197 "Dick Richmond is coming": Andy Throner, interview 05/90. Page 199 "Have you and the others": Peter Aird, interview 06/90. Page 200 "Tony, tell me", page 201 "It was really", page 203 "They still had", page 204 "We want out": Dick Richmond, interview 06/90.

Chapter 10

Page 209 "There should be no": *Synopsis of the Report of the Interdepartmental Review of Canadair Limited*, February 1982, (p. 13). Page 209 "It seems unusual": *Synopsis*, February 1982, (p. 17). Page 210 "The Challenger aircraft": letter from Fred Kearns to Herb Gray, February 24, 1982. Page 210 "We feel that the most important": letter from Fred Kearns to Herb Gray, February 15, 1982. Page 212 "Now, Charles": Charlie Gray, interview 10/90. Page 213 "the aircraft selected": memo from John Lawson to Fred Kearns, November 25, 1982. Page 214 "full consideration of all" letter from Herb Gray to Guy Desmarais, August 25, 1982. Page 214 "Fred, I think", page 215 "Peter, deep down": Peter Aird, interview 06/90. Page 217 "The Challenger is another": *Shieldings Investments Limited Report on Canadair*, October 1982, (p. 34). Page 221 "A contract is a contract": Peter Aird, interview, 06/90.

Chapter 11

Page 226 "They say the Challenger", page 227 "If Canadair is smart", "Hell, yes": Eric Malling, interview 06/90. Page 230 "Look, don't come here to my office": Mike Lavoie, interview 06/90. Page 232 "They said there was gold": memo from Justin Battle to Jacques Ouelett, April 23, 1983. Page 232 "Mr. Chrétien", page 233 "Good show": Eric Malling, interview 06/90. Page 234 "Taxpayers are all": "Shareholders Report", *the fifth estate*, CBC, broadcast April 13, 1983. Page 235 "No interviews": Jacques Ouelett, interview 05/90.

Page 236 "No matter what": letter to the editor, *Montreal Gazette*, May 11, 1983, (p. B-2). Page 237 "He was shocked": Harry Halton, interview 11/89.

Chapter 12

Page 241 "They contend that": "Canadair Challenger 600 Operator Survey" by Robert Parrish, *Business & Commercial Aviation*, September, 1983, (p. 37). Page 241 "Hey Joel": Bill Juvonen, interview 02/90. Page 242 "The Challenger has become": "Requiem for the Challenger", *Wings*, May/June 1983, (p. 6). Page 242 "The mess at Canadair": "The Goings-On at Canadair", *Canadian Aviation*, June 1983. (p. 4). Page 243 "John, there's a hit list", page 243 "Don't worry, John": John Mackenzie, interview 06/90. Page 244 "We're now faced": Address to Canadair Challenger Operators by Gil Bennett, August 14, 1983. Page 246 "I must state emphatically": memo from Jim Taylor to Gil Bennett, July 14, 1983. Page 246 "With due respect": memo from Gil Bennett to Jim Taylor, January 14, 1984. Page 247 "Could you come up to Montreal": Bill Juvonen, interview 06/90. Page 248 "I have been left": memo from Jim Taylor to Gil Bennett, September 10, 1984.

INDEX